D1104287

# Racism in America

Recent Titles in the
# CONTEMPORARY WORLD ISSUES
Series

*Transgender: A Reference Handbook*
Aaron Devor and Ardel Haefele-Thomas

*Eating Disorders in America: A Reference Handbook*
David E. Newton

*Natural Disasters: A Reference Handbook*
David E. Newton

*Immigration Reform: A Reference Handbook*
Michael C. LeMay

*Vegetarianism and Veganism: A Reference Handbook*
David E. Newton

*The American Congress: A Reference Handbook*
Sara L. Hagedorn and Michael C. LeMay

*Disability: A Reference Handbook*
Michael Rembis

*Gender Inequality: A Reference Handbook*
David E. Newton

*Media, Journalism, and "Fake News": A Reference Handbook*
Amy M. Damico

*Birth Control: A Reference Handbook*
David E. Newton

*Bullying: A Reference Handbook*
Jessie Klein

*Domestic Violence and Abuse: A Reference Handbook*
Laura L. Finley

*Torture and Enhanced Interrogation: A Reference Handbook*
Christina Ann-Marie DiEdoardo

Books in the **Contemporary World Issues** series address vital issues in today's society such as genetic engineering, pollution, and biodiversity. Written by professional writers, scholars, and nonacademic experts, these books are authoritative, clearly written, up-to-date, and objective. They provide a good starting point for research by high school and college students, scholars, and general readers as well as by legislators, businesspeople, activists, and others.

Each book, carefully organized and easy to use, contains an overview of the subject, a detailed chronology, biographical sketches, facts and data and/or documents and other primary source material, a forum of authoritative perspective essays, annotated lists of print and nonprint resources, and an index.

Readers of books in the Contemporary World Issues series will find the information they need in order to have a better understanding of the social, political, environmental, and economic issues facing the world today.

Chesapeake College
.earning Resource Center
Wye Mills, MD 21679

# Racism in America

## A REFERENCE HANDBOOK

Steven L. Foy

ABC-CLIO®

An Imprint of ABC-CLIO, LLC
Santa Barbara, California • Denver, Colorado

E
184
.A1
F69
2020
c.2

Copyright © 2020 by ABC-CLIO, LLC

All rights reserved. No part of this publication may be reproduced, stored in a retrieval system, or transmitted, in any form or by any means, electronic, mechanical, photocopying, recording, or otherwise, except for the inclusion of brief quotations in a review, without prior permission in writing from the publisher.

Library of Congress Cataloging in Publication Control Number: 2019051182

ISBN: 978-1-4408-5640-2 (print)
       978-1-4408-5641-9 (ebook)

24  23  22  21  20      1  2  3  4  5

This book is also available as an eBook.

ABC-CLIO
An Imprint of ABC-CLIO, LLC

ABC-CLIO, LLC
147 Castilian Drive
Santa Barbara, California 93117
www.abc-clio.com

This book is printed on acid-free paper ∞

Manufactured in the United States of America

# Contents

*Racism in America: A Reference Handbook* recognizes the need for a holistic look at racism, considering interpersonal and institutional processes and outcomes. Interpersonal racism (the type that occurs between people in their everyday words and actions) is particularly visible and, consequently, is what people usually think about when they think about racism. However, racism goes far beyond the interactions between individuals. It plays a substantial role in and through institutions like the government, the education system, the health care system, and the banking industry via formal rules (e.g., laws that limit access to members of a certain racial group) and informal norms (e.g., a bank's unwritten but patterned practice of denying loans to minorities). That institutionalized nature of racism is the particular focus of this book.

Chapter 1 explains the foundational underpinnings of racism in America, noting how it provided the language and justification for economic expansion and stratification. Racism rendered the forced removal of indigenous people from North American lands and the enslavement of Africans somehow rational in the eyes of the general public and then permeated every major American structure. The chapter discusses how racism became inherent to the institutional DNA of science, religion, immigration, governance, labor, education, transportation, housing, criminal justice, health care, the arts, sports, and consumer markets.

Chapter 2 follows the progression of racism within these institutions into the present day. The chapter recognizes the important milestones by which racial progress has been made but places racial progress in the context of the continued perpetuation of racial stratification in the United States. Each step forward has been met with contestation by proponents of the status quo. Each attempt to correct the injustices of the path has been forestalled or undercut by new injustices. The chapter concludes with a discussion of how we might move closer to racial equality while recognizing that as long as people prioritize self-interest, they will use their group associations and the power derived from them to obtain social advantages—even if doing so impedes others' life, liberty, and pursuit of happiness.

Chapter 3 features the voices of thoughtful experts in the fight against racial injustice, highlighting the unique perspectives that arise from academia, the practice of law, community organizing, art, and journalism. They cover a variety of important topics that range from the theoretical (pushing back against naive narratives of racial progress) to the institutional (noting the ways in which racism permeates the media landscape, law enforcement, immigration enforcement, urban policy, the treatment of indigenous people) and the personal (laying bare the ways in which racism and the fight against it weigh on people in their everyday experiences).

Consistent with the institutional perspective on racism at the heart of this book, Chapter 4 profiles organizations and groups known for particular contributions toward the continuation or remission of racist practices in America, including the American Civil Liberties Union, Black Lives Matter, the Black Panther Party for Self-Defense, the Ku Klux Klan, the National Association for the Advancement of Colored People, the Nation of Islam, the Southern Christian Leadership Conference, the Student Nonviolent Coordinating Committee, The Sentencing Project, and the United Farm Workers' Movement.

Chapters 5 and 6 emphasize some of the raw empirical evidence behind the book's larger claims about the persistence and institutionalized nature of American racism. Chapter 5 directs the reader to speeches from important contributors to conversations around American racial stratification, historical documents that evidence the use of racism within specific institutions, and statistical data from governmental institutions that highlight the persistence of racial inequality. Chapter 6 provides resources for future research, drawing primarily on major peer-reviewed books and journal articles with additional clarification via technical reports.

The book concludes with two chapters that clarify the big picture. Chapter 7 places the governmental policies, court decisions, uprisings, protests, counterprotests, and other major events corresponding to the rise of and contestation against racism in America into context, providing a timeline of events. Finally, a glossary features key terms of relevance to the discussion at hand. At times, the language is raw and characteristic of words used historically that do not befit present-day conversation, but the attempt is to be descriptive and explanatory without being gratuitous.

Like any good book, this one is full of triumphs and tragedies. It features ostensible heroes who display their fallibility and villains who make unexpectedly progressive decisions when it suits them. Perhaps more than anything else, though, this book reminds the reader that the story of America is a cautionary tale about how a nation can be founded on seemingly idealistic principles and yet ultimately be anchored by the same prejudices and discriminatory tendencies that have always plagued humankind.

# Racism in America

# 1 Background and History

## Introduction

This book is grounded in three major premises at the forefront of contemporary research. First, race is socially constructed (created through human interaction and not objectively real), but it results in real consequences through racism. Genetic differences between alleged racial groups are minimal, leading most scientists studying human variation to conclude that there is insufficient evidence to support the existence of biological races (Smedley and Smedley 2005; Sussman 2016). Many scholars argue that the concept of race first entered the American context not through scientific evidence but rather through the ideas of western European colonists who used it to differentiate themselves from the African people whom they exploited and enslaved (Smedley and Smedley 2018). Despite its arbitrary invention, race is still used by the powerful to exploit the disadvantaged.

Second, although everyone is capable of racial prejudice (including racial minorities), racial groups differ in their power to systematically discriminate against the targets of their prejudice. In the American context, white people have a unique ability to act on racial prejudice. As former president of Spelman

Art instruction at the Carlisle Indian School (1901–1903). Federally funded boarding schools like this one separated Native Americans from their families and forcibly assimilated them to European culture. (Library of Congress)

College and psychologist Beverly Tatum (1997:10) puts it, "People of color are not racist because they do not systematically benefit from racism. . . . Reserving the term racist for only the behaviors committed by Whites in the context of a White-dominated society is a way of acknowledging the ever present power differential afforded Whites by the culture and institutions that make up the system of advantage and continue to reinforce notions of White supremacy." This is not to say that the average white person is inherently bad but rather that the average white person benefits from economic, political, and social advantages that are frequently denied to racial minorities. For example, according to a 2016 report from the Corporation for Economic Development and the Institute for Policy Studies, it would take 228 years for African American families to reach the average wealth of white families (Asante-Muhammed et al. 2016). Advantages like this make it possible for whites to discriminate against the targets of their prejudice through institutions to an extent that other racial groups cannot.

Third, while some evidence suggests that prejudice and institutional racism have declined in modern America, these declines may have been overstated. On the one hand, there have been indications of progress; for example, answers in response to the General Social Survey's racial-attitudes scale have reflected greater support for racial integration over time (DiMaggio, Evans, and Bryson 1996). So few whites agreed that black and white children should go to separate schools by 1985 that the survey stopped including a question about this (Bobo et al. 2012). Barack Obama became the first African American to be elected president of the United States in 2008, Sonia Sotomayor became the first Latina confirmed for the Supreme Court in 2009, and the 114th Congress was the most diverse in history, demonstrating progress in dismantling institutional barriers against minority representation in politics (Krogstad 2015; Nagourney 2008; Venkataraman 2009). On the other hand, more than half of African Americans surveyed by the Pew Research Center (2016) perceived that African Americans are treated less fairly than whites in dealing with police, in courts, when applying for a mortgage loan, and in the workplace. Meanwhile, racial gaps in income (DeNavas-Walt and Proctor 2015), health (Phelan and Link 2015), and educational achievement (Stanford Center for Education Policy Analysis 2016) persist. This chapter explains how race became the tremendously stratifying force that it is today, tracing its origins to and continuation through many of the major institutions in American life.

## The Origins of American Racism

> In the modern world we have become so accustomed to thinking within a framework of race and ethnicity that we are quite unable to conceive of a past that may not have had this framework. (Ivan Hannaford 1996:4)

### Clearing the Land

Despite how commonly they are now discussed, systems of social stratification based on race are relatively new. Prior to and in the early years of European colonialism, characteristics like religion and social class typically determined who was advantaged or disadvantaged in many societies (Anderson 2012; PBS 2003; Stam and Spence 1983). While evidence from classical antiquity reveals pictorial and written negative representations of darker-skinned people, Greek and Roman whites traded with and intermarried with Egyptian, Nubian, Ethiopian, and Carthaginian blacks, and most of their slaves were conquered whites (Snowden 1991; Thompson 1993). Cox (2000) also suggests that explicitly racial conflict was largely absent from ancient civilizations. However, as Spain, Portugal, Italy, France, Germany, the Netherlands, and Great Britain sought to expand their empires into North America (among other places), the concept of racial categorization as a primary basis for hierarchy began to make its way into the lexicon of each (Smedley and Smedley 2018). For example, during the late 1660s, the

English shifted from framing Africans as "heathen," due to their not being Christians, to framing them as "black," due to their pigmentation (Wood 2003:32).

Stratification based on racial categorization was no accident. It allowed European colonizers to address three goals: (1) to justify removal of the people already inhabiting the land they wished to occupy, (2) to secure and maintain a stable labor force, and (3) to divide and conquer groups that otherwise might band together against European colonization. Regarding the first goal, Europeans held a long-standing assumption that they had the right to settle on whatever land they discovered—an assumption that would continue with the constitutional establishment of the United States and be formally articulated in the Supreme Court's decision in *Johnson and Graham's Lessee v. William M'Intosh* (Miller 2011). In *Johnson v. M'Intosh* (1823), the Supreme Court argued that "according to every theory of property," Native Americans had neither individual nor collective rights to land, that conquest under title from the Crown constituted a right to land by colonists, and that Native Americans were only compensated for land out of political expediency—not acknowledgment of any Native American property rights. Moreover, major U.S. decision-makers would eventually describe their assumed right to colonization of North America as divinely granted—their "manifest destiny to overspread the continent allotted by Providence for the free development of our yearly multiplying millions" (O'Sullivan 1845:2).

Europeans' presumed right to colonize Native Americans' lands was predicated on the idea that Native Americans' racial inferiority necessitated either their acculturation or their removal (Berger 2009; Mills 1999). Even the famous Enlightenment philosopher John Locke believed that, although humans are naturally endowed with certain rights, Native Americans no longer warranted these rights because they were not using their land properly and opposed European expansion onto that land (Sussman 2016). Colonizers considered sociopolitical structures in America that preceded their arrival as something less than civilization and the Native Americans who created them as something less than civilized. In this way, the colonizers framed their conquest as altruism that justified their seizure of land and attempts to assimilate Native Americans into European culture. The colonizers represented Native American practices of living as "a flattering foil for American society and culture" and their own culture as a way to save these "fatally and racially inferior" people (Berger 2009:591). Evidence indicates that traders and others who had regular individual contact with Native Americans held more complex and charitable views of them, but farmers tended to picture them as "lying, thieving, murdering savage[s], pagan in religion, racially stupid except for a kind of animal cunning," and that view carried greater weight (Simpson and Yinger 1985:48).

A major way in which the U.S. government attempted to assimilate Native Americans from 1810 through 1917 was by funding boarding schools run by Christian missionaries to separate their children from their families, tribes, and cultures. For example, the Treaty of Fort Laramie (1868) stipulated that Native children would be compelled to attend school—supposedly to civilize them. The schools frequently incorporated physical and sexual abuse (EagleWoman and Rice 2016). The first such school resembled an army training camp, and its superintendent, Lieutenant Richard Henry Pratt, described its philosophy as "Kill the Indian, save the man" (EagleWoman and Rice 2016:4).

These boarding schools repressed Native American culture in a variety of intentional ways. The students were often forced to cut their hair, change their clothing, use English names in place of their own names, and abandon traditional religious practices in favor of Christian ones. They were also expected to learn English and were punished for speaking their native languages (National Museum of the American Indian 2007).

Such processes implied that Native Americans were incapable of meeting basic standards of societal acceptability—that they needed an authoritative, guiding hand. Similar paternalism appeared in court cases during the late 1800s. In the 1886 case *United States v. Kagama*, the Supreme Court argued that "these Indian tribes are wards of the nation . . . dependent largely for their daily food; dependent for their political rights. . . . From their very weakness and helplessness . . . there arises the duty of protection, and with it the power." That same logic underpinned colonial justifications for taking over the land held by these tribes.

In another assimilative move, the Dawes Severalty Act of 1887 undermined Native American traditions of communal land use by apportioning Native American lands into individual homesteads. This furthered colonial expansion efforts, as any remaining land after apportionments had been made could be sold to U.S. citizens (Otis 1973).

When acculturation proved insufficient to wholly free up land for colonization, a number of removal techniques were implemented. Thomas Jefferson described those occupying lands wanted for colonization as "pest[s]" whom he aimed to "get clear of" (Prucha 1984:120). Writing to then Indiana Territory governor William Henry Harrison, he suggested that "we push our trading houses, and be glad to see the good and influential individuals among them run in debt, because we observe that when these debts get beyond what the individuals can pay, they become willing to lop them off by a cessation of lands" (Prucha 1984:120).

Then, there were efforts to eliminate the buffalo population in the Great Plains—an important source of food and other materials for Natives there. William T. Sherman, commanding general of the U.S. army after the Civil War, welcomed civilian buffalo hunters and even provided them with letters of introduction to western commanders that would grant them access to military scouts, weapons, and other equipment (Smits 1994). Many of the officers serving under him supported this approach; Lieutenant General John M. Schofield, commander of the Department of the Missouri, would later reflect in his memoirs that he "wanted no other occupation in life than to ward off the savage and kill off his food until there should no longer be an Indian frontier in our beautiful country" (Smits 1994:316).

Another strategy was forced removal. Congress passed the 1830 Indian Removal Act under President Andrew Jackson, but Thomas Jefferson was the one who devised its forced removal plan in the first place. In 1803, he wrote to Indiana Territory governor William Henry Harrison that the Native Americans should either assimilate as U.S. citizens or "remove beyond the Mississippi" (Miller 2006:90). His actions suggested that the latter was his true aim; in 1808, a Cherokee delegation offered to become U.S. citizens, but Jefferson placed unbearable conditions on obtaining citizenship with the expectation that the Cherokee would refuse (Miller 2006). Under the authority of the Indian Removal Act, Cherokee leader Major Ridge signed the Treaty of New Echota in 1835, ceding Cherokee land to the United States in exchange for less valuable land further west and cash. Although Ridge did not have approval from the Cherokee government to sign the treaty, the U.S. military acted anyway, forcibly moving the Cherokee to the west during a brutal winter from 1838 through 1839. Over 4,000 Cherokees died marching down what became known as the Trail of Tears (Taylor-Colbert 2004; Wilkins 1989).

Then, there was slavery. Although most slaves in the American colonies were black, Native Americans were also enslaved and, at times, in consequential numbers. For example, Ethridge (2010:258) notes that Creek slavers selling to European colonists facilitated the "virtual depopulation of the whole of the Florida peninsula." Although enslavement of Native Americans was less common in New York and Pennsylvania (due to a lack of cooperation with the Iroquois who often accepted members of other tribes rather than selling them to the colonies), all of the colonies brought in Native American slaves (Gallay 2015).

Ultimately, if assimilation, forced removal, or enslavement did not eradicate Native American resistance to colonization, violence was always an option. Early on, Lord Jeffrey Amherst, Crown governor of Virginia, referred to Native Americans as "vermine" and called for their complete annihilation (Means 1992). Georgia commissioner Hiram Price presented the destruction of the Native Americans as the consequence of their failure to assimilate, saying "one of two things must eventually take place, to wit, either civilization or extermination of the Indian. Savage and civilized life cannot live and prosper on the same ground. One of the two must die" (Strickland 1986:726).

Significant casualties mounted as Native Americans divided in support for warring European nations. Colonizing European powers like England had long engaged in protracted wars against each other over territorial claims in North America, such as during the 1754–1763 French and Indian War. Often, these wars were conducted alongside Native trading partners, who also experienced casualties. As time went on, many Northern tribes began to see the growing American nation as an even more significant danger than the traditional colonial powers (Calloway 1995). When the American Revolution erupted, a number of tribes supported the British, including the Mohawks and most of the Cayugas, Chickasaws, Choctaws, Mingoes, Onondagas, Senecas, and Wiandots (Calloway 1995, 2008).

At times, outright massacre was legally sanctioned and state supported. Georgia's state legislature justified the murder of the Creek by declaring them outlaws via a 1789 statute that said "the Creek Indians shall be considered as without the protection of the state, but it shall be lawful for the Government and people of the same, to put to death or capture the said Indians wheresoever they may be found within the limits of this state" (Strickland 1986:720). In a letter to Alexander von Humboldt, Thomas Jefferson (1813) argued that the English seduced the Natives to massacre U.S. women and children, concluding that "this will oblige us now to pursue them to extermination, or drive them to new seats beyond our reach." These justifications were especially transparent in some cases, as in when the victims were clearly neither outlaws nor combatants. For example, in 1890, the U.S. military killed approximately 300 Hunkpapa Lakota at Wounded Knee, many of whom were children (EagleWoman and Rice 2016). Some newspapers, such as California newspapers during the mid-1800s, actively encouraged genocidal practices against local Native Americans (Madley 2016).

Taken together, these strategies of acculturation, removal, and killing fit Raphael Lemkin's (1944) original definition of genocide. Lemkin (1944) describes genocide as a process by which actions are taken to eliminate a group's culture, language, religion, and other aspects that once differentiated them as unique as well as their very lives. Strikingly, the term "genocide" is derived from the merger of the Latin word "cide," which means killing, and the Greek word "genos," which means race or tribe (Lemkin 1944). Thus, the process by which Native Americans were assimilated, spatially removed, or killed was one tied to racism even at a definitional baseline. American genocidal practices were dramatically effective; it is estimated that, from the mid-fifteenth century to 1910, the Native American population in North America declined from approximately 15 million to about 200,000 (Ball 1987). In fact, they served as a model for future genocides; Adolf Hitler drew from Native American reservations in designing concentration camps and "often praised to his inner circle the efficiency of America's extermination—by starvation and uneven combat—of the red savages who could not be tamed by captivity" (Toland 1991:702).

These actions intentionally furthered the goal of seizing Native lands for continued expansion. Thomas Jefferson argued that once the Native Americans neared extinction, the United States would be poised to exercise its discovery rights and take their land (Miller 2006). As intended, millions of acres of Native land passed into U.S. hands; for example, between 1887 (when the Dawes Act divided reservations into individual subplots and gave non-Natives the leftover "surplus" land) and

1934, Native American landholdings diminished from 138 million acres to 48 million acres (Ball 1987).


## Securing Labor

Racial categorization also provided a stable labor force for white European colonists. Enslavement extends back for millennia but was not primarily predicated on race until the rise of European colonization (Smedley and Smedley 2018). Even early on in European colonization, the English typically did not enslave Christians, and slaves could secure their freedom through conversion to Christianity (PBS 2017). At the beginning of European colonization in North America, there were also examples of Africans who shared a number of similarities with white indentured servants. In Virginia, for example, black and white laborers alike were referred to as "waged men" and fulfilled fixed contracts (Allen 1997:52). Upon completion of their contracts, they received land and supplies to begin their lives as free people (PBS 2017).

Laborers were also subject to many of the same abuses. For example, wills from as far back as 1623 list both black and white servants as real estate. However, there were some important distinctions. For example, Virginia court records from the 1640s reveal evidence of white servants being punished for running away with additional years of service, whereas black servants were punished for the same offense with servitude for life (Anderson 2012). Moreover, the legal status and conditions of service would soon change across racial groups as demand for labor increased; in 1641, Massachusetts officially legalized slavery, and other colonies would follow (Allen 1997; PBS 2017). In 1705, the Virginia General Assembly declared that "all servants imported and brought into the Country . . . who were not Christians in their native Country . . . shall be accounted and be slaves" (PBS 2017). White servants could still eventually pay off their debts through their labor, but black slaves became the property of their owners (Myrdal 2000). Moreover, by 1670, children of female slaves became slaves themselves by default (Baptist 2014). Although Africans comprised the majority of slaves in colonial America, there were examples of other enslaved racial and ethnic minorities. For example, there were numerous East Indian slaves in the Chesapeake region. The low status accorded East Indians can be found in how they would sometimes represent their ancestors as Native American to increase the likelihood of having freedom petitions approved (Brown and Sims 2006).

The enslavement of racial minorities, in general, and black Africans, in particular, provided a permanent and, through reproduction, self-replicating workforce for the widespread production of tobacco. Tobacco was an important staple in colonies like Maryland and Virginia, which exported it extensively to Europe and used it for a variety of purposes domestically (Baptist 2014; Scharf 1881). In Maryland, for example, "the land on which the houses were built, and the houses that were built upon it, subscriptions to public undertakings or charitable purposes, fines for offenses, salaries of public officers and the clergy were all paid in tobacco" (Scharf 1881:766). Slavery was further buoyed by the invention of the cotton gin in 1793. The cotton gin's efficiency made formerly inconsequential cotton important enough to supplant tobacco as the leading cash crop in the South. The increased profitability brought by the cotton gin dramatically increased demand for labor; by 1860, one-third of Southerners were slaves (Dattel 2011; Schur 2016; Simpson and Yinger 1985). As Marx (1976:915) puts it, this bent toward wealth maximization was characterized by "the conversion of Africa into a preserve for the commercial hunting of black skins."

If the need for labor provided the demand, white supremacy provided the justification by which black indentured servants became differentiated from white indentured servants as slaves. Under white supremacy, "blackness" became synonymous with "slaveability" in the service of capitalism (Smith 2012:68). As Smith (2012:69) puts it, "Anti-Blackness enables people who are not Black to accept their lot in life because they can feel that at least they are not at the very bottom of the racial hierarchy: at least they are not property; at least they are not slaveable."

This construction of "slaveability" relied on a steady narrative of dehumanization. Edward Long (1774) referred to people of African descent as lacking in morality and mental capacity, comprising a different species from Europeans, and more like orangutans than whites. Long argued that Africa was barbaric and that Africans were better off as slaves in America than as free people in their place of origin (Olusoga 2015). Similarly, W. Winwood Reade (1864:23) argued that "the Negro imitates the white man as the ape imitates the Negro. The result in both cases is a caricature." These views were also common to the founders of the United States. Thomas Jefferson (1999) described black people as foul smelling and lacking in reason, arguing that male orangutans preferred black women to female orangutans. Even those who objected to retaining a captive black labor force justified that view in racist terms. Benjamin Franklin asked in a 1751 essay: "Why increase the Sons of Africa, by Planting them in America, where we have so fair an Opportunity, by excluding all Blacks and Tawneys, of increasing the lovely White and Red? But perhaps I am partial to the Complexion of my Country, for such Kind of Partiality is natural to Mankind" (Isaacson 2003:152).

Constructing blacks as inherently different from whites allowed whites to feel justified in securing their forced labor indefinitely. As University of York professor of history emeritus James Walvin put it, "The British don't become slave traders and slavers because they are racist; they became racist because they use slaves for great profit in the Americas and devise a set of attitudes towards black people that justifies what they've done. The real engine behind the slave system is economics" (Skufca 2015). However, once established, racial discrimination continued to operate not only for economic reasons but also for a variety of other reasons. Slavery would be officially abolished in 1865 (U.S. Constitutional Amendment XIII), but institutional racism would remain a tool of American whites to perpetuate not only economic but also social advantages.

### Discouraging Organized Rebellion

In addition to justifying land seizure and labor acquisition, racial hierarchies aided these European powers in colonizing new lands from the fifteenth century onward in another important way. Racial caste systems divided inhabitants of colonial lands and pitted them against one another, encouraging mutual distrust and demotivating coordinated rebellion. For example, the Spanish constructed categories like "chapeton," "creole," "mestizo," "mulatto," "terceron," "quadroon," and "zambo" to differentiate based on skin tone, with darker-skinned individuals experiencing a far more difficult path to professional advancement in the military, in the church, and in politics (Roscher 1904:20–21). Further, Spanish officials issued documents confirming people they deemed of mixed race and potential to foment uprisings as white, giving them a more privileged classification as incentive not to rebel (Roscher 1904).

Similarly, race allowed wealthy landowners in the early British colonies to divide and conquer by sowing enmity among European indentured servants toward African indentured servants (Zinn 2015). During the seventeenth century, black and white servants ate, slept, and worked together under similar circumstances, and they often intermarried (Morgan 2003; Parent 2003). Noted historian Kenneth Stampp (1989) remarked at how unconcerned black and white servants appeared to be with their visible physical differences. In fact, children of mixed race were frequently born to black mothers, and, at first, this occurred rather uneventfully (Higgenbotham and Kopytoff 2003).

However, in the 1660s, Maryland and Virginia began instituting legal distinctions that helped white servants see themselves as temporary workers and black servants as chattel (Stampp 1989). For example, as of 1705, slave owners could whip any servant, but the Virginia assembly outlawed whipping white, Christian servants while they were naked. Other laws directed planters to reserve access to certain trades to whites. Such distinctions enabled white servants to see themselves as potential members of the upper class rather than economically lower-class people with potential for solidarity with black slaves (Thandeka 1998). As Zinn (2015:50) put it, "Their race made them think of themselves as planters and aristocrats, while their actual economic and social condition was dire."

## Institutional Venues of Racism

Racism, having been established as a major organizer of social stratification, became "structured into the rhythms of everyday [American] life" (Feagin 2001:2). A major contribution of the social sciences in general and sociology in particular has been the recognition that racism is not just interpersonal (occurring between individuals in ways that reveal individual prejudice and discrimination) but also institutional (emanating from a variety of structures from governments to homeowners' associations that constrain or enable actors based on race) (Wellman 1993). In keeping with this, we now turn to the institutions that gave structure to American racism. The American racial hierarchy gained legitimacy from scientific and religious institutions and was reinforced in a variety of institutional venues, including the legal system, the education system, places of employment, housing, transportation, the health care system, the criminal justice system, the environment, the food distribution system (impacting food security), the media, the arts, sports, and the marketing of consumer goods.

### Justifying the Racial Hierarchy

*Science and Pseudoscience: Alleged Physical and Mental Differences*

Todorov (1993) distinguishes between racism (behavior born of contempt) and racialism (ideological views about the existence of different racial groups). While racism is not dependent on racialism, racialism provides the seemingly logical underpinnings for racism. Racialism begins with the initial claim that races exist in the first place and are accompanied by clear physical distinctions. Todorov (1993) suggests that, from this perspective, racial groups are seen as similar to horses and donkeys—closely related enough for procreation but uniquely different. Humans were divided into racial groups in a manner that was hardly neutral. Racialists see membership in a particular racial group as dictating one's culture and, by extension, one's behavior and values (Todorov 1993). European and, by extension, American pseudoscience allowed racialists to present specious claims about the alleged superiority of whites as objective truths.

Some believed that racial groups actually constituted wholly separate species (Haller 1972). Others, such as Johann Blumenbach, Charles-Louis de Secondat, Baron de La Brède et de Montesquieu, Carl Linnaeus, and Georges-Louis Leclerc, Comte de Comte de Buffon, argued that racial groups stemmed from common ancestry but became distinct as a result of differences in social conditions and climate. For example, Buffon argued that the "most beautiful and fit humans" came from places with a climate between 40 and 50 degrees (e.g., Germany, Italy, Switzerland, Ukraine, and, conveniently, his own nation of France) (Sussman 2016:17). Common to these explanations was a shared defense of Europeans and European Americans as superior.

Racialism gained traction, at least in part, because of scientific claims of racial difference emanating from Europe and echoing in America. By infiltrating science, racism had the opportunity to take on the trappings of fact and respectability—to become the increasingly less-questioned status quo. Pseudoscience led those like French anatomist Georges Cuvier who once considered slavery immoral and arguments about brain differences between racial groups ludicrous to speak ten years later with certainty that racial groups featured "systematic anatomical differences" that "probably determined their moral and intellectual faculties" (Douglas 2008:33).

Johann Blumenbach, one of the earliest racial classifiers in the eighteenth century, took issue with racialists and believed that humans shared a common origin. He saw Africans as accomplished, intelligent, and beautiful in a time when they were often castigated as inferior. Yet even he suggested (1) that there were real distinctions between, as he termed them, "Caucasians," "Mongolians," "Ethiopians," "Americans," and "Malays" and (2) that the Caucasian skull was the most beautiful from which "the others diverge" (Bhopal 2007; Blumenbach 1865:269). Although Blumenbach did not appear to intentionally put forth this typology in order to justify stratification, the result was a classification system that would be used for precisely that purpose. Others would build on Blumenbach's work, reifying his categories through skull, hair, skin color, and other measurements (Haller 1996).

American scientist Samuel Morton argued that Caucasians had the biggest skulls and, therefore, the most brain capacity (Gould 1978). Diagrams of human faces across different racial groups were compared with orangutans, and blacks were alleged to be most similar due to an alleged "elongation of the snout" and lower facial line (Haller 1996:11). Lower facial lines were argued to be marks of stupidity (Haller 1996). Anatomical indicators of this nature provided ammunition for the re-entrenchment of racialist ideas. Modern science, however, would all but abandon such notions. An attempt to map racial groups looks quite different if based on genetics than if based on bone structure or skin type or other features, and there are greater differences among individuals within racial groups than between racial groups (Todorov 2000).

Yet scientists also defended slavery by pointing to differences between racial groups in susceptibility to certain physical illnesses and conditions. They wrote of blacks' resistance to malaria. They wrote of the extent to which their bodies were better adapted to warmer than colder climates given their proclivity toward respiratory infections, their greater risk of frostbite, and their tendency to sleep with their heads toward the fire rather than their feet (Savitt 1981). Based on these arguments, ensuring that black slaves remained at work in the South was framed as a benevolent gesture; as one South Carolinian doctor stated, "The African races are very susceptible of cold, and are as incapable of enduring a northern climate, as a white population are of supporting the torrid sun of Africa" (Savitt 1981:35).

Just as pseudoscience lent faulty credence to arguments that racial groups fundamentally differ physically and in terms of intellectual capacity, it also opportunistically buttressed suggestions that blacks in America were more susceptible to mental illness as justification for their continued enslavement. American doctor Samuel A. Cartwright argued that when slaves ran away, they fled not because of the inherent injustices of slavery but, rather, because of "drapetomania." In 1851, he argued that drapetomania occurs when slaves are treated too cruelly or too well and, particularly, when "the white man . . . [tries to make] the negro anything else than 'the submissive knee-bender . . .' by trying to raise him to a level with himself, or by putting himself on an equality with the negro" (Cartwright 2004:34). Physicians advocated for the surgical removal of the big toes of those supposedly affected by the disease in the belief that it would keep them from running away. In other words, the medical community was representing runaway slaves as not indicative of a problem with the institution of slavery but, rather, a problem with slave masters being insufficiently patriarchal and slaves attempting to act above their rightful station.

Similarly, Cartwright provided justification for continued enslavement through his alleged discovery of "dysaesthesia aethiopis" (Cartwright 2004:35). Cartwright argued that this was a disease specific to blacks and was "much more prevalent among free negroes living in clusters by themselves, than among slaves on our plantations and attacks only such slaves as live like free negroes in regard to diet, drinks, and exercise" and arose from sloth (Cartwright 2004:35). Supposedly, dysaesthesia aethiopis caused blacks to "break, waste, and destroy everything they handle," including abuse of animals and destruction of private property (Cartwright 2004:35). Conveniently, slavery provided a presumed antidote to this danger by continually engaging blacks in hard labor.

Pseudoscientific explanations of racial difference also provided racist defenses for both sides of debates about whether members of different racial groups should intermarry. On the one hand, Georges-Louis Leclerc, Comte de Buffon argued, in 1849, that relationships between racial groups could "wash the skin of the Negro" through "mixing with the blood of the White" over a couple hundred years (Quoy and Gaimard 1824:18). On the other hand, most twentieth-century American scientists writing about interracial relationships expressed negativity toward the subject, and some even represented Anglo-Saxons mixing with the Irish as "dilution" of the "American race" (Farber 2003:167). Southern physicians saw "mulattos" or "hybrids" as physically weaker, prone to disease, and morally debased (Haller 1972). However, marriages between recent immigrant Irish, Scottish, and English white women and African American men could be overlooked during the late 1800s given the relatively low social status of both (Mills and Miller 2017).

*Religion: Alleged Moral Differences*

Pseudoscience arguing that racial differences were innate, biological, and indicative of health drew from questionable empirical research but, nevertheless, proceeded from expectations of legitimacy set by the scientific method. Similarly, religious arguments of racial difference, although arising from questionable interpretations of religious doctrine, presented a basis for legitimacy from divine dictates and inspiration.

Appeals to faith were as important to justifying racial hierarchy as appeals to science. Some of the most widely touted reasons for the origins of racial difference as well as the supposed reasonableness of racial hierarchy came from religion and, specifically, from Christianity. In the seventeenth and eighteenth centuries, degeneration theory suggested that all people were descendants of Adam and Eve, but nonwhites (whether through life conditions, God's will, or some other mechanism) were flawed creations. Whites (and, particularly, European Christian whites) were seen as superior and tasked with controlling and leading everyone else (Sussman 2016). Others suggested that blacks were the descendants of Ham, the son of Noah. According to the Old Testament biblical account in Genesis 9:24, Ham "saw his father's nakedness" (*The Holy Bible* 1993) while Noah was drunk with wine. Recovering from his intoxication, Noah said to Ham, in Genesis 9:25, "Cursed be Canaan! The lowest of slaves will he be to his brothers" (*The Holy Bible* 1993). That curse was construed to extend to his progeny, and his progeny were alleged to be Africans (Myrdal 2000). For example, South Carolinian Episcopalian clergy member Frederick Dalcho argued that "the descendants of Canaan [Ham's son], the Africans, were to be the 'servants of servants . . . the lowest state of servitude, slaves'" and argued that, because there was no biblical prophecy of that curse's removal, it should remain in place to this day (Morrison 1980:18).

Christianity was frequently used to uphold slavery. Religious leaders pointed to a number of biblical situations in which slavery was said to exist but was seemingly not condemned by God. In the Old Testament, major figures, like Abraham, had slaves (Genesis 21:9–10); the Ten Commandments mentioned slavery (Exodus 20:10, 17); and, in Leviticus 25:44–46, there is a description of slaves being bought and sold, kept as personal property, and inherited by family members (*Christianity Today* 1992; Morrison 1980). In the New Testament, the apostle Paul not only told slaves to obey their masters in a letter to the Ephesians (6:5–8) but also returned an escaped slave, Philemon, to his master (*Christianity Today* 1992). Meanwhile, Christ himself healed a slave without mentioning any problems with his position of forced servitude (Luke 7:1–10) (Morrison 1980).

Even Cartwright's aforementioned description of the disease drapetomania, which was said to occur when blacks were not sufficiently controlled, drew its authority as much from religion as from science. Cartwright (2004) argued that if slaves followed the Bible's call for them to remain submissive to their owners, then they would not be susceptible to drapetomania. Moreover, he argued that any attempt by whites to raise blacks to an equal station would be in opposition to God's will (Cartwright 2004).

Christianity was also used to uphold the brutal treatment of slaves. Dalcho (1823) suggested that, because the Bible did not provide examples under which leaving slavery would be acceptable, blacks should remain slaves regardless of how abusive their masters were. The *Richmond Enquirer* suggested that some punishment may be in order for killing slaves but pointed to a biblical account of Moses representing the murder of a slave as punishable by a fine but not worthy of capital punishment. However, the paper then went on to editorialize that an owner who killed a slave might already be sufficiently punished by the economic loss resulting from no longer having that slave available for work (Morrison 1980).

The fact that the Bible attests to the inherent equality of humans posed a potential problem to the prospect of enslaving black people. After all, a number of verses argue that all people are sinners and that God does not show partiality (e.g., Romans 2:11) (*The Holy Bible* 1993). Yet slave owners were undeterred, turning to 1 Corinthians 7:20's demand for every person to "abide in the same calling wherein he was called" (Morrison 1980:25). From this passage, slave owners suggested that, if people were already slaves (both individually and collectively), then they must remain as such to appease God—even if they converted to Christianity.

A common early debate among Christian colonists in America concerned whether baptism whitened. Slave owners had ample economic incentive to promote an interpretation of Christianity that held black people as perpetual servants regardless of their religious classification. Oddly, such arguments were often couched in the language of fairness. In 1664, Maryland's legislature passed a law to ensure that all black people serving as slaves would be obliged to continue serving until death; the text of that law justified lifetime servitude regardless of religious membership by arguing that, if blacks did not serve for life, they might pretend to have converted to Christianity for the sake of freedom, cheating their masters.

## Perpetuating the Racial Hierarchy

### Immigration

The influx of immigrants from a variety of countries in the nineteenth century posed new questions about racial boundaries. When the Irish fled to America after a catastrophic potato famine in the 1840s, some called them "white negroes," and white Protestants born in the United States were inclined to think of them as nonwhite, inferior, savage, and apelike (Cleaver 1997:160; Ignatiev 1995; Woodham-Smith 1992). Moreover, popular accounts seemed to blame the Irish for their perceived liabilities. James Silk Buckingham (1842:223–224), a British author who wrote a number of travel books, summed it up as follows:

> It is not to be wondered at, that the Americans conceive a very low estimate of the Irish people generally, when they have such unfortunate specimens of the nation as these almost constantly before their eyes . . . the large majority are not merely ignorant and poor—which might be their misfortune rather than their fault—but they are drunken, dirty, indolent, and riotous, so as to be objects of dislike and fear to all in whose neighborhood they congregate. . . . And yet, the remedy is within their own reach—to be clean, sober, and industrious, is surely within the power of every man.

The Irish were also stereotyped as criminals; one account suggests that Irish people comprised half of those arrested in New York during the 1840s and 1850s, leading police vans to be called "paddy wagons" (after the popular Irish name "Patrick") and instances of rioting as "donnybrooks," after the Donnybrook district in Dublin (Mulvaney 2017; Stern 1997).

In such a position, one might anticipate that Irish immigrants would form a coalition with other oppressed groups racialized as inferior, but they instead pursued opportunities to assimilate with those already racialized as white. Given that the Irish often sought some of the same jobs as free blacks, they were incentivized to support claims of black inferiority for their own economic benefit (Craughwell 2011). Appeals to racism provided the Irish with a path for coalition with those most interested in policing the boundaries of whiteness. The Irish arrived in sufficient numbers to constitute a substantial voting bloc for the Democratic Party, supporting the party's proslavery stance and condemning free blacks for taking "white jobs" (Cleaver 1997; Murphy 2010). Although a number of Irish immigrants fought for the Union army, memoirs from Irish soldiers do nothing to suggest that they did so in opposition to slavery. For example, one such solider wrote, "It has turned out to be an abolition war, and ninety-nine soldiers out of one hundred say that if the abolitionists are going to have to carry on this war, they will have to get a new army. They say they came out here to fight for the Union, and not for a pack of n—gers" (Ignatiev 1995:103).

Like the Irish, many early Italian immigrants to the United States left to escape poverty, and, thus, they tended to be relatively low in socioeconomic status upon arrival (Choate 2008). As such, they often lived in neighborhoods with, worked with, and were discussed alongside America's existing stigmatized ethnic and racial minorities (Guglielmo 2003). Henry James, a travel writer in the early 1900s observed immigrants coming into Ellis Island and reflected on the Italians as people who "over the whole land, strike us, I'm afraid, as, after the Negro and the Chinaman" (James 1907:462). They also faced unique criminality stereotypes based, in part, on stories about the Mafia (Richards 1999). The U.S. Immigration Commission even released a report in 1911 claiming that violence, robbery, blackmail, and extortion were "inherent in the Italian race" (Belluscio 2006:34).

Like the Irish, Italians faced disproportionate scrutiny by law enforcement, and, when the justice system failed to find them guilty, they could, at times, also find themselves subject to the sort of mob "justice" that African Americans had repeatedly encountered. In 1891, nine Italians acquitted of the murder of New Orleans police chief David Hennessy and two other Italians who happened to be there facing unrelated charges were hauled from jail and lynched. In response, future president Teddy Roosevelt called the situation "a rather good thing" (Falco 2012). *The New York Times* editorialized the victims as "sneaking and cowardly . . . the descendants of bandits and assassins," worse citizens than rattlesnakes, and needing to be lynched to avoid giving "a new license to the Mafia to continue its bloody practices" (*The New York Times* 1891:4).

Skepticism about Catholicism contributed to discrimination against Italian (as well as Irish) immigrants. American Protestants questioned whether the newly arrived Italians would prioritize loyalty to the Pope over loyalty to their new country (Zeitz 2015). Some, like Senator Ira Hersey, referred to Catholic Masses as pagan (Zeitz 2015). Moreover, Italians' Catholicism faced criticism as embodying anti-American ideals; as Burrus (2015) put it, "America was a bottom-up nation that believed in the power of the common man (provided he was white, straight, and male). Catholicism was a top-down religion that discouraged the common man from finding religious truth for himself." In the early 1900s, a newly reinvigorated Ku Klux Klan would target Catholic immigrants as an impediment to their goal of "one hundred percent Americanism" (Zeitz 2015).

Given the skepticism they already faced upon arrival, many Italians chose to keep a low profile. Maintaining that low profile often involved failing to speak out against racial hierarchy at best or collaboration in maintaining racial hierarchy at worst (Richards 1999). Regarding the latter, many Italians quickly recognized the benefits of being racialized as white in their new home. Thus, they defended race-based stratification while staking claim to being white themselves to maximize their social, economic, and political opportunities (Guglielmo 2003). Events like the Italian invasion of Ethiopia would further strain relations between Italian Americans and African Americans (Luconi 2006).

Unlike the Irish and Italians, early Chinese immigrants to the United States were initially welcomed, as their labor was needed to develop the country's railroads and facilitate a burgeoning mining industry developing around the gold rush. However, they quickly became the victims of their own success. When they worked in the mines, their labor was appreciated but only up to the point where it was not perceived as a threat to the employment prospects of existing domestic workers. When Chinese immigrants began to own their own successful small businesses in competition with existing domestic businesses, they faced considerable backlash (Delgado and Stefancic 1992). In response, the U.S. government negotiated the 1880 Chinese Exclusion Treaty to obtain recognition from the Chinese government of its right to "regulate, limit, or suspend" the immigration of Chinese laborers (PBS 2001). The Chinese Exclusion Act of 1882 soon followed, suspending Chinese immigration for ten years (PBS 2001).

In 1892, the Geary Act extended the suspension of Chinese immigration by another ten years, created new infrastructure for border enforcement, and introduced requirements that Chinese immigrants carry certificates of identity and certificates of residence. The Act's namesake, California congressman Thomas Geary, justified the need for these identifying documents by suggesting that it was otherwise impossible to tell one Chinese person from another (Lee 2003). Chinese workers found without a certificate of residence were subject to imprisonment with hard labor and deportation (Geary Act 1892). These legal moves were accompanied by the rise of arguments framing Asian immigration as "the yellow peril," threatening the stability and morality of the existing nation (Yen 2000).

In addition to prohibiting new immigration, the U.S. government worked to reduce the number of Chinese immigrants already in the United States. The Scott Act of 1888 prohibited Chinese laborers who had left the country from returning. It was upheld by the Supreme Court the following year in *Chae Chan Ping v. United States* (1889). However, in time, Asian immigrants would be recruited again for labor via the

Immigration Act of 1965. The U.S. government prioritized well-educated and relatively wealthier Asian immigrants from places like mainland China, Taiwan, and Singapore for skilled labor in scientific and technical fields (Yen 2000).

*Racial Categorization*

As America became more racially and ethnically diverse, legislation to more clearly delineate membership in different racial groups reemerged. Racial categorization laws generally served at least one of two purposes: (1) to establish and/or maintain a racial hierarchy that benefited whites or (2) to prevent future ambiguity over position in the racial hierarchy by preventing whites from marrying members of other racial groups. Virginia's 1924 Racial Integrity Act was a classic example of both. In a March 1924 issue of the *Virginia Health Bulletin*, State Registrar of Vital Statistics W. A. Plecker directly explained the law's intention to preserve discrimination against racial minorities, arguing that there were an estimated 10,000 to 20,000 "near white people, who are known to possess an intermixture of colored blood . . . still enough to prevent them from being white" who "have demanded the admittance of their children into the white schools, and in not a few cases have intermarried with white people" (Plecker 1924:1).

The Racial Integrity Act defined only those who had "no trace whatsoever of any blood other than Caucasian" as white with the exception of those with one-sixteenth or less "blood of the American Indian" ("An Act to Preserve Racial Integrity" 2018). That exception was made only because a number of Virginia residents who traced their lineage back to the first families of the state claimed ancestry from Pocahontas (Maillard 2007). The law also made it illegal for a white person to marry anyone who was not also white or "with no other admixture of blood than white and American Indian" ("An Act to Preserve Racial Integrity" 2018).

Enacting legislation to keep racial groups separate and distinct was hardly new to Americans. Numerous laws had already attempted to keep whites from intermarrying with racial minorities. The Maryland General Assembly passed the first American anti-miscegenation law in 1664, and similar laws followed in Virginia (1691), Massachusetts (1705), North Carolina (1715), South Carolina (1717), Delaware (1721), and Pennsylvania (1725) (African American Registry 2013). In *Dred Scott v. Sandford* (1856), Chief Justice Taney of the Supreme Court suggested that such laws were intended to ensure that, even though African Americans were moving out of enslavement, a barrier would remain between whites and blacks.

The diversification of America through immigration fueled a new wave of attempts to legally enforce racial divides. In 1871, Congressman Andrew King proposed a constitutional amendment banning interracial marriage (Stein 2004). Neither this amendment nor other attempts to introduce similar amendments were successful, but many states passed, expanded on, or enforced anti-miscegenation laws in the decades that followed. These included twenty-nine states that banned marriages between whites and blacks, fourteen states that banned the intermarriage of whites and "Mongoloid persons," three states that banned black and American Indian marriages, and four that forbade white and American Indian marriages (Browning 1951:31). Such laws often proceeded from a strange mix of fear and tradition; it has been alleged that the North Carolina statute forbidding black–American Indian intermarriage resulted from a belief in a legend that the Cherokee of Robeson County were descendants of Crotau Indians who had married white colonists from Sir Walter Raleigh's lost colony, meaning that Cherokee-black intermarriage would constitute white–black intermarriage. Although not all states had anti-miscegenation statutes, many of the states without them had so few nonwhite residents that they were less concerned about the prospect of interracial marriage (Browning 1951).

*Participation in Governance*

Prior to the Civil War, black suffrage was limited in the North; blacks could vote only in Maine, Massachusetts, New Hampshire, Rhode Island, and Vermont or in New York with at least $250 worth of property (National Park Service 2009). Referenda on black voting rights in Connecticut, Kansas, Michigan, New York, Ohio, and Wisconsin failed (Lawson 1999). Moreover, blacks lacked the right to vote throughout the South. However, under the 1867 Military Reconstruction Acts, Congress required the ten former Confederate states that had not yet reentered the Union to hold constitutional conventions in which (1) all black and white male citizens could vote and (2) a state constitution would be approved that included voting rights for black men. Subsequent legislatures in these states were required to ratify the Fourteenth Amendment that conceptually extended citizenship to blacks but did not protect voting rights (National Park Service 2009). It was not until ratification of the Fifteenth Amendment in 1870 that black men were constitutionally enfranchised, and three of the states needed for ratification (Virginia, Mississippi, and Texas) complied only in order to regain their congressional representation (Matthews 2006). Black women (alongside all American women) continued to lack the right to vote until the ratification of the Nineteenth Amendment in 1920 (Marsico 2011).

With expansion of the vote came new opportunities for black men to hold local, state, and national political offices in the South. More than 1,400 black men served as justices of the peace, magistrates, sheriffs, state secretaries of state, representatives in state assemblies, mayors, members of Congress, and in other positions under Reconstruction (National Park Service 2009). Yet this progress was met with threats and actual incidences of violence toward black voters and ballot box manipulation to dilute black voting power. By 1890, Democrats in states like Tennessee and Arkansas had devised new ways to disenfranchise black voters, including the introduction of secret ballots and a poll tax requirement (Perman 2001). Prior to secret balloting, political parties printed and distributed ballots with their candidates' names on them, but secret balloting provisions prohibited the preprinted ballots and required use of complicated official ballots whose use constituted a literacy test of sorts. Poll taxes eliminated voting by those with insufficient financial means. A new wave of exclusionary policies would follow between 1890 and 1908 when Mississippi, South Carolina, Louisiana, North Carolina, Alabama, Virginia, and Georgia all passed constitutional amendments introducing literacy tests to exclude black voters. Literacy tests were often accompanied by grandfather clauses that allowed illiterate whites to bypass them. These grandfather clauses stipulated that voters were not required to pass a literacy test if registered to vote by January 1, 1867 (a date deliberately chosen because it preceded the Military Reconstruction Acts and the Fifteenth Amendment's enfranchisement of blacks) (National Park Service 2009).

Blacks were not the only racial minorities whose right to vote was contested. Mexicans in Arizona, California, New Mexico, Texas, and Nevada who had received citizenship in 1848 under the Treaty of Guadalupe-Hidalgo could technically vote but were kept from exercising that right via English proficiency, literacy, and property requirements. In 1884, the Supreme Court ruled in *Elk v. Wilkins* that a Native American man born in Nebraska was not a citizen and could not vote, because he owed his allegiance to a tribe rather than the United States (American Civil Liberties Union 2005). In post–Civil War California, Chinese immigrants were denied the right to vote even as the Irish and Italians freely exercised it (Relative to Chinese Americans in California 2014). In general, racial and ethnic minorities experienced robust and protracted efforts to deny them the right to vote.

*Education*

From the beginning, primary and secondary education in colonial America served as a mechanism for control of racial minorities. In some cases, education facilitated forced assimilation (as was the case for Native American children who were compulsorily removed from their homes and enrolled in schools where they were directed to abandon their culture in favor of European American culture) with the goal of undercutting Native

American resistance to European colonization (Feagin and Feagin 2011). Education for enslaved Africans was designed to impart only what was necessary for them to labor with maximal efficiency without facilitating goals of escaping (Woodson 2010).

Prior to European colonization, Native Americans had developed extensive informal education systems to reinforce cultural values (such as respect for older adults and leaders) and prepare children to one day take up needed vocations (Yeboah 2005). As colonization proceeded, these educational practices were supplanted by an educational system in which Native American children were expected to dress in a European style, go by European names, and convert to Christianity. If they spoke their native languages, then they faced punishment (Feagin and Feagin 2011). These practices aimed to dissuade future generations from rebelling.

Similarly, educational practices directed at African Americans were designed to impart very specific information for the benefit of whites. Pragmatically, slave owners found it expedient to teach slaves English so that they could more easily follow orders and read the Bible (on whose authority slavery was often justified). However, owners also harbored concerns that knowledge would stoke a desire for freedom, so they pressured legislatures to curtail black education. In the mid-1700s, Southern states passed a variety of laws closing black schools and prohibiting teachers from assisting black learners. Some states went so far as to make it illegal for educated blacks to teach their own children (Woodson 2010). Even so, Nat Turner and Denmark Vesey—orchestrators of a rebellion in which slaves killed more than fifty people and were executed in similar numbers for participating—were literate, stoking white fears further (Irons 2002).

Punishments for reading and writing against one's owner's wishes could be draconian. Some slaves who learned to read were beaten, and one slave in Louisiana recounted how those who learned to write would have a thumb and a finger cut off

(Irons 2002). Even slaves whose owners permitted their literacy took great care to avoid suggesting that their ability to read or write constituted a change in social status. One of Thomas Jefferson's slaves, Hannah, wrote him a letter about the arrival of furniture that concluded: "Master I do not [know if] my ignorant letter will be much encouragement to you as knows I am a poor ignorant creature" (Schiller 2008).

Although integrated secondary schools have technically existed since the establishment of Lowell High School in Massachusetts in 1831, sustained national integration would not occur until many decades later (Howe 2015). Just three years before Lowell High School was built, Thomas Dartmouth Rice began performing in blackface as "Jim Crow," a character who gave a stereotypical portrayal of black slaves as clumsy and stupid (Andrews 2014). States and localities throughout the United States passed Jim Crow laws that, in addition to segregating prisons, the military, and public transportation, segregated public schools. The Supreme Court validated the provision of "separate but equal" facilities for blacks and whites in its 1896 ruling in *H. A. Plessy v. J. H. Ferguson* (Library of Congress 2018).

The Supreme Court's willingness to support segregation did not necessarily imply acceptance of state laws explicitly differentiating between black and white school funding. In fact, the court had previously invalidated a North Carolina law in 1883 that would have given white schools a substantial financial advantage by letting localities allocate white taxes only to white schools and black taxes only to black schools (Klarman 2004). Yet states found a way to differentiate anyway; Alabama passed legislation that apportioned state education funds based on the total number of students in a locality (regardless of race) but let trustees determine what constituted fair distribution. In this way, funding could be diverted to white schools.

Postsecondary education was also deeply embedded in the racial stratification system. A number of colleges and universities were funded by plantation owners using proceeds from the slave trade, and these institutions often owned slaves who constructed the buildings and cared for the grounds. In the early years of Dartmouth College, there were more enslaved black people than students, faculty, administrators, or trustees on campus. Yale used the proceeds from slaves it inherited to pay for its first graduate programs (Smith and Ellis 2017). Yet blacks were barred from attending classes in the South and were restricted in their attendance in the North via quota systems. Moreover, in parts of the North, free blacks were barred from establishing schools for black children, and existing school-houses were subject to arson (Woodson 2010).

These institutions of supposedly higher learning also con-tributed to the maintenance of white supremacy through their instruction. Colleges and universities frequently attempted to justify the morality of the slave trade and lauded it as responsi-ble for America's economic success (Wilder 2013). These same institutions would also be instrumental in furthering pseudo-scientific eugenicist arguments, suggesting that racial and eth-nic minorities were genetically inferior and unfit to marry or procreate with whites. Universities like Harvard, Columbia, Cornell, and Brown would offer courses in eugenics; by 1928, there were 400 such courses enrolling around 20,000 students (Knight 2003).

*Labor after Slavery*

With the passage of the Thirteenth Amendment to the Con-stitution in 1865, slavery became illegal. Newly freed African Americans needed a way to secure food, shelter, and other basic necessities. After consulting with black leaders in Savannah, Georgia, Union general William T. Sherman responded with Special Field Order No. 15. The order called for the provision of forty acres of land seized from Confederates for each former slave along the coasts of South Carolina, Georgia, and Florida. These lands were commissioned to be self-governing and to exclude white inhabitants with the exception of military per-sonnel stationed there. Although a few communities formed in response to this order (such as a group of 1,000 in Skidaway Island, Georgia), Abraham Lincoln's presidential successor, Andrew Johnson, overturned the order and returned the land to its former owners (Gates 2013).

Without the prospect of reparations, many former slaves returned to work on the very plantations where they had been forcibly held—this time as sharecroppers. Former slaves would take out credit to cover food, housing, and farming supplies; sell the crops each harvest; and use the proceeds to repay their debts. However, creditors would often undervalue the crop yield, and landowners could raise the rent as they saw fit. As a result, sharecroppers often found themselves forced to remain in their position, continually paying off the rising debt resulting from the shortfall between the costs to maintain the farm and support themselves and the amount of money they could obtain by selling the crops they grew.

Newly reinstituted laws throughout the South controlling black Americans' behaviors helped ensure the viability of cash crops like cotton; in several states, blacks without written proof of employment could be arrested as vagrants, increasing the pressure to enter into disadvantageous employment situations (Nelson 2015). Conveniently for plantation owners, the penalty for vagrancy was often forced labor on the plantations, ensuring that former slaves would continue to supply labor for the South one way or another. In South Carolina, blacks were even charged a prohibitively expensive yearly tax for the privilege of working in any profession other than farmer or servant (South Carolina 1866). Sharecropping was also one of the few jobs that blacks could get without facing pushback from white workers. Whites engaged in strikes against the employment of blacks as railroad firemen, machinists, carpenters, telephone linemen, cotton mill operatives, and bricklayers (Ayers 2007).

During the 1880s, plantation owners also gained access to a growing convict lease program. Blacks accused of a crime were encouraged to "confess judgment" (similar to a modern plea agreement) (Blackmon 2009:67). To avoid harsher penalties expected upon conviction, blacks could accept responsibility for a crime and be assessed a bond in lieu of a trial. Then, a white landlord could pay the bond and secure the defendant's ostensible freedom in exchange for labor to pay back the bond cost. By passing a slew of laws criminalizing various activities by blacks (such as talking loudly around white women or owning a firearm), Southern states were able to create a substantial pool of potential laborers for white plantations (Blackmon 2009).

Eventually, legislative and technological changes led to the phasing out of widespread sharecropping and an increasing likelihood that blacks would work in factories rather than on farms. In 1938, President Roosevelt signed the Agricultural Adjustment Act that was intended to stabilize crop prices by paying farmers to plant fewer crops, with a portion of the subsidy going to sharecroppers. Reducing the acreage used for crop production resulted in the displacement of many sharecroppers, and landowners often kept the subsidies intended for sharecroppers for themselves. As mechanization (such as the development of mechanical cotton pickers) reduced the need for labor, fewer sharecroppers were employed. Finally, a 1967 minimum wage law intended to reduce black sharecroppers' debts to white plantation owners resulted in the owners hiring fewer sharecroppers for fewer hours to keep them from establishing economic independence (Wright Austin 2006).

Nonagrarian black employment was only somewhat less tenuous; industrialization brought a number of blacks to the North where they competed with recent immigrants for low-paying, difficult, and dangerous jobs in the factories. Both blacks and recent immigrants from places like England, Ireland, and Germany tended to be concentrated in less remunerative, more difficult, and more dangerous vocations; among steelworkers, for example, nearly one-fourth of recent immigrants were injured or killed on the job (Brody 1998). Blacks, in particular, were formally or informally barred from entering a variety of vocations. For example, in the lumber industry, black men were generally chosen for the most physically arduous jobs, while white men were preferred for managerial roles (Jones 2005). Once employed, blacks faced a number of disparities compared to their peers. During the Great Depression, blacks were more likely to be fired and faced unemployment rates two or three times higher than whites. Assistance programs also distributed aid differentially by race; blacks received less from New Deal programs and were even turned away from some soup kitchens (Rosenberg 2006).

Despite sharing some experiences of deprivation based on class position, white workers often forwent opportunities for solidarity with black workers; not only did they enjoy racial advantages in accessing certain positions, but they also saw blacks as undermining white labor movements because they were frequently employed by factory owners as strikebreakers. Instead of inviting the strikebreakers to strike alongside their labor unions and associations, white workers responded by banning blacks from these organizations (Healey and O'Brien 2015). Major labor organizations like the American Federation of Labor also excluded Chinese immigrants and supported literacy tests for immigrants.

In addition to competition and outright hostility from white workers, blacks (as well as other racial and ethnic minorities) had to navigate white employers' racial preferences in hiring. Even as late as in the 1960s, job ads in major newspapers like the *Chicago Tribune* and the *Los Angeles Times* overtly specified that employers wanted white applicants (Darity and Mason 1998). It wasn't until 1964 that the Civil Rights Act promised legal protections against race-based employment discrimination, and it proved as difficult to enforce as to enact (Schenkkan 2014).

### Transportation

American history is filled with examples of how racial minorities' freedom of movement was restricted. Even before the development of public transportation in the United States, under slavery, it was illegal in many places to leave a master's property without a pass. Further, slaves were generally forbidden from traveling from one plantation to another plantation at night (Waldrep 1998).

With the Jim Crow era came formal restrictions on the use of public transportation. Seats on train cars, streetcars, and steamboats were segregated by race, and dining tables for blacks were sometimes behind a curtain or partition to further separate them from tables designated for whites. Public buses were similarly segregated (Klarman 2004). These restrictions led to transportation boycotts throughout the South in Virginia, Georgia, Tennessee, Louisiana, North Carolina, South Carolina, Texas, Florida, and other states, as well as petitions to local political leaders. Blacks also resisted by organizing their own systems of transportation, running everything from wagons to passenger vans (Meier and Rudwick 1969). Meanwhile, those who were not categorized as "colored" but did not necessarily classify themselves as white often found themselves in ambiguous situations. For example, Asian Americans would sometimes sit at the back of the bus and then be told to sit in the white section (Bow 2010).

Black resistance to transportation restrictions would continue for decades, with arguably the most well-known example being the bus boycott that followed Rosa Parks's arrest in Montgomery, Alabama, in 1955. In Alabama, whites had first priority to the middle section of the bus, but blacks could sit there if no white person was standing. Parks was arrested after she refused to give up her seat there to a white passenger. The case was eventually appealed to the Supreme Court, where public transportation segregation was ruled unconstitutional in 1956 (Theoharis 2015).

Transportation systems perpetuated racial hierarchy in the United States in other ways as well. Specific railroad tracks and avenues often served as dividing lines between black and white neighborhoods. During the Jim Crow era, such transportation features were used by banks to determine where they would and would not extend home loans and by local officials to determine who would go to which schools with an eye toward segregation. Further, new highways were built to allow whites to live in suburban areas and commute to cities for work (i.e., white flight). These highways diminished the tax base needed to support infrastructure for remaining residents (generally the poor and people of color) and were often built in ways that deliberately isolated black communities from resources and amenities that were previously much more accessible (Badger and Cameron 2015).

*Housing*

A variety of deliberate practices have created and maintained racial segregation and discrimination in housing. During slavery, black slaves were generally housed in separate quarters from their masters, and the conditions of such housing varied widely. White plantation owners tended to sleep on feather beds, whereas slaves often had no bed at all and slept on mattresses of grass, old clothing, or rags. People of color were permitted to live in cities like Augusta, Georgia, only if they (1) were owned by or working for a white person or (2) obtained a license from City Council that required posting a bond of up to $100 as assurance of good behavior (Douglass et al. 2018).

Governmental programs also contributed to racial segregation in housing. The Great Depression made home purchases and even new apartment rentals inaccessible to families across racial groups, while World War II made construction materials for affordable housing less available as resources were redirected to the war effort. Just as they did in times of plenty, whites also enjoyed relative advantages even in times of want; the U.S. government under President Franklin D. Roosevelt created civilian housing programs, but blacks were excluded from some housing developments, while other housing options were segregated by race. In some areas that had long been multiracial, the Public Works Administration demolished existing buildings and built new segregated spaces. In such spaces, the white-designated areas usually included more amenities like community centers and playgrounds (Rothstein 2017).

The Home Owners' Loan Corporation (HOLC), sponsored by the federal government in 1933 to expand American homeownership, exacerbated the problem by institutionalizing redlining. HOLC assessed neighborhood quality via four grades, with the lowest being red; not only were predominantly black neighborhoods coded red, but even neighborhoods with a relatively small percentage of black residents were assigned the lowest category. Since private banks relied on HOLC assessments of neighborhood quality, obtaining a home loan in a black neighborhood became exceedingly difficult (Massey and Denton 1993).

In 1937, the National Housing Act created the Federal Housing Administration (FHA), which backed 90 percent of the value of the collateral for home loans issued by private banks. This added security allowed banks to lower interest rates and accept down payments as low as 10 percent of the home value, making property ownership much more attainable. Although FHA mortgages were more financially feasible for many families, they too were administered in a discriminatory fashion; the FHA used HOLC neighborhood assessments to determine eligibility and even encouraged neighborhoods to develop covenants barring ethnic and racial minorities from living in white neighborhoods—ostensibly to protect home values (Massey and Denton 1993).

Housing policies favoring whites led to a lower need for white access to public housing. As spaces remained vacant in white-only projects and housing authorities found themselves advertising to fill them, black-only housing projects faced more demand than available space could accommodate, generating long waitlists. Still, blacks continued to be excluded from housing projects designated for whites, and attempts to build additional housing for blacks in or near white neighborhoods frequently faced pushback. For example, in 1976, the Supreme Court ruled that the Chicago Housing Authority (CHA) chose sites in a manner designed to perpetuate racial segregation. The CHA would suggest sites for housing but give local aldermen the right to veto such suggestions in their wards. Thus, almost all sites that would have integrated white neighborhoods were rejected, while only 10 percent of sites in black neighborhoods were rejected (Rothstein 2017). Thus, the trend toward suburbanization was a predominantly white one; by 1980, 65 percent of whites lived in the suburbs as compared with only 34 percent of blacks (Massey and Denton 1993).

*Criminal Justice*

Ostensibly, the criminal justice system is expected to fairly and objectively uphold community standards, but racial minorities have often been subject to both vigilante action outside the formal justice system and discrimination within it. Between 1882 and 1968, 4,743 people were lynched—72.7 percent of whom were black and most of whom lived in the South (NAACP 2018). These lynchings often occurred in response to allegations that a black man raped a white woman—even when there was far more suspicion than evidence (Harvey 2003). The 27.3 percent of lynchings in which the victim was white were often carried out as extralegal punishment for murder, cattle theft, or some other crime. However, whites were also lynched for aiding blacks or for publicly opposing lynchings (NAACP 2018).

The formal criminal justice system provided little respite from racial discrimination for a number of reasons. Crime has often been reported in racially biased ways; for example, rape victims are more likely to report black perpetrators than white perpetrators, making it seem as though black crime represents a higher proportion of overall crime than is accurate. In addition, police surveillance has typically been higher in minority-majority communities, meaning that racial minorities are more likely to be seen (and therefore stopped or arrested) for deviance than whites regardless of rates of commission (Mann 1993).

Sentencing has also reflected racial bias. A meta-analysis of execution rates from 1930 to 1967 and death-sentencing rates from 1967 to 1978 exposed how blacks convicted of homicide actually received more lenient sentences on average in regions other than the South, but blacks convicted of homicide of any victim or rape of a white victim were more likely to be executed in the South. Across all regions, offenders who targeted a white victim were more likely to be executed than offenders who committed a crime against a black victim (Kleck 1981).

Racial discrimination has occurred not only in reporting, surveillance, and sentencing but also over the course of imprisonment. After an 1883 Supreme Court decision tasked localities with enforcement of the 1875 Civil Rights Act, Southern states were able to discriminate against blacks with significantly less federal scrutiny. This had a dramatic impact on the treatment of blacks serving prison sentences. Black prisoners were disproportionately leased to companies to perform manual labor on farms and in mines. The prisoners were expected to meet performance quotas based on their physical fitness and ability while often being underfed, overworked, and denied access to adequate health care. When they failed to meet work quotas, they were routinely whipped, and hundreds died from the harsh conditions or from explosions, fires, and other mining accidents. Even then, segregation continued to be enforced; for example, in Alabama, it was illegal to chain black and white prisoners together (Blackmon 2009).

*Health and Health Care*

As Byrd and Clayton (2001:115) put it, "African Americans, since arriving as slaves, have had the worst health care, the worst health status, and the worst health outcome of any racial or ethnic group in the U.S." When Africans were shipped to the colonies as slaves, if they demonstrated signs that they might not make the journey (such as symptoms of sleeping sickness), they would be thrown overboard. Upon arrival in the colonies, slaves found that medical practices were dangerous for everyone, but they were at particular risk. Weakened by overwork and exposure to the elements in their ramshackle lodgings, slaves were more susceptible to death from common medical practices like bloodletting. They were also experimented on when doctors devised new medications or surgical procedures. Slaves were the unwilling test subjects of experiments on everything from heat exhaustion to tetanus (Washington 2006).

European colonists' arrival in North America also nearly eliminated Native Americans. Colonists introduced them to smallpox, influenza, measles, typhus, malaria, leprosy, cholera, bubonic plague, gonorrhea, and other deadly diseases. Thanks to colonist-initiated epidemics (particularly of smallpox), wars, and political decisions that threatened access to food and security, the Native population was decimated. It is estimated that as much as 95 percent of the original eight to twelve million inhabitants died (Institute of Medicine 2003).

As the years progressed, there were some improvements. After the Civil War, the Freedman's Bureau and other measures finally gave blacks greater access to medical facilities after years of inadequate options and denial of service throughout the health care system (Institute of Medicine 2003). However, unscrupulous practices continued to endanger racial minorities. Medical experimentation continued unabated; in a particularly striking example, from 1932 to the early 1970s, the Public Health Service recruited black men with syphilis by offering to treat their "bad blood." Instead, they were intentionally denied access to treatment for syphilis (such as penicillin, which had been commonly available by the late 1940s) so that scientists could study the progression of the disease (Centers for Disease Control and Prevention 2015). White doctors also recommended procedures that reflected their own racism more so than represented necessary medical intervention (such as sterilization of the "unfit," with racial categorization contributing to the definition of who was seen as unfit) (Institute of Medicine 2003).

A second wave of racial progress in health care came during the period from the last few years of the 1960s to 1980 when hospital desegregation increased access to public hospitals. However, access to private hospitals remained more difficult for racial minorities than for whites given economic disparities. Moreover, incomplete enforcement of civil rights laws allowed discrimination to continue in the treatment of minority patients (Institute of Medicine 2003).

## The Arts

The arts have often been dominated by white representation and characterized by negative depictions of other racial groups. *The Birth of a Nation* was one of the most famous movies in American history, the first to be shown at the White House, and the first to be projected for Supreme Court justices and members of Congress. Yet it portrayed black men (many of whom were represented by white actors wearing blackface) as uncouth, unintelligent, and dangerous. In contrast, Ku Klux Klan members were depicted as gallant heroes for intimidating blacks out of voting and lynching them for pursuing marriage with white women. Subsequent movies with black actors or characters depicted blacks primarily in positions of servitude from slaves to nannies (Stokes 2007).

Other racial minorities were also mocked or sidelined in films. Paralleling blackface, yellowface emerged alongside Chinese American immigration as white actors portrayed Asian characters who reinforced negative stereotypes. White actors satirized Asian American makeup, speech patterns, and clothing styles (Moon 2005). Movies in the early 1900s depicted Arab Americans as violent and dangerous or rich but stupid (Shora 2009). Native Americans were often also depicted as dangerous as well as uncivilized; the prevalence of negative stereotypes about Native Americans in movies was so widespread and objectionable that they actually prompted a delegation of Chippewa to demand more regulations from President Taft and motivated the Shoshone, Cheyenne, and Arapaho to address their concern to the Bureau of Indian Affairs (Aleiss 2005).

Art museums highlight additional problems in the visual arts with racial injustice. Most mainstream museum curators are white, most museum shows feature white artists, and work by African American artists sells for less in the art market than work from equally well-known white artists (Mendelsohn and Thackara 2016). Historically, white figures have tended to be featured front and center in artwork, whereas black figures would appear off to the side or in the background, often in servile roles (Francis-Crow 2017).

In music, racial and ethnic minorities have faced impediments as well. For example, early European immigrants to America disparagingly compared Chinese music to animal sounds (Moon 2005). In the 1950s to 1970s, COINTELPRO (the same FBI program that sent a letter to Martin Luther King Jr. in an attempt to convince him to commit suicide) also followed and surveilled a number of black jazz musicians, investigating them for ties to communism and civil rights activism. For example, the FBI kept tabs on famous bandleader Duke Ellington for almost forty years (Denton 2017).

*Sports*

Racism has also manifested itself in collegiate and professional sports. The majority of sports teams at historically white colleges and universities did not integrate until the 1950s. At the professional level, integration was similarly delayed—until 1945 for the National Football League (when Kenny Washington and Woody Strode joined the Cleveland Rams), until 1947 for Major League Baseball (when African American Jackie Robinson joined the Brooklyn Dodgers' farm team, the Montreal Royals) and the National Basketball Association (when Japanese American Wataru Misaka joined the New York Knicks), until 1958 for the National Hockey League (when Willie O'Ree joined the Boston Bruins), and until 1961 for the Professional Golfers Association (when Charlie Sifford joined). Once on a collegiate or professional sports team, minority athletes often faced stereotypes and ill treatment. For example, dark-skinned players have historically been more often praised for their physical skills, whereas light-skinned players were noticed for their mental abilities. Moreover, racial minority players have been less likely to be selected for athletic leadership positions (such as quarterback on a football team), been paid less for their contributions at the professional level, and been subject to racist taunting (such as in cases where fans throw bananas at African American players) (Foy 2017).

Yet, during the 1960s in particular, a number of athletes used their platforms to push for racial equality. Wilma Rudolph became widely known as the fastest woman in the world after becoming the first American woman to win three track-and-field gold medals in a single year at the 1960 Olympics. With preparations in progress for two homecoming parades to mark her return—one for whites and one for blacks—she made it clear that she would not be participating in a segregated parade. As a result, the one parade that welcomed her back became the first racially integrated event in Clarksville, Tennessee (Chang 2010).

During the 1968 Olympics in Mexico City, Tommie Smith and John Carlos used the medal ceremony in which the former received a gold medal and the latter a bronze medal to give the Black Power salute. As a result, they received death threats and were suspended from the American team, but they made a statement on one of the world's biggest stages about America's failure to provide equal rights regardless of race (Cosgrove 2014).

In some cases, athletes have used the attention paid to their accomplishments to highlight the racist ideologies promulgated by institutions. In 1969, fourteen black University of Wyoming players planned a protest against the racism of the Church of Jesus Christ of Latter-day Saints at a game against the church-owned Brigham Young University. The church still had not officially renounced its doctrine that black people were cursed by God (and, in fact, would not do so until 2013) (Green 2017). When they asked for the permission of their white coach, Lloyd Eaton, he kicked them off the team. However, karma vindicated them to some extent when the football program promptly went from elite status to struggling with the removal of the players (Keeler 2015).

*Consumer Goods and the Reification of Whiteness*

Given how strictly racial classifications have historically been po-
liced, it is perhaps unsurprising that a consumer market emerged
around products reifying whiteness as ideal. Soap commercials
from the late 1800s depicted white children asking black children
why their mothers did not wash them with a particular brand of
soap—implying that the soap would wash their blackness away
(DuRocher 2011). Asian Americans in advertising during this
time period were depicted as scheming and devious, while Native Americans were associated with alcoholism and barbarism
(Davis 2017). In the decades that followed, blacks in American
advertising were often portrayed as little more than props for ads
intended for whites. Even worse, at times, racial minorities were
displayed as products themselves; human zoos in the early 1900s
displayed Sioux tribal members in Cincinnati and Africans in
New York (Davis 2017).

When companies began to more directly market to blacks in
the 1970s, the approach was often fraught with racial stereotypes, as when McDonald's touted itself as a place where tipping was not expected (Cruz 2015). In addition, "g-dropping,"
or the omission of "g" at the end of a word traditionally ending
in "ing," has been mocked as a characteristic of Ebonics, and
ads featuring blacks at McDonald's included lines like "On the
real, kids can really dig gettin' down with McDonald's" (Cruz
2015; Ronkin and Karn 1999).

## Conclusion

Colonialism was instrumental in establishing race as an over-
arching basis for stratification in America. European colonizers
used race to justify their seizure of land, build and maintain
forced labor, and quell resistance to their expansion. In the
years that followed, race patterned social stratification in a variety of contexts, such as science, religion, immigration, education, employment, transportation, housing, criminal justice,
the arts, sports, and the marketing of consumer goods in ways
that perpetuated the existing racial hierarchy to the benefit

of whites. Chapter 2 extends this discussion into present-day problems and controversies stemming from racism in the afore-mentioned contexts and examines potential solutions.

## References

"An Act to Preserve Racial Integrity." Retrieved January 7, 2018. http://www2.vcdh.virginia.edu/lewisandclark/students/projects/monacans/Contemporary_Monacans/racial.html.

African American Registry. 2013. "Anti-Amalgamation Law Passed." Retrieved January 6, 2018. http://www.aaregistry.org/historic_events/view/anti-amalgamation-law-passed.

Aleiss, Angela. 2005. *Making the White Man's Indian: Native Americans and Hollywood Movies.* Westport, CT: Praeger.

Allen, Theodore W. 1997. *The Invention of the White Race: The Origin of Racial Oppression in Anglo-America.* New York, NY: Verso.

American Civil Liberties Union. 2005. "Voting Rights Act Timeline." Retrieved February 2, 2018. https://www.aclu.org/files/assets/voting_rights_act_timeline20111222.pdf.

Anderson, Patrick D. 2012. "Supporting Caste: The Origins of Racism in Colonial Virginia." *Grand Valley Journal of History* 2(1):1–17.

Andrews, Evan. 2014. "Was Jim Crow a Real Person?" Retrieved January 11, 2018. http://www.history.com/news/ask-history/was-jim-crow-a-real-person.

Asante-Muhammed, Dedrick, Chuck Collins, Josh Hoxie, and Emanuel Nieves. 2016. "The Ever-Growing Gap: Without Change, African American and Latino Families Won't Match White Wealth for Centuries." Retrieved September 14, 2016. http://www.ips-dc.org/wp-content/uploads/2016/08/The-Ever-Growing-Gap-CFED_IPS-Final-1.pdf.

Ayers, Edward L. 2007. *The Promise of the New South: Life after Reconstruction.* Oxford, UK: Oxford University Press.

Badger, Emily, and Darla Cameron. 2015. "How Railroads, Highways, and Other Man-Made Lines Racially Divide America's Cities." Retrieved March 5, 2018. https://www .washingtonpost.com/news/wonk/wp/2015/07/16/how-railroads-highways-and-other-man-made-lines-racially-divide-americas-cities/.

Ball, Milner S. 1987. "Constitution, Court, Indian Tribes." *American Bar Foundation Research Journal* 12(1):1–140.

Baptist, Edward E. 2014. *The Half Has Never Been Told: Slavery and the Making of American Capitalism*. New York: Basic Books.

Belluscio, Steven J. 2006. *To Be Suddenly White: Literary Realism and Racial Passing*. Columbia: University of Missouri Press.

Berger, Bethany R. 2009. "Red: Racism and the American Indian." *UCLA Law Review* 56:591–656.

Bhopal, Raj. 2007. "The Beautiful Skull and Blumenbach's Errors: The Birth of the Scientific Concept of Race." *BMJ* 335(7633):1308–1309.

Blackmon, Douglas A. 2009. *Slavery by Another Name: The Re-Enslavement of Black Americans from the Civil War to World War II*. New York: Anchor.

Blumenbach, Johann Friedrich. 1865. *The Anthropological Treatises of Johann Friedrich Blumenbach*, translated by Thomas Bendyshe. London: Longman, Green, Longman, Roberts, and Green.

Bobo, Lawrence D., Camille Z. Charles, Maria Krysan, and Alicia D. Simmons. 2012. "The Real Record on Racial Attitudes," pp. 38–83, in *Social Trends in American Life: Findings from the General Social Survey since 1972*, edited by Peter V. Marsden. Princeton, NJ: Princeton University Press.

Bow, Leslie. 2010. *Partly Colored: Asian Americans and Racial Anomaly in the Segregated South*. New York: New York University Press.

Brody, David. 1998. *Steelworkers in America: The Nonunion Era*. Cambridge, MA: Harvard University Press.

Brown, Thomas F., and Leah C. Sims. 2006. "'To Swear Him Free': Ethnic Memory as Social Capital in Eighteenth-Century Freedom Petitions," pp. 81–108, in *Colonial Chesapeake: New Perspectives*, edited by Debra Meyers and Melanie Perreault. Lanham, MD: Lexington Books.

Browning, James R. 1951. "Anti-Miscegenation Laws in the United States." *Duke Bar Journal* 1(1):26–41.

Buckingham, J. S. 1842. *The Eastern and Western States of America*. London: Fisher, Son, & Co.

Burrus, Trevor. 2015. "Fighting the 'Papists' and the 'Popery': When America Was Anti-Catholic." Retrieved December 30, 2017. https://www.forbes.com/sites/trevorburrus/2015/09/24/fighting-the-papists-and-the-popery-when-america-was-anti-catholic/.

Byrd, W. M., and L. A. Clayton. 2001. "Race, Medicine, and Health Care in the United States: A Historical Survey." *Journal of the National Medical Association* 93(3 Suppl):11S–34S.

Calloway, Collin G. 1995. *The American Revolution in Indian Country: Crisis and Diversity in Native American Communities*. Cambridge, UK: Cambridge University Press.

Calloway, Collin G. 2008. "American Indians and the American Revolution." Retrieved June 29, 2017. https://www.nps.gov/revwar/about_the_revolution/american_indians.html.

Cartwright, Samuel. 2004. "Report on the Diseases and Physical Peculiarities of the Negro Race," pp. 28–39, in *Health, Disease, and Illness: Concepts in Medicine*, edited by Arthur L. Caplan, James J. McCartney, and Dominic A. Sisti. Washington, DC: Georgetown University Press.

Centers for Disease Control and Prevention. 2015. "The Tuskegee Timeline." Retrieved March 24, 2019. https://www.cdc.gov/tuskegee/timeline.htm.

*Chae Chan Ping v. United States.* 1889. 130 U.S. 581.

Chang, Juju. 2010. "Juju's Inspiration: Wilma Rudolph Ran for Her Country, against Discrimination." Retrieved July 1, 2019. https://abcnews.go.com/GMA/Inspirations/jujus-inspiration-runner-wilma-rudolf/story?id=10689219.

Choate, Mark I. 2008. *Emigrant Nation: The Making of Italy Abroad.* Boston, MA: Harvard University Press.

*Christianity Today.* 1992. "Why Did So Many Christians Support Slavery?" Retrieved July 28, 2017. www.christianitytoday.com/history/issues/issue-33/why-christians-supported-slavery.html.

Cleaver, Kathleen Neal. 1997. "The Antidemocratic Power of Whiteness," pp. 157–163, in *Critical White Studies: Looking behind the Mirror,* edited by Richard Delgado and Jean Stefancic. Philadelphia, PA: Temple University Press.

Cosgrove, Ben. 2014. "The Black Power Salute That Rocked the 1968 Olympics." Retrieved July 1, 2019. https://time.com/3880999/black-power-salute-tommie-smith-and-john-carlos-at-the-1968-olympics/.

Cox, Oliver C. 2000. "Race Relations: Its Meaning, Beginning, and Process," pp. 71–78, in *Theories of Race and Racism: A Reader,* edited by Les Beck and John Solomos. New York: Routledge.

Craughwell, Thomas J. 2011. *The Greatest Brigade: How the Irish Brigade Cleared the Way to Victory in the American Civil War.* Beverly, MA: Fair Winds Press.

Cruz, Lenika. 2015. "'Dinnertimin' and 'No Tipping': How Advertisers Targeted Black Consumers in the 1970s." Retrieved April 6, 2018. https://www.theatlantic.com/entertainment/archive/2015/06/casual-racism-and-greater-diversity-in-70s-advertising/394958/.

Dalcho, Frederick. 1823. *Practical Considerations Founded on the Scriptures, Relative to the Slave Population of South Carolina by a South-Carolinian.* Charleston, SC: A. E. Miller.

Darity, Jr., William A., and Patrick L. Mason. 1998. "Evidence on Discrimination in Employment: Codes of Color, Codes of Gender." *Journal of Economic Perspectives* 12(2):63–90.

Dattel, Gene. 2011. *Cotton and Race in the Making of America: The Human Costs of Economic Power.* Lanham, MD: Ivan R. Dee.

Davis, Judy Foster. 2017. "Selling Whiteness? A Critical Review of the Literature on Marketing and Racism." *Journal of Marketing Management.* doi:10.1080/02672 57X.2017.1395902. Retrieved April 11, 2018. https:// www.tandfonline.com/doi/pdf/10.1080/0267257X.2017.1 395902#%5B%7B%22num%22%3A375%2C%22gen% 22%3A0%7D%2C%7B%22name%22%3A%22XYZ%22 %7D%2C61%2C83%2Cnull%5D.

Delgado, Richard, and Jean Stefancic. 1992. "Images of the Outsider in American Law and Culture: Can Free Expression Remedy Systemic Social Ills." *Cornell Law Review* 77(6):1258–1297.

DeNavas-Walt, Carmen, and Bernadette D. Proctor. 2015. "Income and Poverty in the United States: 2014." Retrieved September 27, 2016. http://www.census.gov/content/dam/ Census/library/publications/2015/demo/p60-252.pdf.

Denton, Jack. 2017. "The FBI's Long, Alarming History of Investigating Black Musicians." *Pacific Standard.* Retrieved May 25, 2018. https://psmag.com/social-justice/ the-fbis-long-history-of-investigating-black-musicians.

DiMaggio, Paul, John Evans, and Bethany Bryson. 1996. "Have Americans' Social Attitudes Become More Polarized?" *American Journal of Sociology* 102(3):690–755.

Douglas, Bronwen. 2008. "Climate to Crania: Science and the Racialization of Human Difference," pp. 33–98, in *Foreign Bodies: Oceania and the Science of Race 1750–1940,* edited by Bronwen Douglas and Chris Ballard. Canberra: Australian National University.

Douglass, Frederick, Harriet Jacobs, Solomon Northup, Willie Lynch, Nat Turner, Sojourner Truth, Mary Prince, William Craft, Ellen Craft, Louis Hughes, Jacob D. Green, Booker T. Washington, Olaudah Equiano, Elizabeth Keckley, William Still, Sarah H. Bradford, Josiah Henson, Charles Ball, Austin Steward, Henry Bibb, L. S. Thompson, Kate Drumgoold, Lucy A. Delaney, Moses Grandy, John Gabriel Stedman, Henry Box Brown, Margaretta Matilda Odell, Thomas S. Gaines, Brantz Mayer, Aphra Behn, Theodore Canot, Daniel Drayton, Thomas Clarkson, F. G. De Fontaine, John Dixon Long, Stephen Smith, Joseph Mountain, Ida B. Wells-Barnett, and Works Project Administration. 2018. *The Unchained: Powerful Life Stories of Former Slaves.* Madrid, Spain: Madison and Adams Press.

DuRocher, Kristina. 2011. *Raising Racists: The Socialization of White Children in the Jim Crow South.* Lexington: The University Press of Kentucky.

EagleWoman, Angelique, and G. William Rice. 2016. "American Indian Children and U.S. Indian Policy." *Tribal Law Journal* 16:1–29.

Ethridge, Robbie. 2010. "The Making of a Militaristic Slaving Society: The Chickasaws and the Colonial Slave Trade," pp. 251–276, in *Indian Slavery in Colonial America*, edited by Alan Gallay. Lincoln, NE: The University of Nebraska.

Falco, Ed. 2012. "When Italian Immigrants Were 'The Other.'" Retrieved November 18, 2017. http://www.cnn .com/2012/07/10/opinion/falco-italian-immigrants/index .html

Farber, Paul. 2003. "Race-Mixing and Science in the United States." *Endeavour* 27(4):166–170.

Feagin, Joe R. 2001. *Racist America: Roots, Current Realities, & Future Reparations.* New York: Routledge.

Feagin, Joe R., and Clairece Booher Feagin. 2011. *Racial and Ethnic Relations,* 9th ed. New York: Pearson.

Foy, Steven L. 2017. "Race and Sports," in *Wiley Blackwell Encyclopedia of Sociology*, 2nd ed., edited by George Ritzer. London: Wiley-Blackwell.

Francis-Crow, Alana. 2017. "Museums: It's a White Man's World." Retrieved April 11, 2018. https://femmagazine .com/its-a-white-mans-world/.

Gallay, Alan. 2015. "Indian Slavery in the Americas." Retrieved March 23, 2019. http://ap.gilderlehrman.org/ essay/indian-slavery-americas.

Gates, Jr., Henry Louis. 2013. "The Truth behind '40 Acres and a Mule.'" Retrieved January 29, 2018. http://www .pbs.org/wnet/african-americans-many-rivers-to-cross/ history/the-truth-behind-40-acres-and-a-mule/.

Geary Act. 1892. Public Law 52-60. 27 Statutes at Large 25.

Gould, Stephen Jay. 1978. "Morton's Rankings of Races by Cranial Capacity." *Science* 200(4341):503–509.

Green, Emma. 2017. "When Mormons Aspired to Be a 'White and Delightsome' People." Retrieved July 1, 2019. https://www.theatlantic.com/politics/archive/2017/09/ mormons-race-max-perry-mueller/539994/.

Guglielmo, Jennifer. 2003. "Introduction: White Lies, Dark Truths," pp. 1–16, in *Are Italians White? How Race Is Made in America*, edited by Jennifer Guglielmo and Salvatore Salerno. New York: Routledge.

Haller, Jr., John S. 1972. "The Negro and the Southern Physician: A Study of Medical and Racial Attitudes 1800–1860." *Medical History* 16(3):238–253.

Haller, Jr., John S. 1996. *Outcasts from Evolution: Scientific Attitudes of Racial Inferiority, 1859–1900*. Carbondale: Southern Illinois University Press.

Hannaford, Ivan. 1996. *Race: The History of an Idea in the West*. Baltimore, MD: Johns Hopkins University Press.

Harvey, Paul. 2003. "'A Servant of Servants Shall He Be': The Construction of Race in American Religious Mythologies," pp. 13–27, in *Religion and the Creation of Race and Ethnicity: An Introduction*, edited by Craig R. Prentiss. New York: New York University Press.

Healey, Joseph F., and Eileen O'Brien. 2015. *Race, Ethnicity, Gender, and Class: The Sociology of Group Conflict and Change.* Thousand Oaks, CA: Sage.

Higgenbotham, Jr., A. Leon, and Barbara K. Kopytoff. 2003. "Racial Purity and Interracial Sex in the Law of Colonial and Antebellum Virginia," pp. 81–139, in *Interracialism: Black-White Intermarriage in American History, Literature, and Law*, edited by Werner Sollors. New York NY: Oxford University Press

*The Holy Bible: New International Version.* 1993. Grand Rapids, MI: Zondervan.

Howe, Jr., Richard P. 2015. *Lowell.* Charleston, SC: Arcadia Publishing.

Ignatiev, Noel. 1995. *How the Irish Became White.* New York: Routledge.

Institute of Medicine. 2003. *Unequal Treatment: Confronting Racial and Ethnic Disparities in Health Care.* Washington, DC: The National Academies Press.

Irons, Peter. 2002. *Jim Crow's Children: The Broken Promise of the Brown Decision.* New York: Penguin Books.

Isaacson, Walter. 2003. *Benjamin Franklin: An American Life.* New York, NY: Simon & Schuster Paperbacks.

James, Henry. 1907. *The American Scene.* London, England: Chapman & Hall.

Jefferson, Thomas. 1813. "Thomas Jefferson to Alexander von Humboldt, 6 December 1813." Retrieved June 28, 2017. https://founders.archives.gov/documents/Jefferson/03-07-02-0011.

Jefferson, Thomas. 1999. *Notes on the State of Virginia.* New York: Penguin.

*Johnson and Graham's Lessee v. William M'Intosh*. 1823. 21 U.S. 543.

Jones, William P. 2005. *The Tribe of Black Ulysses: African American Lumber Workers in the Jim Crow South*. Urbana: University of Illinois Press.

Keeler, Sean. 2015. "'We Were Villains': How Wyoming's Black 14 Blazed the Trail for Missouri Protests." Retrieved July 1, 2019. https://www.theguardian.com/sport/2015/nov/11/we-were-villains-how-wyomings-black-14-blazed-the-trail-for-missouri-protests.

Klarman, Michael J. 2004. *From Jim Crow to Civil Rights: The Supreme Court and the Struggle for Racial Equality*. New York: Oxford University Press.

Kleck, Gary. 1981. "Racial Discrimination in Criminal Sentencing: A Critical Evaluation of the Evidence with Additional Evidence on the Death Penalty." *American Sociological Review* 46(6):783–805.

Knight, Peter. 2003. *Conspiracy Theories in American History: An Encyclopedia*. Santa Barbara, CA: ABC-CLIO.

Krogstad, Jens Manuel. 2015. "114th Congress Is Most Diverse Ever." Retrieved September 16, 2016. http://www.pewresearch.org/fact-tank/2015/01/12/114th-congress-is-most-diverse-ever/.

Lawson, Steven F. 1999. *Black Ballots: Voting Rights in the South, 1944–1969*. Lanham, MD: Lexington Books.

Lee, Erika. 2003. *At America's Gates: Chinese Immigration during the Exclusion Era, 1882–1943*. Chapel Hill: University of North Carolina Press.

Lemkin, Raphael. 1944. *Axis Rule in Occupied Europe: Laws of Occupation, Analysis of Government, Proposals for Redress*. Washington, DC: Carnegie Endowment for International Peace.

Library of Congress. 2018. "Brown v. Board at Fifty: 'With an Even Hand.'" Retrieved January 26, 2018. https://www.loc.gov/exhibits/brown/brown-segregation.html.

Long, Edward. 1774. *History of Jamaica.* London: T. Lowndes.

Luconi, Stefano. 2006. "'The Venom of Racial Intolerance': Italian Americans and Jews in the United States in the Aftermath of Fascist Racial Laws." *Revue Française D'études Américaines* 1(107):107–119.

Madley, Benjamin. 2016. *An American Genocide: The United States and the California Indian Catastrophe, 1846–1873.* New Haven, CT: Yale University Press.

Maillard, Kevin Noble. 2007. "The Pocahontas Exception: The Exemption of American Indian Ancestry from Racial Purity Law." *Michigan Journal of Race & Law* 12(107):1–42.

Mann, Coramae Richey. 1993. *Unequal Justice: A Question of Color.* Bloomington: Indiana University Press.

Marsico, Katie. 2011. *Women's Right to Vote: America's Suffrage Movement.* Salt Lake City, UT: Benchmark Books.

Marx, Karl. 1976. *Capital: Volume 1: A Critique of Political Economy.* New York: Penguin Books.

Massey, Douglas S., and Nancy A. Denton. 1993. *American Apartheid: Segregation and the Making of the Underclass.* Cambridge, MA: Harvard University Press.

Matthews, John Mabry. 2006. *Legislative and Judicial History of the Fifteenth Amendment.* Clark, NJ: The Lawbook Exchange, Ltd.

Means, Russell. 1992. "The Same Old Song," pp. 19–34, in *Marxism and Native Americans*, edited by Ward Churchill. Boston, MA: South End Press.

Meier, August, and Elliott Rudwick. 1969. "The Boycott Movement against Jim Crow Streetcars in the South, 1900–1906." *The Journal of American History* 55(4):756–775.

Mendelsohn, Meredith, and Tess Thackara. 2016. "How Advocates of African-American Art Are Advancing Racial Equality in the Art World." Retrieved April 11, 2018. https://www.artsy.net/article/artsy-editorial-in-black-artists-pursuit-of-equality-these-17-art-world-leaders-are-changing-the-game.

Miller, Robert J. 2006. *Native America, Discovered and Conquered: Thomas Jefferson, Lewis & Clark, and Manifest Destiny.* Westport, CT: Praeger.

Miller, Robert J. 2011. "American Indians, the Doctrine of Discovery, and Manifest Destiny." *Wyoming Law Review* 11(2):329–349.

Mills, Charles W. 1999. *The Racial Contract.* Ithaca, NY: Cornell University Press.

Mills, John Thomas, and DeMond Shondell Miller. 2017. "America: The Miscegenous Nation," pp. 205–224, in *Race in America: How a Pseudoscientific Concept Shaped Human Interaction*, edited by Patricia Reid-Merritt. Santa Barbara, CA: Praeger.

Moon, Krystyn R. 2005. *Yellowface: Creating the Chinese in American Popular Music and Performance, 1850s-1920s.* New Brunswick, NJ: Rutgers University Press.

Morgan, Edmund S. 2003. *American Slavery, American Freedom.* New York: W. W. Norton & Company, Inc.

Morrison, Larry R. 1980. "The Religious Defense of American Slavery before 1830." *Journal of Religious Thought* 37(2):16–29.

Mulvaney, James. 2017. "President Trump's Reference to 'Paddy Wagon' Insults Irish Americans Like Me." Retrieved November 18, 2017. https://www.washingtonpost.com/news/posteverything/wp/2017/08/01/trumps-use-of-paddy-wagon-insults-irish-americans-like-me/.

Murphy, Angela F. 2010. *American Slavery, Irish Freedom: Abolition, Immigrant Citizenship, and the Transatlantic*

*Movement for Irish Repeal.* Baton Rouge: Louisiana State University Press.

Myrdal, Gunnar. 2000. "Racial Beliefs in America," pp. 87–104, in *Theories of Race and Racism: A Reader,* edited by Les Beck and John Solomos. New York: Routledge.

NAACP. 2018. "History of Lynchings." Retrieved March 10, 2018. http://www.naacp.org/history-of-lynchings/.

Nagourney, Adam. 2008. "Obama Elected President as Racial Barrier Falls." Retrieved September 16, 2016. http://www.nytimes.com/2008/11/05/us/politics/05elect.html.

National Museum of the American Indian. 2007. "Boarding Schools: Struggling with Cultural Repression." Retrieved July 1, 2017. www.nmai.si.edu/education/codetalkers/html/chapter3.html.

National Park Service. 2009. "Civil Rights in America: Racial Voting Rights." Retrieved February 2, 2018. https://www.nps.gov/nhl/learn/themes/CivilRights_VotingRights.pdf.

Nelson, Jr., H. Viscount. 2015. *Sharecropping, Ghetto, Slum: A History of Impoverished Blacks in Twentieth-Century America.* Bloomington, IN: Xlibris.

*The New York Times.* 1891. Newspaper editorial. March 16, p. 4.

Olusoga, David. 2015. "The Roots of European Racism Lie in the Slave Trade, Colonialism—And Edward Long." Retrieved June 26, 2017. https://www.theguardian.com/commentisfree/2015/sep/08/european-racism-africa-slavery.

O'Sullivan, John. 1845. "Annexation." *United States Magazine and Democratic Review* 17(1):5–10.

Otis, D. S. 1973. *The Dawes Act and the Allotment of Indian Lands.* Norman: University of Oklahoma Press.

Parent, Anthony S. 2003. *Foul Means: The Formation of a Slave Society in Virginia, 1660–1740.* Chapel Hill: The University of North Carolina Press.

PBS. 2001. "Archives of the West from 1877–1887." Retrieved January 2, 2017. https://www.pbs.org/weta/thewest/resources/archives/seven/chinxact.htm.

PBS. 2003. "Race—The Power of an Illusion." Retrieved January 23, 2017. http://www.pbs.org/race/000_About/002_03-godeeper.htm.

PBS. 2017. "From Indentured Servitude to Slavery." Retrieved January 23, 2017. https://www.pbs.org/wgbh/aia/part1/1narr3.html.

Perman, Michael. 2001. *Struggle for Mastery: Disfranchisement in the South, 1888–1908*. Chapel Hill: The University of North Carolina Press.

Pew Research Center. 2016. "On Views of Race and Inequality, Blacks and Whites Are Worlds Apart." Retrieved September 27, 2016. http://www.pewsocialtrends.org/2016/06/27/on-views-of-race-and-inequality-blacks-and-whites-are-worlds-apart/.

Phelan, Jo C., and Bruce G. Link. 2015. "Is Racism a Fundamental Cause of Inequalities in Health?" *Annual Review of Sociology* 41:311–330.

Plecker, W. A. 1924. "The New Virginia Law to Preserve Racial Integrity." *Virginia Health Bulletin* 16 (Extra No. 2):1–4.

Prucha, Francis Paul. 1984. *The Great Father: The United States Government and the American Indians*. Lincoln: University of Nebraska Press.

Quoy, Jean-René Constant, and Joseph-Paul Gaimard. 1824. "De l'homme: Observations sur la Constitution physique des Papous" ["From the Man: Observations on the Physical Constitution of the Papuans"], pp. 1–11, in *Voyage autour du monde: entrepris par ordre du roi . . . execute sur les corvettes de S. M. l'Uranie et la Physicienne, pendant les années 1817, 1818, 1819 et 1820 [Travel Around the World: Undertaken by Order of the King . . . Executed on the Corvettes of S. M. Urania and the Physics during the Years*

*1817, 1818, 1819, and 1820]*, edited by Louis Claude Desaulses de Freycinet. Paris: Pillet Aîné.

Reade, W. Winwood. 1864. *Savage Africa: Being the Narrative of a Tour in Equatorial, South-Western, and North-Western Africa: With Notes on the Habits of the Gorilla; on the Existence of Unicorns and Tailed Men; on the Slave Trade; on the Origin, Character, and Capabilities of the Negro and on the Future Civilization of Western Africa*. London: Smith, Elder, and Co.

Relative to Chinese Americans in California. 2014. "Senate Concurrent Resolution No. 122." Retrieved February 2, 2018. https://leginfo.legislature.ca.gov/faces/billTextClient .xhtml?bill_id=201320140SCR122.

Richards, David A. J. 1999. *Italian American: The Racializing of an Ethnic Identity*. New York: New York University Press.

Ronkin, Maggie, and Helen E. Karn. 1999. "Mock Ebonics: Linguistic Racism in Parodies of Ebonics on the Internet." *Journal of Sociolinguistics* 3(3):360–380.

Roscher, Wilhelm. 1904. *The Spanish Colonial System*. New York: Henry Holt and Company.

Rosenberg, Jonathan. 2006. *How Far the Promised Land? World Affairs and the American Civil Rights Movement from the First World War to Vietnam*. Princeton, NJ: Princeton University Press.

Rothstein, Richard. 2017. *The Color of Law: A Forgotten History of How Our Government Segregated America*. New York: Liveright.

Savitt, Todd L. 1981. *Medicine and Slavery: The Diseases and Health Care of Blacks in Antebellum Virginia*. Champaign: University of Illinois Press.

Scharf, J. Thomas. 1881. *History of Baltimore City and County from the Earliest Period to the Present Day: Including Biographical Sketches of Their Representative Men*. Philadelphia, PA: Louis H. Everts.

Schenkkan, Robert. 2014. "LBJ's Second Great Battle: Enforcing the Civil Rights Act." Retrieved February 12, 2018. http://www.latimes.com/nation/la-oe-schenkkan-civil-rights-lyndon-johnson-20140629-story.html.

Schiller, Ben. 2008. "Learning Their Letters: Critical Literacy, Epistolary Culture, and Slavery in the Antebellum South." *The Southern Quarterly* 45(3):11–29.

Schur, Joan Brodsky. 2016. "Eli Whitney's Patent for the Cotton Gin." Retrieved June 3, 2017. https://www.archives.gov/education/lessons/cotton-gin-patent.

*Scott v. Sandford.* 1856. 60 U.S. (19 How.) 393.

Shora, Nawar. 2009. *The Arab-American Handbook: A Guide to the Arab, Arab-American, and Muslim Worlds.* Seattle, WA: Cune Press.

Simpson, George Eaton, and J. Milton Yinger. 1985. *Racial and Cultural Minorities: An Analysis of Prejudice and Discrimination.* New York: Springer Science + Business Media.

Skufca, Lawrence Christopher. 2015. "Racism: A History." Retrieved November 13, 2019. https://camdencivilrights project.com/2015/10/27/racism-a-history-2007-2/.

Smedley, Audrey, and Brian D. Smedley. 2005. "Race as Biology Is Fiction, Racism as a Social Problem Is Real: Anthropological and Historical Perspectives on the Social Construction of Race." *American Psychologist* 60(1):16–26.

Smedley, Audrey, and Brian D. Smedley. 2018. *Race in North America: Origin and Evolution of a Worldview.* New York, NY: Routledge.

Smith, Andrea. 2012. "Indigeneity, Settler Colonialism, White Supremacy," pp. 66–90, in *Racial Formation in the Twenty-First Century,* edited by Daniel Martinez HoSang, Oneka LaBennett, and Laura Pulido. Berkeley, CA: University of California Press.

Smith, Stephen, and Kate Ellis. 2017. "Shackled Legacy: History Shows Slavery Helped Build Many U.S. Colleges and Universities." Retrieved January 11, 2018. https://www.apmreports.org/story/2017/09/04/shackled-legacy.

Smits, David D. 1994. "The Frontier Army and the Destruction of the Buffalo: 1865–1883." *The Western Historical Quarterly* 25(3):312–338.

Snowden, Jr., Frank M. 1991. *Before Color Prejudice: The Ancient View of Blacks.* Boston, MA: Harvard University Press.

South Carolina. 1866. *Acts of the General Assembly of the State of South Carolina, Passed at the Sessions of 1864–1865.* Columbia, SC: Julian A. Selby, Printer to the State.

Stam, Robert, and Louise Spence. 1983. "Colonialism, Racism and Representation—An Introduction." *Screen* 24(2):2–20.

Stampp, Kenneth M. 1989. *Peculiar Institution: Slavery in the Ante-Bellum South.* New York: Vintage Books.

Stanford Center for Education Policy Analysis. 2016. "Racial and Ethnic Achievement Gaps." Retrieved September 27, 2016. http://cepa.stanford.edu/educational-opportunity-monitoring-project/achievement-gaps/race/.

Stein, Edward. 2004. "Past and Present Proposed Amendments to the United States Constitution Regarding Marriage." *Washington University Law Review* 82(3):611–685.

Stern, William J. 1997. "How Dagger John Saved New York's Irish." *City Journal.* Retrieved November 18, 2017. https://www.city-journal.org/html/how-dagger-john-saved-new-york%E2%80%99s-irish-11934.html.

Stokes, Melvyn. 2007. *D. W. Griffith's The Birth of a Nation: A History of "The Most Controversial Motion Picture of All Time."* Oxford, UK: Oxford University Press.

Strickland, Rennard J. 1986. "Genocide-at-Law: An Historic and Contemporary View of the Native American Experience." *University of Kansas Law Review* 34(4):713–755.

Sussman, Robert Wald. 2016. *The Myth of Race: The Troubling Persistence of an Unscientific Idea.* Boston, MA: Harvard University Press.

Tatum, Beverly. 1997. *Why Are All the Black Kids Sitting Together in the Cafeteria? And Other Conversations about Race.* New York: Basic Books.

Taylor-Colbert, Alice. 2004. "Major Ridge (ca. 1771–1839)." *New Georgia Encyclopedia.* Retrieved June 30, 2017. http://www.georgiaencyclopedia.org/articles/history-archaeology/major-ridge-ca-1771-1839.

Thandeka. 1998. "The Whiting of Euro-Americans: A Divide and Conquer Strategy." *World: The Journal of the Unitarian Universalist Association* 12(4):14–20.

Theoharis, Jeanne. 2015. *The Rebellious Life of Mrs. Rosa Parks.* Boston, MA: Beacon Press.

Thompson, Lloyd. 1993. "Roman Perceptions of Blacks." *Electronic Antiquity* 1(4). Retrieved January 28, 2017. https://scholar.lib.vt.edu/ejournals/ElAnt/V1N4/thompson.html.

Todorov, Tzvetan. 1993. *On Human Diversity: Nationalism, Racism, and Exoticism in French Thought.* Cambridge, MA: Harvard University Press.

Todorov, Tzvetan. 2000. "Race and Racism," pp. 64–70, in *Theories of Race and Racism: A Reader*, edited by Lee Back and John Solomos. New York, NY: Routledge.

Toland, John. 1991. *Adolf Hitler: The Definitive Biography.* New York: Anchor.

Treaty of Fort Laramie. 1868. Retrieved June 28, 2017. https://www.ourdocuments.gov/doc.php?flash=true&doc=42.

*United States v. Kagama.* 1886. 118 U.S. 375.

U.S. Constitutional Amendment XIII.

Venkataraman, Nitya. 2009. "Senate Votes Sonia Sotomayor as First Hispanic Supreme Court Justice." Retrieved

September 16, 2016. http://abcnews.go.com/Politics/
SoniaSotomayor/story?id=8260207&page=1.

Waldrep, Christopher. 1998. *Roots of Disorder: Race and Criminal Justice in the American South, 1817–1880*. Urbana and Chicago: University of Illinois Press.

Washington, Harriet A. 2006. *Medical Apartheid: The Dark History of Medical Experimentation on Black Americans from Colonial Times to the Present*. New York: Harlem Moon.

Wellman, David T. 1993. *Portraits of White Racism*. Cambridge, UK: Cambridge University Press.

Wilder, Craig Steven. 2013. *Ebony and Ivy: Race, Slavery, and the Troubled History of America's Universities*. New York: Bloomsbury Press.

Wilkins, Thurman. 1989. *Cherokee Tragedy: The Ridge Family and the Decimation of a People*. Norman: University of Oklahoma Press.

Wood, Peter H. 2003. *Strange New Land: Africans in Colonial America*. Oxford, UK: Oxford University Press.

Woodham-Smith, Cecil. 1992. *The Great Hunger: Ireland: 1845–1849*. London, England: Penguin Books.

Woodson, Carter G. 2010. *The Education of the Negro Prior to 1861: A History of the Education of the Colored People of the United States from the Beginning of Slavery to the Civil War*. Whitefish, MT: Kessinger Publishing.

Wright Austin, Sharon D. 2006. *The Transformation of Plantation Politics: Black Politics, Concentrated Poverty, and Social Capital in the Mississippi Delta*. Albany: State University of New York Press.

Yeboah, Alberta. 2005. "Education among Native Americans in the Periods before and after Contact with Europeans: An Overview." Retrieved January 10, 2018. https://www2.ed.gov/rschstat/research/pubs/oieresearch/conference/yeboah_200502.doc.

Yen, Rhoda J. 2000. "Racial Stereotyping of Asians and Asian Americans and Its Effect on Criminal Justice: A Reflection on the Wayne Lo Case." *Asian American Law Journal* 7(1):1–28.

Zeitz, Josh. 2015. "When America Hated Catholics." Retrieved December 30, 2017. https://www.politico.com/ magazine/story/2015/09/when-america-hated-catholics-213177.

Zinn, Howard. 2015. *A People's History of the United States.* New York: Harper Perennial Modern Classics.

# 2  Problems, Controversies, and Solutions

## Acknowledging the Past and Recognizing the Presence of Racism in America

As Chapter 1 highlighted, the rise of racism as an organizer of social stratification in America was no anomaly. Institutional racism in America was a tool carefully and intentionally crafted—first by European colonialists for specific and calculated reasons to obtain land, secure labor, and maintain control by subverting potential uprisings and later by American whites to perpetuate their own economic and social advantages. Yet white Americans have often ignored or attempted to explain away the continued presence of racism as a stratifying factor in the modern United States. Even at the height of the civil rights movement, more than half of whites polled by Gallup believed that blacks were treated the same way as whites (Newport, Ludwig, and Kearney 2001). Recent data points to a continued racial divide over the existence of racism; a 2017 Gallup poll indicated that 82 percent of blacks but only 56 percent of whites considered racism against black Americans to be widespread (Struyk 2017). Moreover, in a Pew Research Center (2017a) survey, almost as many whites (46 percent) believed that people seeing discrimination when it did not actually exist was a bigger contemporary problem than people failing to see

The Kingdom Day Parade honoring Dr. Martin Luther King Jr., in Los Angeles, California, January 19, 2015. Marchers held signs reading "Black Lives Matter," calling attention to police brutality against blacks. (Joe Sohm/Dreamstime.com)

discrimination where it actually did exist (49 percent). Comparatively, only 13 percent of blacks and 30 percent of Hispanics saw unjustifiable claims of discrimination as the bigger problem (Pew Research Center 2017a).

## Downplaying Racism

Tim Wise (2008) summarizes a few of the ways in which people attempt to justify or downplay racism in the United States: (1) minimization, (2) rationalization, (3) deflection, and (4) claims of competing victimization. Minimization includes downplaying the effects of racism and attributing racism primarily to flawed individuals rather than to intentional institutional processes. For example, some argue that minorities facing clear instances of prejudice or discrimination are "playing the race card" or being overly sensitive (Bonilla-Silva 2013). Rationalization involves accepting the presence of racial bias but attributing it to rational causes. For example, one might acknowledge being afraid of people of a particular racial group but justify this by referring back to a previous robbery by someone of that racial group. Even if the vast majority of people identified as being of the same racial group are law abiding, they all become seen negatively based on a specific example or set of examples.

Deflection and claims of competing victimization also serve as means by which the negative treatment of racial minorities becomes downplayed. Some inappropriately deflect responsibility for negative outcomes generated by racism to the victims (e.g., by assuming that people are unemployed because they are lazy rather than recognizing the potential for hiring discrimination to make the job search more difficult for some people than others). Similarly, people from a particular racial group may be singled out for negative treatment based on race, but an explanation might be provided to make it seem as though the reason is not racial discrimination. (For example, Hispanics may be unreasonably surveilled on the basis of citizenship status even though other groups generally avoid scrutiny of their legal standing to be in the United States.) Claims of competing victimization involve attempts to shift the conversation from focusing on how racism impacts socially disadvantaged groups to falsely comparing that impact to the impact of alleged racism toward the dominant group. An example of this can be found in claims of affirmative action as "reverse discrimination" (Wise 2008). More than half of white Americans believe that whites are discriminated against (Gonyea 2017).

## How We Handle Our History

Americans are not always ready to have an honest conversation about present-day American racism. The American public may not universally agree on the extent to which racism is foundational to American society due to a widespread (whether intentional or unintentional) lack of understanding about previous historical events coupled with an inattentiveness to how vestiges of that history continue to negatively impact racial minorities to this day. To take one example, there is ample evidence that slavery was fundamental to Southern states seceding from the Union and ushering in the Civil War. Many Southern states explicitly identified the preservation of slavery as a key goal of secession; South Carolina declared that the potential end of slavery threatened its beliefs and safety, while Mississippi portrayed it as deleterious to commerce and even to civilization (Coates 2015). A newspaper based in Richmond, Virginia, *Southern Punch*, even went so far as to declare, in 1864, that "WE ARE FIGHTING FOR INDEPENDENCE THAT OUR GREAT AND NECESSARY DOMESTIC INSTITUTION OF SLAVERY SHALL BE PRESERVED" (Lozada 2015). Moreover, Confederate veterans openly remarked about having fought to preserve slavery; in addressing why the Civil War took place, Confederate commander John Mosby remarked that he had "never heard of any other cause than slavery" (Coates 2015).

Yet, in research conducted by the Southern Poverty Law Center (2018), for example, only 8 percent of high school seniors identified slavery as the primary reason why the Civil War began, and a review of popular high school history textbooks revealed that the average book addressed less than half of what they considered fundamental to the study of slavery. Teachers in the study noted that they worried about being overly specific about slavery, fearing that this would lead to demoralizing experiences for black students and put white students on the defensive. The downplaying of even slavery in educational curricula—one of the most blatant and known examples of institutional racism in America—suggests that future generations may be inadequately informed about the racist underpinnings of American institutions. The fact that more than 80 percent of American teachers are white reduces the likelihood that this will easily change (Costello 2018).

White aversion to acknowledging historical racism has significant implications for how we interpret present-day realities; for example, 51 percent of Americans continue to see the Confederate flag as more a symbol of Southern pride than as a symbol of racism. When racial classification is taken into account, we see that whites are the primary holdout; 60 percent of white, non-Hispanic Americans, 45 percent of Hispanics, and only 15 percent of black, non-Hispanics believe that the Confederate flag is primarily a symbol of Southern pride (Jones 2017). Thus, a candid assessment of the problems racism continues to pose in America coupled with a thoughtful consideration of what solutions might be feasible is necessary and is particularly necessary for a primarily white audience.

Chapter 1 established America's racist foundations, identifying institutions from which racism emerged and within which it was nurtured and reified. This chapter revisits those institutions and demonstrates the extent to which racism continues to manifest itself. Having established the continuity of American racism, this chapter concludes with a consideration of what has been done and what can still be done to combat it.

## Land, Labor, and the Maintenance of the Status Quo Revisited

Chapter 1 began with a framework for the motivations underlying how racism became a cornerstone of racial stratification—namely, interest in clearing the land for colonial expansion, a desire to secure labor, and a need to prevent rebellion by turning those who might resist against each other. As we explore the problems and controversies surrounding racism in the modern context, it is important to note that those motivations have lived on in various ways.

## Clearing the Land Again: The Racialization of Eminent Domain

When European colonists drove Native Americans from their land and claimed it for their own, they set a precedent of destruction and replacement that would reverberate into the present day. Theodor Herzl, an early and major supporter of the formation of an Israeli state in Palestine, would describe settler capitalism in this way: "If I wish to substitute a new building for an old one, I must demolish before I construct" (Wolfe 2006). That sentiment took literal form again in the 1930s as states gave themselves the authority to sell "blighted" property to private companies for "urban renewal" (Somin 2011). Decades of action along these lines found affirmation in the 2005 Supreme Court case *Kelo v. City of New London.* The court ruled that the government could condemn private property and transfer it to private developers as long as there was some benefit to the public. However, private developers have been able to take over public lands seized through eminent domain without actually demonstrating public benefit.

Eminent domain disproportionately targeted communities of color and, particularly, poor blacks; in fact, James Baldwin referred to urban renewal as "Negro removal" (Somin 2011:6). From the passage of the 1949 Urban Renewal Act to 1973, more than two-thirds of those who lost their homes were black. In their dissenting opinions in *Kelo v. City of New London,* Justices O'Connor and Thomas warned that eminent domain abuses would occur more frequently in less powerful communities, and, indeed, the problem continues to this day (U.S. Commission on Civil Rights 2014). For example, in 2010, the New York Court of Appeals allowed Columbia University to expand its campus into significant tracts of land in a nearby primarily black neighborhood (Somin 2011). Often, residents who manage to retain their homes in areas where many have been displaced via eminent domain find that urban renewal has raised property values (and, in parallel, property taxes and rent costs), pricing them out of their neighborhoods (U.S. Commission on Civil Rights 2014).

This is just one example of gentrification—a method by which areas seen as decaying or falling apart are renovated to appeal to more economically advantaged people, creating new economic spaces for enterprise and entrepreneurship but pricing lower-income residents out of their communities.

### Securing Labor Again

The early American colonial economy largely relied on indentured servitude or enslavement to ensure a sufficient labor force while maximizing profit. Though slavery officially ended in 1865 (U.S. Constitutional Amendment XIII), a more recent trend to ensure that a large workforce continues to labor for low wages has been through more informal "race typing" of jobs (Reich, Gordon, and Edwards 1973). Relying on widely held societal stereotypes about racial minorities, employers may make hiring decisions en masse that undercut their ability to obtain high-status jobs, making it more likely that they will take up lower-status jobs for which there is greater numerical need (Stewart and Perlow 2001). Evidence suggests that uneven racial representation across high-status jobs is much more a product of race typing than of skill differentials between groups (see, for example, Kaufman 2002). In other words, the problem is not with racial minorities lacking the skills to perform well in high-status jobs—it's that employers believe racial minorities are less capable.

### Discouraging Organized Rebellion Again

Although lower-class workers across racial groups have experienced exploitation, employers have found ways to undercut their coordination for better wages and working conditions by appealing to racism. Given difficulties in obtaining adequate employment due to racial discrimination, blacks took some of the jobs that protesting workers vacated during most major American strikes, fostering antagonism toward them by white strikers. This anger toward black strikebreakers was misdirected given that white workers have been far more commonly employed to break strikes. Even so, as Spero and Harris (1931:527) noted, although "the number of strikes broken by blacks have been few as compared with the number broken by whites," the "presence of a dozen black men in a force of strikebreakers appears to the strikers like a hundred." This occurred even though the strikebreakers themselves may have been unaware of what they were signing up for; the ads recruiting strikebreakers could often be very misleading, focusing on the pay, opportunity for job stability, travel money, and other benefits without any indication of an ongoing strike (Whatley 1993). Still, the fears raised by the specter of racial competition over scarce jobs helped employers destabilize worker attempts at collective action.

## Institutional Venues of Racism Revisited

Against this backdrop, we continue to see persistent examples of racism throughout a variety of societal institutions from science to religion to the arts. We now return to institutions from Chapter 1 where racism has historically abounded to look at the extent to which it currently remains.

### Science and Pseudoscience

The American eugenics movement ostensibly sought to perfect the human race by limiting the gene pool. Harry Clay Sharp, the first doctor to perform an unwanted vasectomy on a prisoner (in an effort to curb criminality in the population), once wrote, "We make choice of the best rams for our sheep. . . . How careful then should we be in begetting of children!" (Black 2012).

Assuming whites to be superior, eugenicists believed that they could better humanity by trying to prevent members of different racial groups from reproducing. For example, nonprofit eugenicist funder Pioneer Fund specifically sought to protect the genes of those "descended predominantly from white persons who settled in the original thirteen states" (Urban 2008:166). An unnamed magazine thought to be *The Nation* reported in 1960 that the Pioneer Fund's founder, Wickliffe Draper, was primarily occupied with trying to "prove simply that Negroes were inferior . . . and . . . to promote some program to send them all to Africa" (Tucker 2002:71).

American history is rife with eugenicist practices to limit reproduction in instances with racial implications. As the Chicago Committee to End Sterilization Abuse (1977) argued, although some increase in sterilization could be explained by a rise in women wanting to limit the number of children they had, many other women were manipulated into agreement. Those convinced to undergo sterilization under questionable circumstances tended to be "the poor, the Black, the Latino, the American Indian—those already abused by our health care system" (Chicago Committee to End Sterilization Abuse 1977). In fact, twice as many black women had been sterilized in 1977 as white women. Reports from Los Angeles during the 1970s revealed examples of Chicana women being asked to sign consent forms to undergo sterilization while heavily medicated and on their way to deliver via caesarian section or told that sterilization was a temporary birth control option rather than permanent (Chicago Committee to End Sterilization Abuse 1977).

Further, the U.S. government funded a number of programs disproportionately targeting nonwhite people for sterilization. About a third of Puerto Rican women of child-bearing age were sterilized between the 1930s and 1970s with partial funding from the U.S. Department of Health, Education, and Welfare (Louis de Malave 1999). The Peace Corps even performed mass vasectomies in New Delhi, India (Beal 2008).

Institutional support and funding for eugenicist thinking are not simply vestiges of an antiquated past. For example, the Pioneer Fund continues to contribute substantial funding to scientists seeking to prove black intellectual inferiority. Suggestions by eugenicists that promoting reproduction among those with "good" genes and dis-incentivizing reproduction among those with "bad" genes would improve humanity assumed that particular genetic factors could be reliably linked to undesirable traits. Measures of intelligence provided eugenicists with seemingly objective evidence to claim that whites were more worthy than members of another group to pass their genetic profiles on to future generations. Claims of black intellectual inferiority, like Samuel Cartwright's claims many years before about drapetomania allegedly causing slaves to run away, were couched in patriarchal terms. When Nobel Prize–winning physicist William Shockley was criticized as racist for concluding blacks had lower IQs due to genetic differences, he countered that failure to subscribe to his conclusions could have far-lasting consequences: "If those Negroes with the fewest Caucasian genes are in fact the most prolific and also the least intelligent, then genetic enslavement will be the destiny of the next generation" (Shockley 1972). Many of the researchers cited in Charles Murray and Richard Herrnstein's (1994) book *The Bell Curve* to support the claim that IQ differences are partially attributable to race, including William Shockley and Arthur Jensen, received funding from the Pioneer Fund. The fund also contributed over $1 million in grants to J. Philippe Rushton, who claimed that blacks were less intelligent than whites because they had larger genitalia and that genitalia size was inversely proportionate with IQ (Southern Poverty Law Center 2018).

The *American Renaissance* newsletter (another major beneficiary of Pioneer Fund grants) has promoted similar arguments about white genetic superiority. Founded in 1990, the newsletter openly decries "high birth rates among blacks and Hispanics" and has organized conferences bringing together a plethora of scientists pushing an agenda that racial difference is genetic (The JBHE Foundation, Inc. 1998). Even Dinesh D'Souza, who referred to then president Barack Obama as "ghetto" (D'Souza 2015) and argued that "the American slave *was* treated like property, which is to say, pretty well" (D'Souza 1995, emphasis in original), objected to how fellow participants in the *American Renaissance*'s 1998 conference claimed that blacks were innately inferior to members of other racial groups (The JBHE Foundation, Inc. 1998).

Current politicians and governmental officials have also echoed eugenicist rhetoric. In July 2016, Steve Bannon (who eventually worked for a time as chief strategist for President Donald Trump) suggested that blacks murdered by police officers may have deserved it because they were "naturally aggressive and violent" (Evans 2018). In March 2017, white U.S. representative Steve King tweeted his agreement with a Dutch nationalist that "we can't restore our civilization with somebody else's babies" (Hemmer 2017). In January 2018, a Kansas state representative was videoed, arguing that blacks were genetically predisposed to using marijuana (Lopez 2018). While this sort of rhetoric is generally condemned and followed by an obligatory apology, its continual reappearance suggests that eugenicist ideas remain at least somewhat entrenched.

Eugenicist ideas have also continued to result in detrimental action toward people of color. Even as recently as from 2006 to 2010, the California Department of Corrections and Rehabilitation illegally sterilized 148 women, and, although their demographic data was not publicly available, all of the women willing to talk with investigators from the Center for Investigative Reporting about their sterilizations were racial minorities (Rivas 2013).

### Religion

Historically, as discussed in Chapter 1, religion (specifically Christianity) was used to justify slavery. Though few would echo that justification now, direct appeals to racism by religious movements have yet to entirely subside. Bob Jones University, a Christian fundamentalist institution, even enforced an interracial dating ban until 2000, arguing that racial groups should be separated because God had separate plans for each (*Christianity Today* 2000). Even more recently, in 2014, 10 percent of respondents polled by Public Religion Research Institute agreed that businesses should be allowed to refuse service to black people on religious grounds (Cox, Navarro-Rivera, and Jones 2014).

For a number of reasons, religion in America may contribute to racism. In general, religiosity in the Judeo-Christian tradition tends to promote conservative values, favoring conformity and tradition (Saroglou, Delpierre, and Dernelle 2004). Indeed, 85 percent of American conservatives are Christian (Pew Research Center 2018). Conservative values, in turn, are associated with prejudice, in general, and with ethnocentrism and racism, in particular (Hall, Matz, and Wood 2010).

Recent research suggests that religion may be reinforcing racism by segregating racial groups from one another and fostering an in-group versus out-group mentality about race. Religious congregations in which at least 20 percent of attendees are not part of the racial majority are relatively rare (Dougherty, Martí, and Martinez 2015). As Martin Luther King Jr. decried, "It is appalling that the most segregated hour of Christian America is eleven o'clock on Sunday morning" (King 1960). This may partially explain why Hall, Matz, and Wood (2010) found in a meta-analysis that people who had strong religious in-group identities were more likely to be disparaging toward people from other racial groups. Put more simply, because most congregations are not very racially diverse, churches may reinforce feelings of solidarity with people within one's own racial group and skepticism about, misunderstanding of, or hostility toward members of other racial groups.

Racial segregation of churches may be deliberately reinforced to some extent by what Bracey and Moore (2017:282) refer to as "race tests." Such tests can be used to draw racialized lines around who is accepted and welcome and who is informally excluded. They may include defining certain forms of worship more frequently employed by whites as acceptable in a church space and others more commonly practiced by racial minorities as deviant. In one particularly extreme example, a black respondent in Bracey and Moore's (2017) study described visiting a couple's private home for a house church service and facing a surprised expression when they first saw him. He was then taken on a tour that included viewing photos of Civil War soldiers prominently displayed on the wall, and one of the homeowners explained that they had relatives on both sides of the war but only put up items honoring the Confederate soldiers (Bracey and Moore 2017).

Even when religion has not directly promoted racism, it has, at times, deflected attention from the need for political reform to address racism in favor of an approach that lays the blame for racism at the feet of inadequate religiosity. On the one hand, in August 2017, Reverend Al Sharpton and hundreds of others participated in the "We Shall Not Be Moved" rally. The rally covered a variety of topics, but countering structural racism and the rise of white supremacy politically was an undeniable component. On the other hand, several religious leaders (nearly all of whom served on advisory councils for President Donald Trump) met at the National Press Club in Washington, D.C., to argue that racism was primarily a spiritual problem. Covenant Church founding pastor Mike Hayes stated, "I don't think anything changes until you have a personal encounter with Jesus, which breaks your heart" (Burton 2017). At this same meeting, a number of speakers blamed leftist media for overstating the existence of racism, and one speaker, Day Gardner, president of the National Black Pro Life Union, suggested that blacks should focus less on racial inequality and more on "black-on-black crime" and abortion (Burton 2017).

### Racial Categorization

Attempts to define racial groups legally were historically designed to establish and maintain a racial hierarchy that benefited whites. The three-fifths compromise defined slaves as three-fifths of a person for legislative representation, allowing white Southerners to hold additional seats in the U.S. House of Representatives (Waldstreicher 2009). Virginia's 1924 Racial Integrity Act included strict definitions of race and criminalized interracial marriages to reduce ambiguity surrounding who could take advantage of white privilege. During World War II, the Secret Service used Census Bureau data to locate people of Japanese descent and intern them (Granick 2017). However, over time, official racial categorizations have also been used to identify and address the needs of racial minorities.

Consider, for example, the pan-ethnic label "Hispanic," included in the U.S. Census for the first time in 1970 (Cohn 2010). Although the label was not particularly informative in describing ethnicity—after all, it encompasses people with quite varied countries of origin—it was useful to politically further the advancement of people often racialized together as nonwhite and discriminated against as such. Christina Mora (2014) notes how the political weight of pointing to a large and growing population of Hispanic potential voters allowed for more effective advocacy to address labor inequities, housing problems, poverty, educational discrimination, and other issues faced by those who took on the label. For example, Mexican Americans might have been able to effectively work toward the reduction of immigration restrictions alone, but their concerns could be more powerfully conveyed if represented as important to a constituency as large as the group defined as Hispanics. Similarly, census race categorization has also allowed for targeted responses to income inequality, wealth inequality, and other issues faced by racial minorities.

Despite these indications of progress, racial categorization continues to be used to perpetuate stratification in some cases. Take, for example, Asian Americans. Due to American prioritization on facilitating the immigration of Asian Americans with demonstrably high skills for scientific and technical positions following the passage of the Immigration and Nationality Act of 1965, post-1965 Asian immigrants tended to be relatively wealthy and highly educated (Nadeem et al. 2015). Asian immigrants to the United States were praised for their drive to achieve and their academic prowess in news segments on *NBC Nightly News*, *60 Minutes*, and the *McNeil/Lehrer Report* as well as in stories in *U.S. News and World Report*, *Time*, *Newsweek*, and the *New Republic* (Tataki 1989).

In the wake of these events, William Petersen, a demographer and sociology professor, wrote a story for *The New York Times* entitled "Success Story, Japanese-American Style," in which he described how Japanese Americans, despite facing prejudice and discrimination, achieved higher incomes and even higher life expectancies than whites (Petersen 1966). As a result, he dubbed them the "model minority"—an example for other immigrating groups to which to aspire. Arguments like this allowed mainstream Americans, ignoring the selection effects that provided Asian immigrants with advantages relative to other immigrants, to assign blame to blacks and Hispanics for not doing as well economically on average. The model minority label also had negative repercussions for Asian Americans themselves given its lack of attention to the substantial variation among groups within that classification. For example, some Asian immigrants were more likely to come from experiences of substantial poverty, such as the Bhutanese, the Hmong, the Vietnamese, and Filipino farmworkers (Chow 2017; Yen 2000).

Some scholars have suggested that the acceptance of Asian Americans as "racial bourgeoisie" has come at a cost (Matsuda 1997). Matsuda (1997) argues that universities have used secret quotas to limit the number of Asians and remain primarily white. At the same time, conservative opponents of affirmative action have opportunistically used that treatment of Asian Americans to perpetuate further injustice against other racial minorities by attempting to dismantle affirmative action (Matsuda 1997).

Recent controversies over racial categorization in the census underscore both how fluid racial categories can be and how important ultimate conclusions about how to conceptualize race at the policy level matter. When it became possible to choose more than one race in 2000 on the census, the National Association for the Advancement of Colored People (NAACP) and the Japanese Citizens League protested that the change could diminish civil rights enforcement (Moore 2001). Controversy has also surrounded discussion of adding a racial category to the census for people with Middle Eastern or North African ancestry. On the one hand, groups like the Arab American Institute initially expressed support for the addition, and Arab American Institute executive director Maya Berry issued a statement calling the lack of inclusion of the category in the 2020 census a "severe blow" to adequately estimating the population of Middle Eastern and North African Americans. The Obama administration had suggested that such a category could be used to enforce the Voting Rights Act; create affirmative action plans; assist minority-owned businesses with federal grants and loans; and address discrimination in housing, employment, lending, and other areas (Korte 2016). On the other hand, a number of former advocates have expressed concern that the Trump administration might use the information gained from including a Middle Eastern and North African race category to enforce travel bans against countries like Iran, Libya, Syria, and Yemen (Wang 2018).

## Immigration

As discussed in Chapter 1, once America was established and its borders were firmly delineated, the nation quickly took a skeptical view of any newly arrived immigrants. From the Irish and Italians, who were initially lumped together as more racially similar to blacks than whites, to the Chinese who were appreciated for contributing to the mining industry until they were viewed as creating too much competition for white workers, those arriving in the United States faced the vitriol and fear of those who were struggling to maintain their own livelihoods and felt no incentive to share the nation's abundance.

This mentality remains persistent today and is particularly evident in attitudes about undocumented immigrants. Polling suggests that most Americans believe undocumented immigrants take jobs away from U.S. citizens, and that belief is more common at lower-income ranges than among high-income respondents (Rasmussen Reports 2017). Although certain works are negatively impacted by increases in immigration—namely prior immigrants and American citizens who did not complete at least a high school education—the long-term impact of immigration on wages and employment is fairly minimal, and increases in immigration generally benefit economic growth. High-skilled immigrants have contributed substantially to entrepreneurship and technological innovation, while low-skilled workers have provided needed labor in a number of economic sectors in which hiring demands are high, from food preparation to construction (The National Academies of Sciences, Engineering, and Medicine 2016).

Despite these benefits, undocumented adults knowingly breaking immigration laws are not the only immigrants who face pushback for entry into the United States. Anywhere from 13 to 34 percent of Americans are opposed to allowing undocumented immigrants to remain in the country even if they arrived as children, earned a high school diploma or served in the military, and were not convicted of any serious crimes. Moreover, Gallup has consistently found that the majority of Americans are not in favor of increasing *legal* immigration— preferring to keep numbers steady or decrease opportunities to immigrate legally (Kurtzleben 2018).

There remains a clear and persistent racial component to immigration opposition. For example, in a nationally representative experiment, Brader, Valentino, and Suhay (2008) found that whites were more opposed to Latino immigration than to European immigration when given news about the costs of increased immigration. Parallels can be found in concerns about the coming of a "demographic bomb"—the idea that current racial minorities will have children at a quicker pace than whites, leading to whites becoming racial minorities themselves. Fox News political commentator John Gibson framed this in particularly white nationalistic terms, telling his white viewers, "Do your duty. Make more babies . . . half of the kids in this country under five years old are minorities. By far the greatest number are Hispanic. You know what that means? Twenty-five years, and the majority of the population is Hispanic. Why is that? Well, the Hispanics are having more kids than others. Notably . . . white people are having fewer" (Calabresi 2006).

Although immigrants from the Middle East have been traditionally racialized as white, as previously mentioned, under the Obama administration, the Census Bureau debated adding a racial category that included people of Middle Eastern and North African heritage intended to go beyond the ethnic attribution of "Arab" (Korte 2016). If we think about the extent to which immigrants from the Middle East are racialized in discriminatory ways that parallel the experiences of blacks and Hispanics in the United States, then restrictions on Middle Eastern immigration can be seen as institutionally racist as well. In 2017, President Donald Trump issued Executive Order 13769, which indefinitely suspended Syrian refugee immigration to the United States and temporarily suspended entry for immigrants from Iran, Iraq, Somalia, Sudan, Syria, and Yemen. After it was challenged in court and the Trump administration faced a temporary restraining order, officials revisited the language and, after other iterations, eventually arrived at Presidential Proclamation 9645, which was upheld by the Supreme Court in *Trump v. Hawaii*. It kept much of the substance of the original executive order but no longer mentioned Sudan. Currently, it categorically denies immigrant and diversity visas to people coming from Iran, Libya, North Korea, Somalia, Syria, and Yemen (unless a waiver is granted) and restricts other visa types for people coming from Iran, Libya, North Korea, Syria, Venezuela, and Yemen (U.S. Department of State 2019). In 2018, 37,000 visa applications were denied as a direct result of these actions (Al Jazeera 2019).

## Participation in Governance

Historically, there were a number of impediments to minority participation in governance at the national, state, and local levels. The ability to vote and hold office was originally limited to white men and, in most states, required property ownership as well (The University of Texas at Austin College of Liberal Arts 2005). Although all racial groups now have the right to vote and hold office, a number of other factors have contributed to racial inequality in this realm.

One of the most contentious issues surrounding race and participation in government has been implementation of Section 5 of the 1965 Voting Rights Act. The Voting Rights Act not only guaranteed the right to vote regardless of race but also implemented specific protections to keep states with a history of racial discrimination in voting policy from future offending. Section 5 of the act established that states (or political subdivisions of a state) with a history of racial discrimination in voting were subject to approval by the attorney general or, after lawsuit, by the U.S. District Court for the District of Columbia. Section 4 established the criteria by which states and localities were chosen for oversight—any in which fewer than 50 percent of people with voting age were registered to vote or had voted as of November 1, 1964, and in which a test or device restricted people from registering to vote or voting as of November 1, 1964, could not implement new election procedures unless they were. This brought the election procedures of Alabama, Alaska, Georgia, Louisiana, Mississippi, South Carolina, and Virginia as well as sections of Arizona, Hawaii, Idaho, and North Carolina under federal oversight. Although Section 5 was originally intended only as a temporary five-year legislation, Congress found it necessary to extend it repeatedly thereafter, adjusting certain aspects such as the formula by which states and localities were chosen for electoral oversight. Most recently, Congress extended it in 2006 for an additional twenty-five years (U.S. Department of Justice 2017).

In 2013, everything changed. In a narrow 5–4 vote, the Supreme Court ruled in *Shelby County v. Holder* that Section 4 of the Voting Rights Act—the section that had established the coverage formula that determined which states and localities were subject to Section 5's oversight rules—was unconstitutional. Several states immediately instituted new election procedures. For example, Texas and North Carolina reinstituted voter identification laws that had previously been blocked (Liptak 2013; Newkirk 2017). When the U.S. Fourth Circuit Court of Appeals struck down North Carolina's voter ID law, the decision noted that the law "target[ed] African-Americans with almost surgical precision" (*North Carolina State Conference of the NAACP v. McCrory* 2016).

The *Shelby County v. Holder* ruling left Congress free to establish a new coverage formula based on more recent data to determine oversight rules governing Section 5 of the Voting Rights Act, but disagreements over the specifics have left states previously required to gain approval for their election procedure changes free to continue changing their electoral policies ever since. Numerous bills have been drafted, but none have made it through the legislative process successfully. For example, the Voting Rights Amendment Act of 2017 enjoyed bipartisan cosponsorship in the House of Representatives but has yet to move beyond the Subcommittee on the Constitution and Civil Justice (H. Res. 3239 2017). That subcommittee is also where Representative Eleanor Norton's Resolution 751 "Calling on Congress to Enact a New Preclearance Formula for the Voting Rights Act of 1965 and Condemning Voter Suppression Laws Enacted by States and Political Subdivisions" has remained since March of 2018 (H. Res. 751 2018).

Minority voting has also been significantly impacted by gerrymandering. In an effort to effect more diverse representation in line with minority political preferences, Democratic legislatures tended to draw some congressional districts with high percentages of black voters. Such districts were challenged by white voters as "racial gerrymandering" in the 1993 Supreme Court case of *Shaw v. Reno* but were upheld by the court (Pitts 2018). Since then, Republicans found that, depending on how they drew up majority-minority districts, they could use the consolidation of black voting power in a small number of districts to dilute black voting power. If enough blacks could be districted together, then black voting power in the rest of the state would be diminished. Given that blacks tend to vote for Democrats, this also had the (intended) effect of diluting Democratic representation. However, recent court decisions have placed limits on racially discriminatory gerrymandering. In *Virginia House of Delegates v. Bethune-Hill, No. 18-281*, the Supreme Court allowed a district court decision striking down a redistricting plan that diluted black voting power in Virginia to stand (Liptak 2019).

Aside from racialized barriers to full participation in voting, we also continue to face racial disparities in access to political office. A readily apparent example is how the United States has had only one president who did not identify as white (Barack Obama) (Demby 2017). Although diversity has improved over time in Congress, 81 percent of Congress members are white despite racial minorities comprising 38 percent of the U.S. population (Bialik and Krogstad 2017). When we consider who holds elected office at all levels of government, 97 percent of Republican officials and 79 percent of Democratic officials are white. This lack of diversity is exacerbated by the difficulties that political candidates who are racial minorities have competing with whites for access to fundraising networks; partially as a result, racial minorities constitute only 4 percent of Republican candidates and 18 percent of Democratic candidates. Moreover, the fact that incumbents are more likely to win elections than newcomers means that the primarily white elected officials already in office have substantial advantages in facing off against racial minority challengers (Lardieri 2017).

## Education

Horace Mann famously described education as "a great equalizer of conditions of men—the balance wheel of the social machinery" (Growe and Montgomery 2003). The veracity of this claim in the context of racial equality is worth vetting. Data from Duke University's Campus Life and Learning Project provides partial support for this view; although Latino and black students came to college with significantly lower standardized test scores than white and Asian students and earned a lower GPA (grade point average) during their first year of college, the GPA gap narrowed substantially in subsequent years. Moreover, there were no significant differences between multiracial, white, Asian, black, and Latino students in degree attainment (Martin, Spenner, and Mustillo 2016).

Yet a variety of impediments to racial equality in education persist. At the K-12 level, non-special education classes are 80 percent larger in predominantly minority schools than in predominantly white schools. Teachers in predominantly minority schools also have lower average levels of education themselves and are less-highly trained in the fields in which they teach, contributing to lower standardized test scores among minority students (Darling-Hammond 1998).

Instructional staff in K-12 classes systematically differentiate between students of various racial groups in assignment to educational tracks and administration of punishment. Black students are more likely to be assigned to lower educational tracks and lower ability groups than white students, leading to learning gaps (Tyson 2011). There are also substantial differences between racial groups in likelihood to take Advanced Placement classes. Using PSAT scores to predict potential, six out of ten Asian students identified as having a 60 percent or higher likelihood of success in an AP science course actually took one as compared to four out of ten whites, four out of ten Hispanics/Latinos, three out of ten blacks, and three out of ten American Indians/Alaskan Natives (College Board 2014). Part of the reason for this may lie in teacher expectations and whether teachers motivate students to enroll in more difficult courses or not based on those expectations. A recent study indicated that nonblack teachers have much lower expectations than black teachers for black students' academic success (particularly in the case of black male students) (Gershenson, Holt, and Papageorge 2016).

Regarding punishment, according to data from the Kentucky School Discipline Study, black students were 7.57 times as likely to face suspension as whites, while Latinos were more than twice as likely. Although Asians were less likely to be suspended than whites, overall, nonwhite students were about 2.61 times more likely to face suspension than whites (Morris and Perry 2016). Black students are also much more likely to be expelled, subjected to corporal punishment, or referred to law enforcement following a school infraction than other students (U.S. Government Accountability Office 2018).

Some concern has also emerged around the capacity for the education system to weaken cultural awareness and stigmatize cultural practices among racial minorities. Indeed, as noted in Chapter 1, the American education system has a long history of assimilating racial minorities, most notably in the case of Native Americans. In more recent years, educational institutions have persisted in trying to curb racial minorities' cultural practices. One example is prohibitions on hairstyles and head coverings. Evidence suggests that dreadlocks have been worn as early as 3,000 to 4,000 years ago in places like ancient India and Greece, but they were popularized by Jamaicans and became seen as symbols of black pride and strength in the face of discrimination (Robinson 2018). Thus, the decision by certain schools to not allow dreadlocks has clear racial implications. In one highly publicized example, black, six-year-old Clinton Stanley Jr. was denied entry into A Book's Christian Academy on his first day of school because of his dreadlocks; the school's handbook prohibited the hairstyle explicitly and compared it to "Mohawks, . . . unnatural color, or unnatural designs" (Yancey-Bragg 2018). Black female students have also been punished for wearing braid extensions (Nittle 2018).

Similarly, most Muslim Americans identify as a race other than white (with 51 percent of third-generation or later immigrants identifying as black), and their use of a hijab has, at times, been called into question by schools (Pew Research Center 2017b). For example, Benjamin Franklin Science Academy in Oklahoma agreed to allow hijabs as a religious exception to the dress code but only after suspending an eleven-year-old twice for wearing one and subsequently facing a five-year lawsuit (Arter 2008). More recently, a teacher in Nashville, Tennessee, was suspended for ripping a hijab off of a student's head and telling her that her hair was too pretty to be covered (Pirani 2017).

Language has been similarly contested in a manner that indicates racial bias. Although more than thirty-seven million Latinos speak Spanish at home in the United States, Latino students have been suspended for using it at school (Krogstad and Lopez 2017; Reid 2005). As recently as in 2016, a school bus driver banned speaking in Spanish on the bus and, when an eighth-grade Latino student failed to comply, poured a bottle of water on him (Gonzalez 2016).

**The Labor Market**

Racial disparities are particularly apparent in employment, beginning with the hiring process. A major reason why we know this is because of audit studies. Audit studies are designed to determine whether testers matched on as many characteristics as possible (e.g., gender, height, work experience, educational experience) attempting to participate in everyday activities in various institutional settings experience equal treatment and/or outcomes. In an audit study of entry-level jobs in Wisconsin, Devah Pager (2003) found that not only were white applicants more likely to receive a callback than similarly qualified black applicants but also white applicants disclosing a drug felony were more likely to be contacted about a job than black applicants presented with no criminal history. Something as simple as a black-sounding name can derail an application; an audit study of jobs in Boston and Chicago revealed that white-sounding names elicited 50 percent more interview opportunities than black-sounding names (Bertrand and Mullainathan 2004).

Even employers who signal an interest in diversity may still be prone to racial bias; in another audit study, Kang et al. (2016) looked at how minority job candidates fared when they submitted their résumés as per usual versus when they "whitened" them by removing or deemphasizing racial cues. Not only did employers in general prefer whitened applications but so too did employers with explicit diversity statements (Kang et al. 2016). It's no surprise, then, that, even with recent declines in black unemployment, blacks still face 1.85 times higher unemployment than whites (Long 2018).

Once hired, employees of color continue to face impediments to full equality according to a variety of measures. The economic disparities are blatant: a black man at the 50th percentile of income among blacks has the same income as a white man at the 27th percentile of income among whites (Bayer and Charles 2018). Considering race and gender in tandem, the results become especially stark. For every $1 that a white man earns on average, an Asian woman earns $0.87, a white woman earns $0.79, a black woman earns $0.63, a Native American woman earns $0.57, and a Latina woman earns $0.54 (Connley 2018). This is not simply a product of differences in educational attainment; for example, black women are underpaid relative to white men at every level of education. It also cannot be explained away simply by suggesting that racial minorities are choosing careers that pay less, as, for example, black women earn less than white men in not only lower-paying jobs (as social workers, retail salespersons, and elementary school teachers) but also in relatively lucrative fields as accountants, physicians, lawyers, and financial managers (Wilson et al. 2017).

Income differences, although instructive, do not entirely account for racial discrimination in pay. It is possible that members of Group A make more money on average than members of Group B but are still facing unfair treatment, meaning that their income advantage would be even bigger relative to members of other groups in a nondiscriminatory environment. For example, in a survey conducted for the National Public Radio, the Robert Wood Johnson Foundation, and Harvard University's T. H. Chan School of Public Health (2017), researchers found that, although Asian Americans in the sample had the highest average incomes, 25 percent of Asian Americans reported having been discriminated against in job pay and promotion.

Promotion decisions often reflect discriminatory tendencies that prioritize white men. The Ascend Foundation's Executive Parity Index (EPI) provides a ratio of representation in managerial positions to professional workforce representation outside of administration. Only white and Hispanic men enjoy advantages in access to managerial jobs. White men have an EPI rating of 1.81 (indicating 81 percent overrepresentation in management), whereas Hispanic men have a much lower but still advantageous EPI rating of 1.07. Other groups (white women at 0.65, black men at 0.63, Asian men at 0.56, Hispanic women at 0.49, black women at 0.30, and Asian women at 0.24) are at a substantial disadvantage when it comes to managerial hiring (Gee 2018). The problem is especially pronounced at the highest levels of industry; for example, there are only three black CEOs in the Fortune 500. On Fortune 500 corporate boards, fewer than 10 percent of members are black, while about 6 percent are Hispanic and about 6 percent are Asian or Asian American (Donnelly 2018).

Day-to-day treatment of racial minorities in the workplace also illustrates the persistence of structural racism. In a recent Pew Research Center poll, 62 percent of blacks in STEM (science, technology, engineering, and mathematics) jobs, 50 percent of blacks in non-STEM jobs, 42 percent of Hispanics in STEM jobs, and 42 percent of Hispanics in non-STEM jobs answered that they had experienced racial discrimination at work (Funk and Parker 2018). Further, although only 31 percent of U.S. adults agreed that "[facing] discrimination in recruitment, hiring, and promotions" was a major reason for blacks and Hispanics being underrepresented in STEM jobs, 72 percent of blacks agreed with this statement. Black workers also face higher scrutiny from managers, making it more likely that they will be caught making mistakes on the job (Cavounidis and Lang 2015).

Even in positions of supervision and authority, racial minorities find their judgment and competence questioned. For example, academia, black female professors face the lowest average student evaluations and experience more frequent challenges to their authority than other professors. An author of a chapter on the plight of black women in academia described a personal example of this when a student derailed one of her classes on the first day of a new semester by detailing how another professor had set up his syllabus, publicly offering to show it to her "so you can learn how to do one" (Pitt et al. 2015). In a study of female faculty of color, Pittman (2010) found that white, male students were the ones who most often challenged such faculty's research acumen, teaching ability, and general authority and who most often displayed aggressive or threatening behavior. The degree to which faculty of color (and, especially, female faculty of color) are undercut by their students (and, particularly, their white, male students) is especially problematic given that faculty of color teach more than any other faculty (Pittman 2010).

Racial minorities who are leaders in their companies may also be penalized for encouraging additional diversification of their workplaces. Those who engage in "diversity-valuing behaviors," such as promoting racial minorities or recruiting more diverse hiring pools, are viewed as less competent by their bosses and peers. White, male executives, on the other hand, do not face the same consequences (Hekman et al. 2017).

Racial discrimination also occurs when decisions are made about whom to fire. When it comes to how job performance factors in, blacks are more likely to be fired than colleagues of other racial classifications for making mistakes on the job (Cavounidis and Lang 2015). Regardless of performance, when the business cycle progresses from a period of growing gross domestic product (GDP) to a period of declining GDP, research suggests that blacks and immigrants are especially likely to be fired (Couch and Fairlie 2010; Xu 2018). Among immigrants, Hispanic immigrants are fired with particular frequency in an economic downturn (Xu 2018).

As a result of racial discrimination in hiring, treatment, and firing, people of color may make attempts to outwardly assimilate to white workplace culture or navigate white expectations. Latino/Latina workers may try to hide their accents, while black workers may work longer hours to signal differentiation from stereotypes about black laziness or style their hair in ways considered more appropriate by white bosses (Wingfield 2015). Code-switching (talking and acting in ways that reflect the dominant culture) becomes a way to navigate white work spaces at the loss of individual authenticity (Cheeks 2018).

Diversity trainings, while intended to improve interracial interactions in the workplace, may contribute to some of the very processes they seek to curb. For example, many diversity training sessions challenge participants to discuss their negative racial attitudes aloud. However, the desire to provide a safe space for talking through such attitudes can lead to people of color feeling an expectation to avoid reacting too negatively to the racist stereotypes expressed by their white coworkers. After all, these coworkers are seen as putting themselves in a vulnerable place by confronting their tendencies toward racial prejudice, and it may be assumed that they would become defensive and less likely to participate if challenged. Yet the openness extended to whites in order to encourage them to honestly process their animus limits opportunities for people of color to react honestly (Wingfield 2015). The result is the stifling of legitimate objections and challenges to discrimination.

### Transportation

The average American spends more each year on transportation than on food, education, or health care. Among people of color, expenditures on transportation can reach as high as a third of their annual incomes. Yet the experience of transportation can differ substantially based on racial discrimination. Take, for example, buying a car. The National Fair Housing Alliance recently concluded an audit study of car-buying experiences in Virginia by sending a white tester and a nonwhite tester with a better credit rating to each dealership. Their 2018 reporting of those findings indicated that nonwhites with higher credit scores were offered higher prices than whites in 62.5 percent of cases and fewer financing options in 75 percent of cases. When discrimination occurred (i.e., in cases in which a white tester with a lower credit score was offered a better deal than a nonwhite tester with a higher credit score), nonwhite car buyers were offered, on average, loans that would have cost them about $2,662.56 more than what was offered to less-qualified whites (Rice and Schwartz 2018).

Part of the reason why people of color are more likely to be offered unfavorable loan rates is that loans made through car dealerships are offered by independent lenders but are also subject to what are known as "dealer participation" markups. A dealer is allowed to increase the interest rate of a loan in order to recoup costs for his or her services in making a deal with the customer on behalf of the lender. The amount of that markup is subject to a degree of discretion and usually is not explicitly disclosed to the consumer, meaning that, when you buy a car, you may not know what loan rate you actually qualified for (as compared to what loan rate you were quoted based on the extent to which the dealer inflated the cost) (Davis and

Frank 2011). This allows car dealers to discriminate against people of color in a relatively subtle manner.

Steps have been taken by the federal government to address such discrimination. In 2013, the Consumer Financial Protection Bureau released a reminder that discriminating on the basis of race, religion, age, or sex in auto lending is illegal under the Equal Credit Opportunity Act. The release also noted that auto lenders are responsible for ensuring that dealers do not use lending rates in a discriminatory manner. The increased oversight motivated a number of auto lenders to make changes to their practices voluntarily, such as when BB&T bank moved to a model of offering all auto loans as flat-fee loans without any interest rate markups from one customer to another. However, when leadership at the Consumer Financial Protection Bureau changed under President Trump, BB&T went back to using interest rate markups (Nova 2018). In addition, on May 21, 2018, President Trump signed into law S. J. Res. 57 (2018), which stated that the Consumer Financial Protection Bureau's guidance on the illegality of auto loan discrimination based on race, religion, age, or sex would have "no force or effect." It is unsurprising, then, that car loan discrimination persists.

Public transportation brings its own problems. In an effort to lure suburban white commuters from their cars back to public transportation, some transit providers have prioritized new, comfortable, energy-efficient buses and trains for their neighborhoods. Transit companies are aware that those who cannot afford a car (who also are more likely to be people of color) may be reliant on public transportation and will, therefore, be more likely to accept it if buses and trains that run in their neighborhoods are outdated, dirty, or ill equipped. In this way, people of color in cities often end up paying a greater proportion of their income for transportation than whites while receiving lower-quality services (Bullard 2004).

Uber and Lyft—peer transportation companies that pay independent contractors to work essentially as taxi drivers using their own vehicles—crowdsource transportation. Theoretically, that could mean that there could be more racially egalitarian transportation options, but, unfortunately, the unregulated nature of these companies' operations has led to even more discrimination than present in other forms of transportation. In one recent audit study of peer transportation companies, passengers hailed around 1,500 rides in Seattle and Boston. Passengers with black-sounding names had their trips canceled more frequently than passengers with white-sounding names (Ge et al. 2016).

## Housing

As with public transportation, audit studies have given us a clear window into racial discrimination in the housing market. From 2000 to 2002, the Department of Housing and Urban Development conducted a series of almost 5,500 audits in almost thirty areas of the United States, finding that blacks faced discrimination in about one-fifth of searches for a home to rent or buy, while Hispanics faced such discrimination in one-fourth of searches, and Native Americans faced housing discrimination at an even higher rate. Asian Americans were not statistically significantly more likely to face housing discrimination than whites when trying to rent a home but did face statistically significant discrimination when attempting to purchase one. People of color more frequently were given less information about housing units, fewer opportunities to tour homes, and less help with loan options (Pager and Shepherd 2008).

Compared to whites, blacks looking to rent were told about 11.4 percent fewer available units and shown 4.2 percent fewer, while Hispanics were told about 12.5 percent fewer and shown 7.5 percent fewer, and Asian Americans were told about 9.8 percent fewer and shown 6.6 percent fewer. Also, compared to whites, blacks looking to buy a home were told about 17 percent fewer units and shown 17.7 percent fewer, while Asian Americans were told about 15.5 percent fewer units and shown 18.8 percent fewer (U.S. Department of Housing and

Urban Development 2013). People of color were also more likely to be directed to available units in poorer neighborhoods (Pager and Shepherd 2008). Such discrimination is even more common when those seeking housing use vernacular that is interpreted as "lower class" (e.g., Massey and Lundy 2001). More recent research has also demonstrated discrimination in renting experienced by Arab Americans; in one audit study of responses to roommate-ads on Craigslist, people with Arab American–sounding names were 40 percent less likely on average to be chosen as roommates even when controlling for educational background, socioeconomic status, and English proficiency (Gaddis and Ghoshal 2015).

Once housed, people of color may also experience discrimination by landlords and residential associations. This can range from slower or less adequate responses to maintenance issues up to outright harassment or threats (Roscigno, Karafin, and Tester 2009). It can also involve decisions to give tenants additional time when they fall behind on rent or to proceed with an eviction. In a study of 1,086 Milwaukee, Wisconsin, rental households, Greenberg, Gershenson, and Desmond (2016) found that Hispanics at risk of eviction were twice as likely to actually be evicted if they lived in majority-white neighborhoods as they were if they lived in majority nonwhite neighborhoods. Further, white landlords were more likely than Hispanic landlords to evict Hispanic tenants (Greenberg, Gershenson, and Desmond 2016).

Beyond the aforementioned examples of discrimination, people of color are also more susceptible to environmental racism. A recent report from scientists at the Environmental Protection Agency's (EPA) National Center for Environmental Assessment concluded that nonwhites faced 1.28 times higher environmental burden from particular matter-emitting facilities (e.g., polluting factories) than whites, while blacks faced a 1.54 times higher burden. The average black resident faced a higher environmental burden than the average person below the poverty line, indicating that economic position could not explain away the impact of racism in the location of pollution-emitting facilities (Mikati et al. 2018). In general, people of color are more likely to experience lower air quality than whites, including exposure to nitrogen dioxide (Milman 2017). They are also more likely to live near Superfund sites (i.e., places targeted by the EPA for extensive cleanup after a particularly toxic chemical spill). This contributes to higher cancer rates in majority nonwhite neighborhoods (Amin 2017).

In a widely publicized recent example, large protests met the attempt to build the Dakota Access Pipeline through Standing Rock Sioux and Cheyenne River Sioux lands. As Standing Rock Sioux Tribal Council chairman David Archambault II argued in a 2014 meeting with representatives from the Dakota Access Pipeline (DAPL) and Energy Transfer Partners, the pipeline would violate the Fort Laramie treaties of 1851 and 1868. The pipeline was also proposed to go through 380 archaeological sites and could not be guaranteed not to leak oil into the water used by people who lived nearby, particularly given that 200 of the pipelines operated by proposed DAPL operator Sunoco Logistics had leaked between 2010 and 2016 (Estes 2019). Thanks to the tribes' push for a full environmental study, operation of the pipeline was delayed, but, at Donald Trump's request, the Army Corps of Engineers greenlighted the pipeline's completion without the study (Meyer 2017).

### Criminal Justice

Racism in the criminal justice system begins even before anyone is arrested or charged with a crime in the decisions made regarding whether or not to consider an individual as suspicious and worth questioning. Take, for example, Charlottesville, Virginia—recently made infamous for being the site of the convergence of a large number of white supremacists for a rally at the University of Virginia at which a protestor was run over by a car. A report to the Charlottesville City Council in 2018 indicated that, although blacks constituted less than one-fifth of the city's population, they accounted for 91 of 125 investigative detentions in 2017 (Di Maro 2018). Similarly, in the first half of 2018, of 5,064 recorded New York Police Department stops, 58 percent of suspects were black, 31 percent were Latino, and only 9 percent were white (New York Civil Liberties Union 2018). Traffic stops reveal a similar pattern; in a review of twenty million such cases, blacks were twice as likely to be pulled over and more likely to be subsequently searched than whites. There is ample evidence that discrimination is at the root of these differences, as they occurred despite blacks being both less likely to drive and less likely to have contraband when stopped (Baumgartner, Epp, and Shoub 2018). Moreover, a report from researchers at the Institute for Municipal and Regional Policy at Central Connecticut University revealed that blacks and Hispanics were more likely to be pulled over by police during the day but not at night (when their skin tone would be less identifiable) (Ross et al. 2017).

When members of one particular group are more frequently surveilled, stopped, questioned, and searched than members of other groups, the likelihood of their being arrested goes up dramatically even if members of that group are no more or less law abiding than members of any other group. One example that bears this out is the case of illegal drug use. Although surveys suggest that whites, blacks, and Hispanics have relatively similar rates of illegal drug use, whites are arrested less likely—in part, because they have higher socioeconomic statuses on average, which means that the spaces in which they buy, sell, and use drugs are less frequented by police (The Sentencing Project 2015).

Not only are police more likely to target racial minorities themselves, but they are also more likely to be called to detain racial minorities by members of the public. In recent years, there have been a number of examples of whites reporting black people to the police for engaging in normal, everyday activities. Recently, whites have called the police in response to blacks sitting in a Starbucks without ordering yet, eating lunch in a common room at a university, barbequing in a public park, wearing socks in a public pool, and "[skipping] holes and [taking] an extended break after the 9th hole at a golf club" (Anderson 2018; Associated Press 2018).

When police decide to detain an individual, race plays a role in how that person is treated. This includes the use of basic decorum in initial interactions; in an Oakland, California, analysis of how police talk to motorists whom they stop, police officers (regardless of their race or the severity of the alleged offense) used more respectful language toward white motorists than toward black motorists (Voigt et al. 2017). Examples of respectful language included addressing the motorist formally (e.g., sir or ma'am), apologizing for the inconvenience of stopping the motorist, or thanking the motorist for cooperating. Racial differences also play a role in officers' decisions about whether or not to handcuff a suspect; in one study of officers making at least one stop during a thirteen-month period of study, 26 percent handcuffed at least one white person, whereas 72 percent handcuffed at least one black person when not making an arrest (SPARQ 2016).

More concerning is the extent to which race also impacts the likelihood that an officer will engage in violence. National data collected from multiple police departments around the country from 2011 to 2015 revealed that police used force against blacks more frequently than against whites every year, including use of dogs, pepper spray, and Tasers (Goff et al. 2016). Blacks and Hispanics are also disproportionately subject to SWAT team raids (American Civil Liberties Union 2014). Although blacks constitute just over 13 percent of the American population and Hispanics constitute a little more than 18 percent, black and Hispanic men are both twice as likely as white men to be killed by police (U.S. Census Bureau 2017). Numerous black people (and especially black men) have been killed by police officers under questionable circumstances. There was Eric Garner, who died in a police chokehold while shouting that he couldn't breathe. There was Tamir Rice, who was killed at twelve years of age supposedly because he was carrying a gun; the gun was a toy. Philando Castile actually had a gun and a license to carry it but was shot to death during a traffic stop despite alerting the officer to the fact that the gun was in the car (Hobson 2016). Fear of such instances has led some black men to wear formal clothes when outside of their homes to signal that they are "safe" and not "thugs" (Yi 2015).

This does not necessarily confirm that police are prone to more racist tendencies than anyone else. For example, participants in social psychology experiments have been asked to press one button to shoot video-simulated suspects if they are armed and another to not shoot if they are unarmed. On average, they were both more accurate in choosing to shoot armed targets when those targets were black and more accurate in choosing not to shoot targets when they were white (The Sentencing Project 2015). Although such a tendency transcends occupation, police wield unique institutional power and have unique opportunities to exercise their discretion in the use of force. They also have a greater degree of protection from prosecution when they exercise that discretion.

When police kill, they rarely face serious consequences, primarily because of how infrequently they are charged with murder or manslaughter. Data from a study of police crime reveals that, despite there being approximately 1,000 police shootings per year in the United States, only 80 officers were arrested on charges of murder or manslaughter after shooting someone while on duty from 2005 to 2017. In those eighty cases, 39 percent of the officers facing charges were not convicted, 26 percent had a case still pending, and only 35 percent were convicted (Stinson 2017).

While a slight majority of the public (54 percent) see the deaths of blacks in interactions with police in recent years as indicative of a broader problem, officers themselves are less inclined to suggest that racism in police departments is pervasive and institutional (Gramlich 2017). In a national poll from Pew Research Center, 72 percent of white officers saw recent deaths of blacks during interactions with police as isolated events rather than signs of a more widespread problem (as opposed to 43 percent of black officers). Perhaps more tellingly, 92 percent of white officers believed that the United States had already made sufficient changes to provide blacks with equal rights to whites as compared to only 29 percent of black officers (Gramlich 2017). Thus, black officers are more likely to see racism in police departments as systemic and underaddressed than their white colleagues.

If charged with a crime, racial minorities face additional impediments to equal treatment. Black defendants face higher bails for pretrial release than whites, and the less experienced the judge, the bigger the disparities (suggesting that, given lack of experience on the job, racial stereotypes substantially influence decision-making about bail assignment) (Arnold, Dobbie, and Yang 2018). Although the findings are not universal, multiple studies reveal that racial minorities are also offered plea bargains less frequently than whites. When they are offered plea bargains, the terms are less favorable on average than they are for whites (Banks 2017). Not only does the inability to obtain a reasonable plea bargain opportunity subject one to the stress and complexity of a trial, but the outcomes of those trials are themselves tinged with racial discrimination.

When pretrial negotiations fail and cases proceed to trial, racial minorities face substantial disadvantages in adjudication. First, there is the issue of who judges; despite comprising a third of the population, white men make up 58 percent of judges in state courts (where more than 95 percent of court cases are heard). In contrast, women of color collectively account for only 8 percent of state judges while representing one-fifth of the population (Jawando and Anderson 2016).

Although there is an expectation that defendants in criminal cases will be tried by a jury of their peers, insofar as race is concerned, this is less likely for defendants who are racial minorities. It is illegal to exclude people from juries on the basis of race (given the 1986 Supreme Court ruling in *Batson v. Kentucky*), but that has not kept prosecutors from finding ways to exclude black and Hispanic jurors via supposedly "race-neutral" policies. Prosecutors have successfully excluded racial minorities from juries for everything from speaking Spanish to being affiliated with a traditionally black college or university (The Equal Justice Initiative 2010). Diverse juries make fewer mistakes in deliberation, are more likely to consider the potential role of racism in a case, and are more lenient than all-white juries toward black defendants (Sommers 2006).

Evidence of statistical significance is mixed regarding disparities in conviction rates, but a number of studies suggest that people viewing the facts of a case are more likely to support conviction when defendants are Latino or black (Sommers 2007). Even more troubling, when exonerations are taken into account, innocent blacks are twelve times more likely than whites to be convicted of a drug crime, seven times more likely to be convicted of murder, and three and a half times more likely to be convicted of sexual assault (Gross, Possley, and Stephens 2017).

When it comes to sentencing, additional disparities arise. In a national analysis of sentencing differences by race, the United States Sentencing Commission (2017) found that black defendants are given about 19 percent longer sentences on average than white defendants in similar circumstances. Not only are racial minorities disadvantaged as defendants in the sentencing process, but they are also disadvantaged as family members of victims seeking justice. Fewer than half of murder victims in the United States are white, but 80 percent of people on death row killed a white person. Black defendants are more likely to be sentenced to the death penalty if convicted of killing a white woman than if convicted of killing someone from any other combination of racial group and gender designation (Amnesty International 2003; Baumgartner and Lyman 2016).

The disproportionately black prison population is subject to additional harms imposed by the prison system and its negotiations with corporations. When British Petroleum was responsible for the biggest oil spill in history, the company hired primarily black prisoners to reduce labor costs and get access to various tax breaks during the cleanup process. This led NAACP president Ben Jealous to send a public letter protesting the disproportionate number of black people doing the "most physically difficult, lowest paying jobs, with the most significant exposure to toxins" (Young 2010).

## Health and Health Care

Racial minorities in America also face substantial health disadvantages. They have higher disease rates and, even when this is not the case, may experience diseases with greater severity (e.g., blacks experience more "persistent, severe, disabling, and untreated" depression) (Williams and Sternthal 2010). They also have higher mortality rates than whites at all age ranges and are more likely to die from a wide range of health problems (Nelson 2002). Blacks are more likely than whites to die from heart disease, cancer, stroke, diabetes, kidney disease, hypertension, and cirrhosis of the liver (Williams and Mohammed 2009). Latinos are more likely than whites to die from diabetes, hypertension, or cirrhosis of the liver (Williams and Sternthal 2010).

Racial discrimination is at the heart of racial disparities in health. Discrimination is associated with increases in both physical health problems (e.g., high blood pressure) and mental health problems (e.g., stress or anxiety) (Krieger and Sidney 1996). To avoid discrimination by health care professionals, racial minorities may fail to seek preventative care (e.g., cholesterol screenings or flu shots) or rely on alternative health providers with less standardized credentials, further endangering their health (Williams and Mohammed 2009).

Occupational differences also contribute to racial disparities in health. Given that they are more likely to be of lower socioeconomic status, blacks and Hispanics are also more likely to be employed in dangerous jobs in which they are exposed to carcinogens or a high risk of injury (Seabury, Terp, and Boden 2017; Williams and Mohammed 2009). For example, in the 1930s, hundreds of miners in West Virginia (most of whom were black) died from lung cancer after repeatedly inhaling silica dust. Visiting members of the management team from the corporation contracted to do the work wore masks to protect themselves, but they did not issue any such equipment to the workers. Yet, even in such harsh conditions, the day-to-day experience was even worse for black workers than white workers; black workers who survived later testified to Congress that they were denied clean air breaks and forced from bed to work at gunpoint when sick, exposing them to even more of the silica dust (Lancianese 2019).

As a result of years of discriminatory housing policies, homeowners' association decisions, and bank loan decision, racial segregation has persisted, and it has also contributed to health differences. Racial minorities are more likely to live in areas exposed to environmental toxins (an aspect of environmental racism). They are less likely to have access to healthy grocery store options (particularly in more segregated areas with predominantly black populations). They are also more likely to find that their neighborhood pharmacies are insufficiently stocked with medication for severe pain (Mikati et al. 2018; Williams and Collins 2001). Low-income minorities are also more likely to be exposed to be targeted with advertisements about alcohol and tobacco—two products that can contribute to a variety of health problems (Williams and Collins 2001).

Given the health disparities that racial minorities face relative to whites, it is important that they have access to adequate health care. Yet access to health care is another area in which racial minorities are disadvantaged. Asians, Hispanics, blacks, American Indians, and Alaska Natives between birth and sixty-four years of age all access and use health care less than whites in the same age range (Artiga et al. 2016). Studies of blacks, Asian Americans, and Latinos suggest that underutilization stems partially from financial barriers (e.g., lack of insurance) and partially from concerns about being disrespected by medical professionals (American College of Physicians 2003). One way to avoid discrimination is to avoid spaces in which it occurs; if health care professionals are discriminatory, then patients may avoid them. While such a strategy reduces exposure to direct discrimination, it also may negatively impact access to important medical information.

Health care professionals are not substantially different from other Americans in their capacity to believe negative stereotypes about race. For example, on average, health care professionals see black patients as less educated and intelligent and less likely to follow medical advice (American College of Physicians 2003). This may partially explain racial differences to the extent to which patients are offered major treatments. Several studies suggest that racial minorities may be provided with a lower standard of care. In one study of 1.7 million hospital discharges across 500 hospitals, blacks were less likely than whites to be offered a major therapeutic procedure in nearly half of the disease categories assessed (Harris, Andrews, and Elixhauser 1997). This was true even in some cases in which doctor discretion is relatively low (e.g., in the decision to recommend an appendectomy) (Mort, Weisman, and Epstein 1994). When socioeconomic status is controlled for, Hispanics are also less likely than whites to be provided with major treatment for a variety of disease types (Andrews and Elixhauser 2000).

## The Arts

Racism even impacts success in the arts. In theatre, Broadway producers are primarily white; as Stephen Byrd said, in reference to himself and Alia Jones, "We're probably the only African Americans on Broadway who hands-on produce, choose the project, director, etc." (Goff 2013). As for actors, there has been some progress toward diversity. For example, in New York City, from 2015 to 2016, almost two in five roles went to minority actors, and 15 percent of roles went to African Americans. However, over the past decade, Middle Eastern/North African, American Indian, and disabled actors combined accounted for only 2 percent of all roles, while 4 percent of roles went to Latinos and 4 percent went to Asians. On Broadway, the disparity has been less pronounced, with 36 percent of roles going to minorities during the 2015–2016 season. Yet this progress has not extended to all minority groups; during that season, only 5 percent of those roles went to Asian American performers (Fuchs 2018). Moreover, white actors make higher salaries, on average, than actors of other racial groups in Broadway and Off-Broadway productions (Actors' Equity Association 2017).

In the movie industry, similar issues arise. The vast majority of studio heads are white; as famous director Spike Lee put it, "It's easier to be the president of the United States as a black person than to be the head of a studio" (Yuen 2017:32). Similarly, the vast majority of directors and actors behind top-grossing films are white. In a study of the top one hundred films from 2007 to 2014 (excluding 2011), only 5.8 percent of directors were black, while 2.4 percent were Asian. Among actors, 73.1 percent were coded as white, 12.5 percent as black, 5.3 percent as Asian, 4.9 percent as Hispanic/Latino, 2.9 percent as Middle Eastern, and less than 1 percent as American Indian/Alaska Native or Native Hawaiian/Pacific Islander (Smith et al. 2016).

In terms of recognition for individual movie actors, 92.2 percent of acting Oscars have gone to whites, and only one woman of color—Halle Berry—has ever won the award for best actress (Yuen 2017). Berry has since lamented her win as a moment that "meant nothing" given the perpetual lack of recognition of women of color in movies since then (White 2017). Further, no Asian, Latino, or indigenous actor has won an acting Oscar for more than a decade. When actors of color do win such awards, it is often for portrayal of characters in subservient roles (e.g., Hattie McDaniel, the first black actor to win an Academy Award, and Lupita Nyong'o, who won best supporting actress in 2014, both played slaves, while Octavia Spencer won best supporting actress playing a maid) (Yuen 2017).

Television is no different. In recent years, more than 90 percent of showrunners have been white, and racial minority writers contributed between 11 and 20 percent of episodes for 22 percent of scripted shows on cable. Only 20 percent of Emmy Award–winning shows were created by a racial minority during the 2014–2015 season and the 2015–2016 season (up from 0 percent from 2011 through 2012) (Hunt et al. 2018). As for actors, whites get approximately three-fourths of the roles on scripted cable and broadcast shows (Miranda 2017). In addition, only 20 percent of the leads in new scripted broadcast shows for the 2017–2018 season were racial minorities or Hispanic, and that number dipped as low as 9 percent for one network (Holloway 2017).

In the music industry, we see a similar pattern. Since the early twenty-first century, Grammy nominations of racial minorities for best record, album, song, and new artist of the year and appearances of minority artists on Billboard's Hot 100 list have steadily fallen (Keith and Gilat 2015). In 2013, for example, not a single black lead artist achieved a number-one hit on the U.S. Billboard 100 chart (Bruce 2017). In orchestras, all but about 15 percent of the musicians are white. Although the number of Asian/Pacific Islander musicians in orchestras has steadily risen in recent years, the proportion of Hispanic/Latino musicians has risen only slightly, and the proportion of black musicians has hardly changed at all (League of American Orchestras 2016). As for country music, well-regarded artists began receiving memberships to join the Grand Ole Opry in 1925 (a sign of success in the genre), but there have been only three black artists invited since then, and there is currently only one living member of the Country Music Hall of Fame (Charley Pride) (Bargmann 2016). Beyond racial classification, skin tone may play a connected role; Laybourn (2017) found that having lighter skin is associated with one's songs reaching higher Billboard Rap Year-End chart rankings.

## Sports

Unlike a number of other institutions in which racial minorities are underrepresented, there are sports in which they actually comprise the majority of players. Yet this does not necessarily mean that all racial groups are adequately represented across all sports. In addition, diversity among players does not necessarily extend to ownership and management of teams. Further, representation also does not imply that racial minorities are unaffected by prejudicial views and discriminatory treatment in sporting.

When it comes to racial diversity in sports, there is wide variation. On the one hand, whites constitute 80.8 percent of collegiate baseball players and 74.5 percent of collegiate softball players (Lapchick 2017). At the professional level, all but thirty players (95 percent) in the National Hockey League (NHL) were white during the 2018–2019 season (Thomas 2018). On the other hand, in a number of sports, racial minorities are actually overrepresented relative to their numbers in the American population in some sports. Black players are overrepresented in Division I FBS (55.9 percent), Division I men's basketball (53 percent), Division I women's basketball (43.4 percent), the National Basketball Association (NBA) (73.9 percent), the Women's National Basketball Association players (78.1 percent), and the National Football League (NFL) (69.7 percent) (Lapchick 2018b, 2018c, 2019c). Latinos are overrepresented in proportion to their numbers in the American population in Major League Baseball (MLB) (31.9 percent) and Major League Soccer (MLS) (25.1 percent) (Lapchick 2018a, 2019b). One thing that remains consistent across sports is the underrepresentation of Asian Americans and Native Americans (see, for example, Lapchick 2017, 2018a, 2018b, 2019b).

Although some racial minority groups are well represented among players in particular sports, racial minorities, in general, are less likely to be chosen for "skill" positions and less likely to retain those roles. Volz (2015) found that, over a thirteen-year period, between 16 and 28 percent of quarterbacks were black (despite around two-thirds of NFL players being black), and black starting quarterbacks in the NFL were 1.98 to 2.46 times more likely to be replaced the following week than similarly skilled white starting quarterbacks. Similarly, black centers are rare and black kickers have often been exceedingly rare in the NFL. In MLB, Hispanics and blacks (but especially blacks) have often been underrepresented among catchers and pitchers (Kooistra, Mahoney, and Bridges 1993).

Among coaches and owners, there is considerably less diversity. All Football Bowl Subdivision (FBS) conference commissioners are white, as are 86.1 percent of Division I, 87.4 percent of Division II, and 93.4 percent of Division III athletic directors. The vast majority of head coaches at the collegiate level are also white (86.5 percent in Division I, 87.8 percent in Division II, and 91.6 percent in Division III) (Lapchick 2017). All NFL team principal owners are white except for Jacksonville Jaguars owner Shahid Khan (who is Pakistani American) and Buffalo Bills co-owner Kim Pegula (who is Asian American) (Garcia 2018). As of the 2018–2019 season, there was not a single racial minority coaching any of the thirty-one NHL teams (Thomas 2018). The vast majority of coaches and owners of MLB teams, MLS teams, and NBA teams are also white (Lapchick 2018a, 2018b, 2019b, 2019c).

Once on professional sports teams, it is not uncommon for racial minorities to encounter prejudicial views and discriminatory treatment. For some players, this begins with having a scholarship from or being employed by a team with a mascot that portrays a racial minority (typically an American Indian) in a derogatory and stereotypical way. In 2005, the National Collegiate Athletic Association (NCAA) banned all teams from using American Indian mascots in its postseason tournaments, labeling a number of specific mascots as "hostile or abusive," including the Florida State Seminoles and the Illinois' Illini. However, the NCAA lacked the authority to ban such mascots in general; some schools (such as St. John's, which changed nicknames from the "Redmen" to the "Red Storm") voluntarily changed their mascots, while others did not and appealed (ESPN 2005). Both at the collegiate level and at the professional level, teams have faced scrutiny from diverse groups ranging from the Robert Woods Johnson Foundation (which sponsors the RWJF Sports Award) (Besser 2018) to professional academic organizations like the American Sociological Association (2016) and the American Psychological Association (2005).

Beyond stereotypical representation via mascots, instances of racism in sports are on the rise according to the University of Central Florida's Institute for Diversity and Ethics in Sport, impacting athletes from the most celebrated to the least known. Just two years ago, basketball legend LeBron James came home to find that the front gates were defaced with a racial slur (Bromwich 2018). In just the last year, fans of North Arkansas College made monkey noises and crow caws at the players of predominantly black Labette Community College's basketball teams, someone posted a picture of Florida State University's first-ever black head football coach being lynched in the Florida State Football Facebook group, and a team competing in the Cincinnati Premier Youth Basketball League was ejected after its players wore jerseys displaying "coon" and "knee grow" on the back (Lapchick 2019a).

On the other hand, sporting has also—both historically and recently—provided a venue in which to dispel negative racial stereotypes or protest negative treatment of racial minorities. In a recent example, then 49ers quarterback Colin Kaepernick took to a knee during the singing of the national anthem at the NFL games in protest against police brutality faced by black Americans. A number of other players joined the protests in subsequent NFL games despite criticism from certain circles, including even from President Trump. After it looked like Kaepernick would be let go from the 49ers and opted out of his contract, Kaepernick felt that he was blackballed from playing by other teams and filed a collusion lawsuit against the NFL. The NFL was forced to settle for an undisclosed amount after they were unable to get the case dismissed (Mangan 2019).

Under the Trump administration, a number of athletes have refused invitations to be honored at the White House in light of his history of racist remarks and actions. Steph Curry of the NBA's Golden State Warriors voiced his opposition to going to the White House to be honored for his team's championship, explaining that "the things that he's said and the things that he hasn't said at the right times [referring to his hesitancy to condemn white supremacists]—that we won't stand for it." Curry's teammates Kevin Durant and David West expressed similar sentiments (Rapaport 2017). When the NFL's New England Patriots were invited to the White House, Devin McCourty (who is black) refused as well, noting, "I don't feel accepted in the White House. With the president having so many strong opinions and prejudices . . ." and his teammate, Martellus Bennett concurred, noting that America was "[built] on inclusiveness not exclusiveness" (Howard 2017).

## Consumer Goods and the Continued Reification of Whiteness

The reification of whiteness and promotion of stereotypes about racial minorities that historically accompanied the sale of consumer goods have continued into the present era. A number of examples of this can be seen in the marketing of food and beverages. In 2018, Heineken aired a commercial in which a bartender slides a bottle of light beer down the bar past several black people to a light-skinned woman followed by the tagline "sometimes lighter is better" (Snider 2018). Kellogg's released a Corn Pops box with a picture of the cereal pieces as cartoon characters at a mall; the only corn pop with a dark complexion was depicted as a janitor (Smith 2017).

Beauty and hygiene products have also furthered racist themes. A Dove ad depicted three women lined up from darkest to lightest skin tone with the word "before" above the darkest complected woman and "after" above the lightest (Moss 2017). American company Colgate-Palmolive's Darlie toothpaste (originally called Darkie, popular in Asia, and referred to by Chinese consumers as "black man toothpaste") retained its logo of a man in blackface until the 1990s, at which point the man's depiction was toned down, but little else about the branding has changed since then (Thomas 2016).

Technology products have been marketed in a questionable manner as well. Intel released an ad in 2007 for the Core 2 Duo Processor that represented the speed of the processor with black sprinters low to the ground as if about to begin a race. The sprinters were arranged in two rows on either side of a white man standing with his arms crossed as though they were bowing to him, and the caption above it all read, "Multiply computing performance and maximize the power of your employees." The caption reinforced the notion that the lone white man was in charge (Frucci 2007).

In other cases, companies attempted to air progressive ads highlighting racial diversity but experienced a racist backlash—highlighting the continued pervasiveness of racism writ large. For example, Cheerios aired a commercial in which an interracial couple had breakfast with their daughter. It generated so many racist comments on YouTube that it became necessary to close the comments section. Some of those comments referred to the family as "disgusting," expressed surprise that the black father in the ad would stay with his family, referenced pro-Nazi slogans, and referred to "racial genocide" (Goyette 2013).

## Working toward Solutions

Given that racism operates both at the interpersonal level and at the institutional level, potential solutions to racism have been proposed at both levels. Some have suggested that the way forward in combating racism is to create more opportunities for people of different racial groups to get to know one another and to provide educational experiences to help improve people's attitudes toward people of other racial classifications. However, addressing individual prejudice at an interpersonal level may not be sufficient to uproot the more deeply embedded racist foundations of our institutions; thus, others have proposed more far-reaching responses driving toward legal changes and mass demonstrations to challenge racist practices. In this section, we consider the role of all of the aforementioned suggestions and assess how successful each approach has been in addressing racism in America.

## Intergroup Contact

As a result of years of discriminatory housing policies, loan policies, and homeowners' association decisions as well as the tendency for whites to leave neighborhoods that become more racially diverse, many Americans have ended up racially segregated (Massey and Denton 1993). Whites remain particularly segregated from blacks—more so than they are from Hispanics and Asian Americans (Matthew, Rodrigue, and Reeves 2016). One approach that has been frequently proposed to reduce racism is to expose people to greater racial diversity. If lack of contact with people of other racial classifications has led to unfair and incorrect stereotypes, then perhaps exposure to diversity could lead to greater solidarity and cooperation. Social psychologists began pursuing this possibility (applying the Allport hypothesis to race) in the 1930s. One of the first such studies occurred at the University of Alabama, where researchers observed how racial attitudes of white students changed as Northern blacks began attending alongside them. In this particular study, intergroup contact did not have the desired result; in fact, the more time Northern blacks were enrolled, the more negative whites' attitudes were toward blacks. On the other hand, studies of Merchant Marines and Philadelphia police demonstrated that intergroup contact could potentially improve whites' attitudes toward blacks (Pettigrew and Tropp 2005).

Why did intergroup contact seem to improve relations between people of different racial groups in some contexts but not in others? Subsequent research revealed particular circumstances under which intergroup contact was more likely to succeed: when members of each group are of relatively equal status, working toward common goals in intergroup cooperation while explicitly supported by authorities or social institutions (Pettigrew and Tropp 2005). Evidence suggests that the precondition of relatively equal status especially can lead to more productive intergroup contact.

Blacks who might otherwise face prejudice and discrimination may have an easier time with whites in intergroup interactions if they signal equivalent education or income or an ability to perform the task at hand with particular effectiveness. Meanwhile, whites may be more likely to assume that their negative stereotypes about blacks are less applicable in individual cases in which they encounter a black person who gives off high-status cues. For example, *New York Times* columnist and former psychology graduate student Brent Staples described how his presence as a young black man walking through the streets of Chicago led white people to clutch their valuables or cross over to the other side of the street. However, when he began whistling a Beatles song or something from Vivaldi's *Four Seasons*, it demonstrated a knowledge of white culture, made Staples appear less consistent with stereotypes about black men being violent, and led to white people smiling and becoming visibly less tense as they passed (Steele 2011).

While demonstrating equivalent social position may be a viable means for certain individual racial minorities to avoid overt mistreatment in specific situations, it is insufficient as a generally usable, long-term strategy. First, not all racial minorities have the educational credentials or income or other signifiers to sufficiently demonstrate equivalency as judged by whites. Second, maximizing potential for successful intergroup contact from this perspective requires racial minorities to constantly prove their worth when the same expectation is not assumed for whites. Finally, this approach places the burden of resolving racist situations on the victims rather than on the perpetrators of racism.

### Educational Interventions

Another approach to combating racism that is frequently suggested is education. Those with race-based privilege may not understand the advantages they have or the disadvantages that racial minorities face. They may have been brought up with stereotypes that could be dispelled with new information. They may also have been unaware of the benefits to diversity and, therefore, find it difficult to potentially give up personal privilege in exchange for a more broadly diffused societal benefit like racial equality. Even if one has already been socialized into prejudicial attitudes, that which can be learned can also (at least theoretically) be unlearned. Survey data confirms the persistence of an ignorance to racial inequality that might be addressable by education; for example, in a recent national NBC News/SurveyMonkey poll, a plurality of whites (50 percent) answered that whites benefited "not too much" or "not at all" from "societal advantages that blacks do not" despite the overwhelming evidence (much of which has been mentioned in this book) of white privilege in America. In contrast, 84 percent of blacks and 71 percent of Hispanics answered that whites benefit "a great deal" or "a fair amount" from societal advantages not shared by blacks (Arenge, Perry, and Clark 2018).

Similarly, evidence suggests that, when goals are shared among members of a group, diversity is beneficial to decision-making in a variety of contexts (e.g., Page 2007; Smith 1997). Yet, in a recent national Pew Research Center (2018) poll, only 47 percent of Americans who self-identified as Republican or who leaned Republican agreed that diversity made the United States a better place in which to live. In fact, about 17 percent of conservative Republicans said that increasing racial and ethnic diversity actually made America worse (Fingerhut 2018).

Education has the potential to open people's eyes to how negatively impactful experiences of inequality can be for the disadvantaged. Take, for example, Jane Elliott's classic blue eyes/brown eyes experiment devised to help third graders understand what experiencing racial discrimination was like in the wake of Dr. Martin Luther King Jr.'s death in 1968. Elliott began by inventing a claim that intelligence came from melanin in people's eyes, so people with brown eyes were the smartest. She let brown-eyed students drink directly from the water fountain (whereas blue-eyed children had to use a paper cup), go to lunch first, and stay out at recess for longer. The brown-eyed children, emboldened by this, became condescending to the blue-eyed students, and one even told Elliott that she would have been a principal or superintendent by now instead of a teacher if she didn't have blue eyes. In contrast, the blue-eyed children lost confidence and started to decline in their classroom performance. When she reversed the roles and favored blue-eyed children, she found that the blue-eyed children were not as mean and condescending as the brown-eyed children had been when favored, because they did not want others to experience the discrimination that they had recently experienced (Bland 2018).

Endeavors to educate the public about racism have also been undertaken or supported by literature and the arts. A number of classic works have critiqued American racism from Harriet Beecher Stowe's *Uncle Tom's Cabin* (2008) to Alice Walker's *The Color Purple* (1982) and Toni Morrison's *Beloved* (2004). In April 2019, the Antiracist Research and Policy Center at American University launched its first annual National Antiracist Book Festival, featuring a variety of authors like children's book writer Jacqueline Woodson (winner of the National Book Award, the Caldecott Medal, and a variety of other honors) and Pulitzer Prize–winning poet Tyehimba Jess (Antiracist Research and Policy Center 2019). The festival included panels with the authors and a Teaching for Change workshop on antiracist pedagogy in which participants reflected on questions about how to use literature to help children develop positive racial identities and learn to think critically about race and racism (D.C. Area Educators for Social Justice 2019).

In theatre, numerous playwrights have spotlighted systemic racism through their narratives and through their casting choices. Suzan Lori-Parks, the first African American woman to win the Pulitzer Prize for Drama, released the thought-provoking *White Noise* in 2019. In *White Noise*, a black artist with insomnia is attacked by police while simply walking down the street at night and asks his rich, white friend to buy him for forty days so they can be "master and enslaved person, walking the streets. Making a statement. Showing the world how far we've come!" (Soloski 2019). In another recent example, although Lin-Manuel Miranda's massive hit *Hamilton: The Musical* took the setting of colonial America, it featured no slave characters and included a nearly all-minority cast (Churchwell 2016).

There have also been collectivized efforts to combat racist tendencies within the theater community. Stephanie Ybarra (Baltimore Center Stage's artistic director), Roberta Pereira (The Playwrights Realm producing director in New York City), Jacob G. Padrón (Long Wharf Theatre's artistic director), and David Roberts (former Stage Directors and Choreographers Foundation executive director) formed the Artists' Anti-Racism Coalition (AARC). The AARC reviewed Off-Broadway season announcements and sent personal notes to artistic directors asking to talk when they noticed a lack of directors and playwrights of color involved with upcoming productions. They gathered data on the lack of diversity among artists whose plays had been produced in New York City over the last decade. In addition, they organized a People's Institute for Survival and Beyond workshop specifically for people employed in theatre professions to discuss race and racism in New York City theatre (Clement 2019).

There have also been numerous examples recently of visual art addressing racism in America. Take, for example, "Black Like Me: African-American Portraits," a collection of work that comprises a part of the "Black Like Who? Exploring Race and Representation" exhibit at the Birmingham Museum of Art in Alabama. The portraits are presented in response to a quote from Frederick Douglass in which Douglass notes that white artists never seem to be able to paint black portraits "without most grossly exaggerating their distinctive features" (Museum Geographies 2015). Over the past few decades, African American artist Kerry James Marshall has centered black people in his paintings, as he noted that there is commonly an expectation that people of color will see themselves in white protagonists but not a simultaneous expectation that whites will see themselves in racial minority protagonists (Sooke 2014). Less than an hour and a half away, The Legacy Museum: From Enslavement to Mass Incarceration opened in 2018 to educate the public on American racial abuses.

Music has long been connected to the struggle against racial inequality. Gospel songs sung by slaves may have included code words about escape. For example, Harriet Tubman is said to have used the song "Wade in the Water" to advise people fleeing plantations to use the water to avoid detection (Harriet Tubman Historical Society 2019). Similarly, "Follow the Drinking Gourd" referenced how "dead trees will show you the way," because moss grew on the north side of such trees, providing another means of determining which direction was north (Harriet Tubman Historical Society 2019). Music has continued to be an important means by which to contest systemic racism up to the present day, as Jasiri X did in his 2010 song "What If the Tea Party Was Black?" Jasiri X (2010) suggested that the antiestablishment, pro-gun tendencies of the Tea Party were primarily tolerated because its members were white; if they had been black, then they would have been violently combated.

Numerous other examples can be noted. In the music video for the song "Formation," Beyoncé addresses police shootings of young black men and the aftermath of Hurricane Katrina (when the federal government failed to respond to the serious post-disaster needs of minority communities in a timely manner) (Beyoncé 2016). Other parts of the *Lemonade* album's accompanying video feature Sybrina Fulton holding a picture of her son, Trayvon Martin, whose death catalyzed the Black Lives Matter movement, and Malcolm X talking about how black women are disrespected in America (Hawkes 2016). In his 2017 music video for *The Land of the Free*, Joey Bada$$ made a statement about the continuation of systemic racism when he depicted members of the KKK (Ku Klux Klan) revealing themselves to be police officers, judges, and priests (Zaru 2017).

Nevertheless, education is not a panacea; well-educated people are still quite capable of maintaining negative racial attitudes. As Kuppens and Spears (2014) found, although higher-educated people are less likely to express explicit racism, they frequently still exhibit implicit racism. For example, they may not shout a racial slur at someone, but they may also believe that blacks unfairly benefit from affirmative action (despite its relative minor contribution to alleviating the consequences of years of systematic racism).

A serious potential flaw with educational interventions is that they may assume people are willing to be better than they actually are—that faced with the knowledge that racial minorities are being unfairly compensated for their contributions to society, they would support policies to create a more just world. Unfortunately, exposure to new information about racial inequality often results in precisely the opposite reaction. For example, whites told that racial minorities were executed more often than whites were more likely to indicate strong favor for the death penalty (52 percent) than whites who were not told about this disparity (36 percent) (Peffley and Hurwitz 2007). Whites are also less likely to support petitions to end harsh laws or increased police stop-and-frisk tactics when told that blacks are more frequently targeted (Hetey and Eberhardt 2018).

Whites may also respond to educational interventions defensively. As Robin DiAngelo (2011) notes, whites are often able (through residential segregation and other mechanisms) to avoid contexts in which their racial worldviews are threatened. This protects them from racial stress but simultaneously makes it more threatening to experience challenges to those worldviews, leading to "white fragility" (DiAngelo 2011:56). Even well-meaning progressively minded whites who recognize that racism is a problem and acknowledge their own contributions to it can fall prey to defensiveness. Such individuals may have read books or taken classes on the subject and, consequently, view themselves as more or less inoculated from the pernicious effects of racism. Yet their specific experiences of learning about racism may be incomplete or, even if thorough at the time, in need of updating as processes of racism change.

## Governmental Interventions

Most American adults (including a plurality of blacks [48 percent]) see racism as primarily a problem of individual prejudice rather than something "built into laws and institutions" (Pew Research Center 2016). Interventions aimed at exposing people to diversity or educating people about the persistence and insidiousness of racial inequality may have an impact on individual-level discrimination, but these, in and of themselves, may be insufficient to effect widespread change. After all, even as individual-level racial attitudes have ostensibly improved, racial inequality persists. This is likely attributable to a lack of willingness to implement the policies that would support improvement toward racial inequality. Since the early 1970s, white support has, overall, trended upward for integrated schools and interracial marriages. However, support for governmental intervention has been much more mixed; for example, white support has wavered regarding whether the government should ensure that blacks can be served at any hotel or restaurant they can afford. Moreover, whites have actually declined in their support for laws prohibiting racial discrimination in the sale of homes and in the workplace in recent years (Krysan and Moberg 2016). Similarly, national Gallup polling indicates that more than half of Americans support the broad idea of affirmative action for racial minorities, and 71 percent of Americans who responded supported "affirmative action programs designed to increase the number of black and minority students on college campuses" (Newport 2018). Yet, from 2006 to 2018, between 67 and 70 percent of respondents said that college admissions should be decided "solely on merit," and 63 percent said that race should not be a factor at all (in fact, only 9 percent said that race should be a major factor in the process of college admissions) (Newport 2018). Thus, whatever gains we have experienced in understanding and appreciating diversity may not necessarily be translating into support for policies that contribute to racial equality.

This is unfortunate given that governmental intervention has been historically important to the push toward racial equality. Laws like the Civil Rights Act of 1964 (prohibiting discrimination based on race among other factors), the Voting Rights Act of 1965, and the Civil Rights Act of 1968 (prohibiting discrimination in housing) have been particularly impactful. So too were Supreme Court decisions like *Brown v. Board of Education of Topeka* (which prohibited "separate but equal" school segregation) and the Civil Liberties Act of 1987 (which provided reparations, albeit limited ones, to survivors of Japanese descent who had been forced into American internment camps) (Browne-Marshall 2013; Maki, Kitano, and Berthold 1999). Presidential actions like Executive Order 9981 (which desegregated the armed forces) (Taylor 2013), Executive Order 8802 (which made it illegal to bar people from employment in the defense industry based on "race, creed, color, or national origin") (Equal Employment Opportunity Commission 1941), and Executive Order 11246 (which established affirmative action) have also steadily improved structural conditions for racial minorities (Browne-Marshall 2013).

However, political moves that lead to greater racial equality often require an asterisk next to them. Thomas Jefferson was instrumental in the passage of the Slave Trade Act of 1807, which made America's participation in the international slave trade illegal. Yet doing so enriched slaveholders by raising the value of their existing slaves, particularly if those slaves were capable of bearing children to replace them in bondage for subsequent generations. Jefferson recognized this himself and reaped the profits. In a letter to John Wayles Eppes on June 30, 1820, Jefferson once wrote, "I know no error more consuming to an estate than that of stocking farms with men almost exclusively.

I consider a woman who brings a child every two years as more profitable than the best man of the farm. What she produces is an addition to the capital, while his labors disappear in mere consumption." Jefferson also said a number of degrading things about black people in his only published book, *Notes on the State of Virginia* (1853).

Although the Emancipation Proclamation—which promised freedom for slaves in states that had seceded from the Union—has been widely lauded, its abolishment of slavery was hardly absolute (Lincoln 1865). It exempted states that were not contemporaneously in rebellion (Kentucky, Missouri, Maryland, and Delaware), and it applied only to areas that were not yet occupied by the Union army, meaning that the Union needed to win the Civil War for the proclamation to have any substance to it (Guelzo 2004). This being the case, some have criticized the Emancipation Proclamation for being primarily a propaganda tool designed to catalyze the war effort (Hofstadter 2009). W.E.B. Du Bois argued, in a speech before the Inter-Collegiate Socialist Society in 1917, that "if [Lincoln] could keep the Union from being disrupted, he would not only allow slavery to exist but would loyally protect it" (Guelzo 2004:15).

Franklin D. Roosevelt issued Executive Order 8802 to end employment discrimination in the defense industry but only after being threatened with a massive protest by the March on Washington Movement (MOWM). Roosevelt's acquiescence not only allowed him to avoid the personal embarrassment of a march but also resulted in MOWM leaders Asa Philip Randolph (president of the Brotherhood of Sleeping Car Porters) and Walter White (executive secretary of the NAACP) referencing his executive order as a "Second Emancipation Proclamation" (Kersten 2000:18). Further, whereas his wife, Eleanor, joined the NAACP and worked toward the passage of anti-lynching legislation, Franklin Roosevelt remained aloof to avoid losing the support from white Southerners that he knew he would need to push through his New Deal legislation (Little 2019). The New Deal policies Roosevelt sought to protect also distributed resources in racially unjust ways. To take one example, Social Security did not apply to agricultural and domestic jobs (both of which were primarily occupied by blacks) (Reed 2008). Of course, Roosevelt was also responsible for the devastating internment of Japanese Americans during World War II—an internment that he did not extend to German Americans or Italian Americans (Ng 2002).

On the one hand, Lyndon B. Johnson helped get the Civil Rights Act of 1957 passed while Senate majority leader and, as president, signed the Civil Rights Act of 1964 and the Voting Rights Act of 1965 into law. As president, he also instructed the FBI to go after the KKK (Serwer 2014). On the other hand, the authenticity of Johnson's support for civil rights has been called into question. After all, Johnson spent at least the first twenty years of his political career opposing civil right legislation and did not change course until supporting the Civil Rights Act of 1957. National best-selling Johnson biographer Robert Caro once said, in an interview for the Library of Congress's magazine *LCM*, "He always had this true, deep compassion to help poor people and particularly poor people of color, but even stronger than the compassion was his ambition. But when the two aligned, when compassion and ambition finally are pointing in the same direction, then Lyndon Johnson becomes a force for racial justice, unequalled certainly since Lincoln" (Allen 2013). Aside from his reluctance to support civil rights, Johnson was known for using racial epithets in reference to black people on a regular basis and once referred to East Asians as "hordes of barbaric yellow dwarves" (Serwer 2014).

There have been contemporary attempts to continue legislative progress toward racial equality, but these attempts have often been stymied in Congress. Take, for example, the DREAM Act, which was proposed to protect children of immigrants whose parents brought them into the United States illegally from deportation. Although the proposed legislation was designed for children of all racial classifications, those who would have been eligible for its benefits are largely of Mexican origin and Hispanic (López and Krogstad 2017). The DREAM Act failed to make it through Congress on numerous occasions under the Bush and Obama administrations (Alcindor and Stolberg 2017). Similarly, the End Racial and Religious Profiling Act (ERRPA), which would ban racial profiling by law enforcement agencies and agents and allow the Department of Justice or victims of racial profiling to pursue civil action, has languished in the Senate Committee on the Judiciary since February 2017 (S.411-ERRPA 2017). Not only have bills providing reparations for slavery to African Americans never been successful in Congress, but also even a bill to create a commission to develop a reparations proposal has made little progress toward being taken up for a vote since its initial referral to the House Committee on the Judiciary in January of 2017 (H. R. 40 2017).

Legislation contributing to racial equality has also been less common recently given that a number of the protections against racial discrimination already technically exist in law and judicial precedent. Instead, the role of the courts in interpreting legislation and remedying violations has become central to whether governmental intervention is capable of achieving greater racial equality, and, in the courts, there has been some progress. In *Pigford v. Glickman*, black farmers filed a class action lawsuit against the U.S. Department of Agriculture for racial discrimination and failure to address complaints of said discrimination. The 22,721 farmers comprising the class were awarded about $1.06 billion, and, in a subsequent lawsuit (often referred to as *Pigford II*), a settlement of $1.25 billion was reached with additional farmers (Cowan and Feder 2013). *Johnson v. California* clarified that segregating prisoners by race required strict scrutiny (i.e., there would have to be compelling proof that doing so was necessary to achieve an important objective and narrow enough to avoid violating prisoners' right to equal protection under the law) (Browne-Marshall 2013). In another example, *Grutter v. Bollinger, Gratz v. Bollinger, Fisher v.*

*University of Texas*, and *Fisher v. University of Texas II*, the Supreme Court upheld the use of race as a factor in college admissions, allowing affirmative action to proceed (with certain caveats) (Wright and Garces 2018).

Executive orders and memoranda have also been a medium by which racial progress has been indirectly furthered. For example, President Obama used an executive memorandum to set Deferred Action for Childhood Arrivals (DACA) into motion after the aforementioned DREAM Act failed to pass Congress on numerous occasions. Unlike the DREAM Act, which was designed to provide a path to citizenship for children whose parents brought them into the United States illegally, DACA offered only a renewable two-year visa. However, it did provide the opportunity for a large number of primarily Hispanic immigrants to obtain a driver's license, go to college, and get a job in the United States (Shoichet, Cullinane, and Kopan 2017). Obama also issued memoranda promoting diversity and inclusion in national security and national park and forest jobs and creating the My Brother's Keeper Task Force to make "a coordinated Federal effort to improve significantly the expected life outcomes for boys and young men of color (including African Americans, Hispanic Americans, and Native Americans)" (Office of the Press Secretary 2014, 2016, 2017).

Although congressional, presidential, and judicial action racial equality can potentially promote equality, it must be remembered that progress can also be undone through the same mechanisms. For example, in terms of legislation, in 2018, congressional Republicans passed and President Trump signed into law a measure rolling back 2013 guidance from the Consumer Financial Protection Bureau to indirect auto lenders. This guidance had called on lenders to implement a variety of measures to prevent racial (among other forms of) discrimination in the car-buying process (Wren 2018). Moreover, the Trump administration's 2019 budget proposal included a cut in funding for the Department of Housing and Urban Development's Fair Housing Initiatives Program, which addresses housing discrimination complaints (National Low Income Housing Coalition 2018).

The judiciary has also contributed to thwarting racial progress recently. As mentioned previously in this chapter, the decision in *Shelby County v. Holder* struck down a key component of the Voting Rights Act of 1965 designed to protect racial minorities against voting discrimination (Liptak 2013). In another example, the Supreme Court upheld Michigan voters' right to prohibit "sex- and race-based preferences in public education, public employment, and public contracting" in *Schuette v. Coalition to Defend Affirmative Action*, striking a blow against affirmative action (Oyez 2019).

Given the potential for governmental intervention to substantially catalyze or impede racial progress, the vote holds potential be a powerful mechanism for change—positively or negatively. Yet voting and polling aggregate political opinion toward moderation that is often unlikely to quickly or easily move governmental institutions toward racial progress. Moreover, voting embodies power that is diluted by the space between elections. Working within what are institutionally considered to be appropriate parameters, therefore, may be insufficient to effect real change. As we look back through history, some of the most successful attempts to combat racial inequality were only operationalized as governmental policy because of the hard work of activists on the ground. Even then, not all participants in social movements have been adequately acknowledged for their contributions. For example, a number of accounts of 1960s' civil rights movements overlook the Asian American civil rights movement. As University of California at Los Angeles professor Hirabayashi notes, "We may not have the same iconic figures, but I prefer to see Asian American civil rights as an ongoing series of struggles, with the civil rights movement as a very big part of that" (Japanese American Citizens League 2008).

## Direct Disruption

The status quo of racial hierarchy depends on the relatively unquestioning acceptance or allowance of the average person. As a result, a great deal of social change in the United States has proceeded from social movements utilizing tactics that make it more difficult to passively acquiesce to the norm. Demonstrations, protests, strikes, and other such tactics take a problem primarily felt by its victims and make it of relevance to the perpetrators of inequality. Perhaps even more important, these tactics bring awareness to average Americans who may not intentionally or directly perpetuate inequality but benefit from it all the same. It's a strategy that has improved circumstances for the disenfranchised throughout modern American history from the furtherance of racial equality in the 1960s to the call for greater attention to the AIDS epidemic and the legalization of same-sex marriage in more recent decades (Staggenborg 2016).

One recent example of how direct disruption can lead to progress toward racial equality can be found in the work of the Black Lives Matter (BLM) movement. Anita Alvarez was the state attorney for Cook County, Illinois, when unarmed seventeen-year-old Laquan McDonald was shot to death by Chicago police officer Jason Van Dyke. Alvarez did not charge Van Dyke with murder until 400 days later when she learned that dashcam footage from the incident was about to go public. In the footage, Van Dyke was seen firing sixteen bullets into McDonald as he was walking away. Activists protested and called on Alvarez to resign. When she refused, they helped Kim Foxx defeat her in the next Democratic primary (Muwakkil 2016).

BLM protestors also challenged presidential candidates during the 2016 election to focus on racial justice. In particular, they targeted Hillary Clinton over policies she supported that led to mass incarceration of racial minorities during Bill Clinton's presidency and confronted Bernie Sanders over his focus on economic inequality without sufficient specific attention to racial inequality (Lind 2015; Muwakkil 2016). Although it is more difficult to assess the extent to which such action impacted the candidates' subsequent actions, the rhetoric at least changed relatively quickly. The Democratic Party included the following in its platform: "Democrats will promote racial justice through fair, just, and equitable governing of all public-serving institutions and in the formation of public policy. . . . We will push for a societal transformation to make it clear that black lives matter and that there is no place for racism in our country" (Democratic National Committee 2018).

The evidence of BLM's effectiveness appears to support something larger than anecdotal change in specific situations. Overall, Sawyer and Gampta (2018) found that, at points of high struggle in the BLM movement, both whites and blacks were more likely to explicitly express egalitarian racial preferences instead of racial bias toward their own respective groups. Moreover, pro-white implicit attitudes declined across the board (Sawyer and Gampta 2018).

Efforts toward racial justice are never easy—they necessitate entrenched groups with social advantages giving up some of their privilege. They require courage on the part of the disenfranchised and disadvantaged to push for equal recognition and treatment at the possible cost of verbal and even physical abuse. Further, they rely on the average person on the sidelines neither willfully supporting nor intentionally trying to dismantle white supremacy to choose a side, to make the political personal, and to value the whole of humanity over personal goals and aspirations. Yet progress toward racial equality—however imperfect, inconsistent, and frequently backsliding—has been made, and focused continual effort will be necessary to sustain that progress.

Continued perseverance is necessary, as white supremacists have recently enjoyed an amplified voice under Donald Trump's presidency. Trump's former chief strategist Steve Bannon had previously chaired Breitbart (which had long-standing ties to the alt-right and white nationalism) (Okeowo 2016). Trump has faced criticism for failing to adequately denounce white nationalists, including former KKK Grand Wizard David Duke, who formally endorsed him (Carroll 2016). He has also, on numerous occasions, re-tweeted and endorsed false statements by white supremacists, including, for example, claims that the African National Congress was killing white farmers and stealing their land in South Africa (Newkirk 2018). Moreover, Trump has engaged in actions consistent with the aims of white supremacists, including implementing bans on Middle Eastern refugees from a number of countries and working to shift a U.S. government program designed to counter a number of violent ideologies to focus only on Muslim extremism (deemphasizing investigation of white supremacists) (Ainsley, Volz, and Cooke 2017). It is perhaps unsurprising, then, that there has been an uptick in reports to the Anti-Defamation League of racist threats, vandalism, and physical assaults, and the number of anti-Muslim hate groups grew from 34 to 101 from 2015 to 2016 (Okeowo 2016; Southern Poverty Law Center 2019).

White supremacists have also become smarter about representing racism in a manner that is more palatable to mainstream Americans than the raw antagonism of groups like the KKK. Although many white supremacist groups have enacted or threatened violence, others have attempted to present ostensibly nonviolent and seemingly more-inclusive stances to attract more members. However, the heart of the message—pro-white racism—remains consistent. Take, for example, identitarians. Identitarian and National Policy Institute president Richard Spencer (who also coined the term "alt-right") ostensibly disavows violence and argues that people of all political affiliations can be identitarians. However, he also calls for each racial/ethnic group to have its own state and argues that "race is the foundation of identity. . . . So, for an identitarian, identity is the beginning, and identity isn't just race . . . but race is the foundation of identity" (Daniel and Richendollar 2017).

There also continue to be a number of white supremacists who have no problem resorting to violence. Hammerskin Nation, a group of skinheads largely known for its Hammerfest white power concerts, has been known to host "boot parties" in which they throw people on the ground and stomp on them with steel-tipped boots—sometimes to the death (Tenold 2018). The Atomwaffen Division (AWD), which has focused its recruitment efforts on the American military and offered its members military training, has also been tied to violence (Taddonio 2018). Members of AWD engaged in violence in Charlottesville at the Unite the Right rally (where neo-Nazi James Alex Fields Jr. rammed into a crowd of counterprotesters, killing Heather Hayer and injuring thirty-five other people) (Myre 2018; Wamsley 2019).

## References

Actors' Equity Association. 2017. "Looking at Hiring Biases by the Numbers." Retrieved February 9, 2019. https://www.actorsequity.org/news/PR/DiversityStudy/.

Ainsley, Julia Edwards, Dustin Volz, and Kristina Cooke. 2017. "Exclusive: Trump to Focus Counter-Extremism Program Solely on Islam-Sources." Retrieved November 14, 2019. https://www.reuters.com/article/us-usa-trump-extremists-program-exclusiv/exclusive-trump-to-focus-counter-extremism-program-solely-on-islam-sources-idUSKBN15G5VO.

Alcindor, Yamiche, and Sheryl Gay Stolberg. 2017. "After 16 Futile Years, Congress Will Try Again to Legalize 'Dreamers.'" Retrieved January 7, 2019. https://www.nytimes.com/2017/09/05/us/politics/dream-act-daca-trump-congress-dreamers.html.

Al Jazeera. 2019. "State Department Rejects More Than 37,000 Visas Due to Travel Ban." Retrieved February 27, 2019. https://www.aljazeera.com/news/2019/02/state-department-rejects-37000-visas-due-travel-ban-190227210725292.html.

Allen, Erin. 2013. "Last Word: Author Robert Caro on LBJ." Retrieved June 30, 2019. https://blogs.loc.gov/loc/2013/02/last-word-author-robert-caro-on-lbj/.

American Civil Liberties Union. 2014. "War Comes Home: The Excessive Militarization of American Policing." Retrieved December 26, 2018. https://www.aclu.org/sites/default/files/assets/jus14-warcomeshome-report-web-rel1.pdf.

American College of Physicians. 2003. "Racial and Ethnic Disparities in Health Care." Retrieved February 8, 2019. https://www.acponline.org/acp_policy/policies/racial_ethnic_disparities_healthcare_2003.pdf.

American Psychological Association. 2005. "Summary of the APA Resolution Recommending Retirement of American Indian Mascots." Retrieved February 20, 2019. https://www.apa.org/pi/oema/resources/indian-mascots.

American Sociological Association. 2016. "ASA Letter on Baseball Mascots." Retrieved February 20, 2019. http://www.asanet.org/news-events/asa-news/asa-letter-baseball-mascots.

Amin, Raid. 2017. "A Spatial Study of the Location of Superfund Sites and Associated Cancer Risk." *Statistics and Public Policy* 5(1):1–9.

Amnesty International. 2003. "United States of America: Death by Discrimination—The Continuing Role of Race in Capital Cases." Retrieved December 26, 2018. https://www.amnesty.org/en/documents/AMR51/046/2003/en/.

Anderson, Elijah. 2018. "Black Americans Are Asserting Their Rights in 'White Spaces.' That's When Whites Call 911." Retrieved December 19, 2018. https://www.vox.com/the-big-idea/2018/8/10/17672412/911-police-black-white-racism-sociology.

Andrews, Roxanne, and Anne Elixhauser. 2000. "Use of Major Therapeutic Procedures: Are Hispanics Treated Differently Than Non-Hispanic Whites?" *Ethnicity & Disease* 10:384–394.

Antiracist Research and Policy Center. 2019. "National Antiracist Book Festival." Retrieved June 27, 2019. https://www.american.edu/centers/antiracism/book-fair/index.cfm.

Arenge, Andrew, Stephanie Perry, and Dartunorro Clark. 2018. "Poll: 64 Percent of Americans Say Racism Remains a Major Problem." Retrieved January 3, 2018. https://

www.nbcnews.com/politics/politics-news/poll-64-percent-americans-say-racism-remains-major-problem-n877536.

Arnold, David, Will Dobbie, and Crystal S. Yang. 2018. "Racial Bias in Bail Decision." *The Quarterly Journal of Economics* 133(4):1885–1932.

Arter, Melanie. 2008. "Suit Settled on Behalf of Girl Suspended for Wearing Headscarf." Retrieved October 22, 2018. https://www.cnsnews.com/news/article/suit-settled-behalf-girl-suspended-wearing-headscarf.

Artiga, Samantha, Julia Foutz, Elizabeth Cornachione, and Rachel Garfield. 2016. "Key Facts on Health and Health Care by Race and Ethnicity." Retrieved February 8, 2019. https://www.kff.org/report-section/key-facts-on-health-and-health-care-by-race-and-ethnicity-section-2-health-access-and-utilization/.

Associated Press. 2018. "Golf Club Apologizes for Calling Cops on Black Women Members." Retrieved December 19, 2018. https://apnews.com/95e02521b2884a2abd1470fd9b6fecbb?utm_campaign=SocialFlow&utm_source=Twitter&utm_medium=APEastRegion.

Banks, Cyndi. 2017. *Criminal Justice Ethics: Theory and Practice.* Thousand Oaks, CA: Sage.

Bargmann, Joe. 2016. "Will Darius Rucker Break Country Music's Color Barrier Once and for All?" Retrieved February 11, 2019. https://www.dallasobserver.com/music/will-darius-rucker-break-country-music-s-color-barrier-once-and-for-all-8445362.

Baumgartner, Frank R., Derek A. Epp, and Kelsey Shoub. 2018. *Suspect Citizens: What 20 Million Traffic Stops Tell Us about Policing and Race.* New York: Cambridge University Press.

Baumgartner, Frank, and Tim Lyman. 2016. "Louisiana Death Sentenced Cases and Their Reversals, 1976–2015." *The Southern University Law Center Journal of Race, Gender, and Poverty* 7:58–75.

Bayer, Patrick, and Kerwin Kofi Charles. 2018. "Divergent Paths: A New Perspective on Earnings Differences between Black and White Men since 1940." *The Quarterly Journal of Economics* 133(3):1459–1501.

Beal, Frances M. 2008. "Double Jeopardy: To Be Black and Female." *Meridians* 8(2):166–176.

Bertrand, Marianne, and Sendhil Mullainathan. 2004. "Are Emily and Greg More Employable Than Lakisha and Jamal? A Field Experiment on Labor Market Discrimination." *American Economic Review* 94(4):991–1013.

Besser, Richard E. 2018. "Robert Woods Johnson Foundation: We Honored Sports Teams with Racist Mascots. Not Anymore." Retrieved February 20, 2019. https://www .usatoday.com/story/opinion/2018/05/07/kansas-city-chiefs-washington-redskins-racist-mascots-football-rwjf-sports-award-column/584858002/.

Beyoncé. 2016. "Formation." Retrieved June 27, 2019. https://www.youtube.com/watch?v=WDZJPJV__bQ.

Bialik, Kristen, and Jens Manuel Krogstad. 2017. "115th Congress Sets New High for Racial, Ethnic Diversity." Retrieved July 23, 2018. http://www.pewresearch.org/fact-tank/2017/01/24/115th-congress-sets-new-high-for-racial-ethnic-diversity/.

Black, Edwin. 2012. *War against the Weak: Eugenics and America's Campaign to Create a Master Race*. Washington, DC: Dialog Press.

Bland, Karina. 2018. "Blue Eyes, Brown Eyes: What Jane Elliott's Famous Experiment Says about Race 50 Years On." Retrieved January 3, 2019. https://www.azcentral .com/story/news/local/karinabland/2017/11/17/blue-eyes-brown-eyes-jane-elliotts-exercise-race-50-years-later/ 860287001/.

Bonilla-Silva, Eduardo. 2013. *Racism without Racists: Color-Blind Racism and the Persistence of Racial Inequality in America*. Lanham, MA: Rowman & Littlefield.

Bracey, Glenn E., and Wendy Leo Moore. 2017. "'Race Tests': Racial Boundary Maintenance in White Evangelical Churches." *Sociological Inquiry* 87(2):282–302.

Brader, Ted, Nicholas A. Valentino, and Elizabeth Suhay. 2008. "What Triggers Public Opposition to Immigration? Anxiety, Group Cues, and Immigration Threat." *American Journal of Political Science* 52(4):959–978.

Bromwich, Jonah Engel. 2018. "'To Me, It Was Racist': N.B.A. Players Respond to Laura Ingraham's Comments on LeBron James." Retrieved February 20, 2019. https://www .nytimes.com/2018/02/16/sports/basketball/lebron-laura-ingraham.html.

Browne-Marshall, Gloria J. 2013. *Race, Law, and American Society: 1607–Present*, 2nd ed. New York: Routledge.

Bruce, Ryan J. 2017. "AND STILL WE RISE: How Racism Is Positioning Black Artists for Independent Success." Retrieved February 11, 2019. https://www.huffingtonpost .com/entry/and-still-we-rise-how-racism-is-positioning-black_us_58f7bea6e4b071c2617f0204.

Bullard, Robert D. 2004. "Introduction," pp. 1–14 in *Highway Robbery: Transportation Racism & New Routes to Equity*, edited by Robert Doyle Bullard, Glenn Steve Johnson, and Angel O. Torres. Cambridge, MA: South End Press.

Burton, Tara Isabella. 2017. "These Pro-Trump Pastors Held a Press Conference on Racism." Retrieved June 28, 2018. https://www.vox.com/identities/2017/8/29/16216170/ pro-trump-pastors-press-conference-racism-evangelical-charlottesville-sharpton.

Calabresi, Massimo. 2006. "Is Racism Fueling the Immigration Debate?" Retrieved July 2, 2018. http://content.time.com/ time/nation/article/0,8599,1195250,00.html.

Carroll, Rory. 2016. "'Alt-Right' Groups Will 'Revolt' If Trump Shuns White Supremacy, Leaders Say." Retrieved June 29, 2019. https://www.theguardian.com/world/2016/ dec/27/alt-right-donald-trump-white-supremacy-backlash.

Cavounidis, Costas, and Kevin Lang. 2015. "Discrimination and Worker Evaluation." NBER Working Paper No. 21612. Retrieved December 7, 2018. https://www.nber.org/papers/w21612.

Cheeks, Maura. 2018. "How Black Women Describe Navigating Race and Gender in the Workplace." Retrieved November 24, 2018. https://hbr.org/2018/03/how-black-women-describe-navigating-race-and-gender-in-the-workplace.

Chicago Committee to End Sterilization Abuse. 1977. "Sterilization Abuse: A Task for the Women's Movement." Retrieved June 23, 2018. https://www.cwluherstory.org/health/sterlization-abuse-a-task-for-the-womens-movement.

Chow, Kat. 2017. "'Model Minority' Myth Again Used as a Racial Wedge between Asians and Blacks." Retrieved June 26, 2019. https://www.npr.org/sections/codeswitch/2017/04/19/524571669/model-minority-myth-again-used-as-a-racial-wedge-between-asians-and-blacks.

*Christianity Today.* 2000. "Bob Jones University Drops Interracial Dating Ban." Retrieved June 26, 2018. https://www.christianitytoday.com/ct/2000/marchweb-only/53.0.html.

Churchwell, Sarah. 2016. "Why Hamilton Is Making Musical History." Retrieved June 27, 2019. https://www.theguardian.com/stage/2016/nov/05/why-hamilton-is-making-musical-history.

Clement, Olivia. 2019. "Meet the Collective of Theatremakers Working to Undo Racism in the American Theatre." Retrieved June 26, 2019. http://www.playbill.com/article/meet-the-collective-of-theatremakers-working-behind-the-scenes-to-undo-racism-in-our-industry.

Coates, Ta-Nehisi. 2015. "What This Cruel War Was Over." Retrieved June 5, 2018. https://www.theatlantic.com/politics/archive/2015/06/what-this-cruel-war-was-over/396482/.

Cohn, D'Vera. 2010. "Census History: Counting Hispanics." Retrieved July 20, 2018. http://www.pewsocialtrends.org/2010/03/03/census-history-counting-hispanics-2/.

College Board. 2014. "10 Years of Advanced Placement Exam Data Show Significant Gains in Access and Success; Areas for Improvement." Retrieved March 23, 2019. http://media.collegeboard.com/digitalServices/pdf/ap/rtn/10th-annual/10th-annual-ap-report-press-release-english.pdf.

Connley, Courtney. 2018. "Reminder: Today Isn't Equal Pay Day for Black, Latina, or Native American Women." Retrieved November 7, 2018. https://www.cnbc.com/2018/04/10/today-isnt-equal-pay-day-for-black-latina-or-native-american-women.html.

Costello, Maureen. 2018. "Teaching Hard History." Retrieved June 4, 2018. https://www.splcenter.org/20180131/teaching-hard-history#preface.

Couch, Kenneth A., and Robert Fairlie. 2010. "Last Hired, First Fired? Black-White Unemployment and the Business Cycle." Retrieved December 7, 2018. https://www.ncbi.nlm.nih.gov/pmc/articles/PMC3000014/.

Cowan, Tadlock, and Jody Feder. 2013. "The *Pigford* Cases: USDA Settlement of Discrimination Suits by Black Farmers." Retrieved January 4, 2019. http://nationalaglawcenter.org/wp-content/uploads/assets/crs/RS20430.pdf.

Cox, Daniel, Juhem Navarro-Rivera, and Robert P. Jones. 2014. "Americans Oppose Allowing Small Businesses to Refuse Services on Religious Grounds." Retrieved June 28, 2018. https://www.prri.org/research/employer-contraception/.

Daniel, Hayden, and Nathan Richendollar. 2017. "The Charlatan of Charlottesville: An Interview with Richard Spencer." Retrieved June 29, 2019. http://www.wluspectator.com/home/2017/11/14/the-charlatan-of-charlottesville-an-interview-with-richard-spencer.

Darling-Hammond, Linda. 1998. "Unequal Opportunity: Race and Education." Retrieved July 23, 2018. https://www.brookings.edu/articles/unequal-opportunity-race-and-education/.

Davis, Delvin, and Joshua M. Frank. 2011. "Under the Hood: Auto Loan Interest Rate Hikes Inflate Consumer Costs and Loan Losses." Retrieved December 8, 2018. http://www.responsiblelending.org/other-consumer-loans/auto-financing/research-analysis/Under-the-Hood-Auto-Dealer-Rate-Markups-Executive-Summary.pdf.

D.C. Area Educators for Social Justice. 2019. "Powerful Day at the Antiracist Book Festival at American University." Retrieved June 27, 2019. https://www.dcareaeducators4socialjustice.org/stories/antiracist-book-festival-american-university.

Demby, Gene. 2017. "Obama's Racial Legacy: Some Last Words on the First Black President." Retrieved July 23, 2018. https://www.npr.org/sections/codeswitch/2017/01/20/510676874/obamas-racial-legacy-some-last-words-on-the-first-black-president.

Democratic National Committee. 2018. "African Americans." Retrieved January 25, 2019. https://democrats.org/people/african-americans/.

DiAngelo, Robin. 2011. "White Fragility." *International Journal of Critical Pedagogy* 3(3):54–70.

Di Maro, Geremia. 2018. "Data Shows African Americans Subject to 73% of Stop and Frisk Incidents in Charlottesville in 2017." Retrieved December 10, 2018. http://www.cavalierdaily.com/article/2018/03/data-shows-african-americans-subject-to-73-of-stop-and-frisk-incidents-in-charlottesville-in-2017.

Donnelly, Grace. 2018. "The Number of Black CEOs at Fortune 500 Companies Is at Its Lowest since 2002." Retrieved November 14, 2018. http://fortune.com/2018/02/28/black-history-month-black-ceos-fortune-500/.

Dougherty, Kevin D., Gerardo Martí, and Brandon C. Martinez. 2015. "Congregational Diversity and Attendance in a Mainline Protestant Denomination." *Journal for the Scientific Study of Religion* 54(4):668–683.

D'Souza, Dinesh. 1995. *The End of Racism: Finding Values in an Age of Technoaffluence.* New York: Free Press Paperbacks.

D'Souza, Dinesh (@DineshDSouza). 2015. "YOU CAN TAKE THE BOY OUT OF THE GHETTO . . . Watch This Vulgar Man Show His Stuff, While America Cowers in Embarrassment." Twitter, February 18. 7:48 A.M.

Equal Employment Opportunity Commission. 1941. "Executive Order 8802." Retrieved January 7, 2019. https:// www.eeoc.gov/eeoc/history/35th/thelaw/eo-8802.html.

The Equal Justice Initiative. 2010. "Illegal Racial Discrimination in Jury Selection: A Continuing Legacy." Retrieved December 24, 2018. https://eji.org/sites/default/files/illegal-racial-discrimination-in-jury-selection.pdf.

ESPN. 2005. "NCAA American Indian Mascot Ban Will Begin Feb. 1." Retrieved February 20, 2019. http://www.espn.com/college-sports/news/story?id=2125735.

Estes, Nick. 2019. *Our History Is the Future: Standing Rock versus the Dakota Access Pipeline, and the Long Tradition of Indigenous Resistance.* Brooklyn, NY: Verso.

Evans, Gavin. 2018. "The Unwelcome Revival of 'Race Science.'" Retrieved June 26, 2018. https://www.theguardian.com/news/2018/mar/02/the-unwelcome-revival-of-race-science.

Fingerhut, Hannah. 2018. "Most Americans Express Positive Views of Country's Growing Racial and Ethnic Diversity." Retrieved June 14, 2018. http://www.pewresearch.org/fact-tank/2018/06/14/most-americans-express-positive-views-of-countrys-growing-racial-and-ethnic-diversity/.

Frucci, Adam. 2007. "Intel Apologizes for 'Insulting' Sprinter Ad." Retrieved February 21, 2019. https://gizmodo.com/intel-apologizes-for-insulting-sprinter-ad-285278.

Fuchs, Chris. 2018. "Broadway Diversity Improves for All but Asian Americans, Report Finds." Retrieved February 9, 2019. https://www.nbcnews.com/news/asian-america/broadway-diversity-improves-all-asian-americans-report-finds-n838351.

Funk, Cary, and Kim Parker. 2018. "Blacks in STEM Jobs Are Especially Concerned about Diversity and Discrimination in the Workplace." Retrieved November 7, 2018. http://www.pewsocialtrends.org/2018/01/09/blacks-in-stem-jobs-are-especially-concerned-about-diversity-and-discrimination-in-the-workplace/.

Gaddis, S. Michael, and Raj Ghoshal. 2015. "Arab American Housing Discrimination, Ethnic Competition, and the Contact Hypothesis." *The Annals of the American Academy of Political and Social Science* 660(1):282–299.

Garcia, Ahiza. 2018. "These Are the Only Two Owners of Color in the NFL." Retrieved February 14, 2019. https://money.cnn.com/2018/05/18/news/nfl-nba-mlb-owners-diversity/index.html.

Ge, Yanbo, Christopher R. Knittel, Don MacKenzie, and Stephen Zoepf. 2016. "Racial and Gender Discrimination in Transportation Network Companies." NBER Working Paper No. 22776. Cambridge, MA: National Bureau of Economic Research.

Gee, Michael. 2018. "Why Aren't Black Employees Getting More White-Collar Jobs?" Retrieved November 7, 2018. https://hbr.org/2018/02/why-arent-black-employees-getting-more-white-collar-jobs.

Gershenson, Seth, Stephen B. Holt, and Nicholas W. Papageorge. 2016. "Who Believes in Me? The Effect of Student-Teacher Demographic Match on Teacher Expectations." *Economics of Education Review* 52:209–224.

Goff, Keli. 2013. "Black Producers Still Rare on Broadway." Retrieved February 9, 2019. https://www.theroot.com/black-producers-still-rare-on-broadway-1790896185.

Goff, Phillip Atiba, Tracey Lloyd, Amanda Geller, and Steven Raphael. 2016. "National Justice Database Sample City Report." http://policingequity.org/wp-content/uploads/2016/07/EverytownPD.City_.Report-FINAL.pdf.

Gonyea, Don. 2017. "Majority of White Americans Say They Believe Whites Face Discrimination." Retrieved June 4, 2018. https://www.npr.org/2017/10/24/559604836/majority-of-white-americans-think-theyre-discriminated-against.

Gonzalez, Barbara. 2016. "Idaho Bus Driver Pours Water on Latino Student and Demands He Speak English." Retrieved July 23, 2018. http://www.latina.com/lifestyle/our-issues/idaho-bus-driver-pours-water-student-demands-speak-english.

Goyette, Braden. 2013. "Cheerios Commercial Featuring Mixed Race Family Gets Racist Backlash." Retrieved February 20, 2019. https://www.huffingtonpost.com/2013/05/31/cheerios-commercial-racist-backlash_n_3363507.html.

Gramlich, John. 2017. "Black and White Officers See Many Key Aspects of Policing Differently." Retrieved January 12, 2017. http://www.pewresearch.org/fact-tank/2017/01/12/black-and-white-officers-see-many-key-aspects-of-policing-differently/.

Granick, Jennifer Stisa. 2017. *American Spies: Modern Surveillance, Why You Should Care, and What to Do about It.* Cambridge, UK: Cambridge University Press.

Greenberg, Deena, Carl Gershenson, and Matthew Desmond. 2016. "Discrimination in Evictions: Empirical Evidence and Legal Challenges." *Harvard Civil Rights-Civil Liberties Law Review* 51(1):115–158.

Gross, Samuel R., Maurice Possley, and Klara Stephens. 2017. "Race and Wrongful Convictions in the United States."

Retrieved December 25, 2018. https://www.law.umich
.edu/special/exoneration/Documents/Race_and_Wrongful_
Convictions.pdf.

Growe, Roslin, and Paula S. Montgomery. 2003. "Educational
Equity in America: Is Education the Great Equalizer?"
Retrieved July 23, 2018. https://files.eric.ed.gov/fulltext/
EJ842412.pdf.

Guelzo, Allen C. 2004. "How Abe Lincoln Lost the Black
Vote: Lincoln and Emancipation in the African American
Mind." *Journal of the Abraham Lincoln Association*
25(1):1–22.

Hall, Deborah L., David C. Matz, and Wendy Wood. 2010.
"Why Don't We Practice What We Preach? A Meta-Analytic
Review of Religious Racism." *Personality and Social Psychology
Review* 14(1):126–139.

Harriet Tubman Historical Society. 2019. "Songs of the
Underground Railroad." Retrieved June 27, 2019. http://
www.harriet-tubman.org/songs-of-the-underground-
railroad/.

Harris, D. R., R. Andrews, and A. Elixhauser. 1997. "Racial
and Gender Differences in Use of Procedures for Black and
White Hospitalized Adults." *Ethnicity & Disease* 7:91–102.

Hawkes, Rebecca. 2016. "Beyoncé's New Album: Why Is It
Called Lemonade, What Do the Lyrics Mean, Plus All You
Need to Know." Retrieved June 27, 2019. https://www
.telegraph.co.uk/music/news/beyoncs-new-album-why-is-
it-called-lemonade-plus-everything-else/.

Hekman, David R., Stefanie K. Johnson, Maw-Der Foo, and
Wei Yang. 2017. "Does Diversity-Valuing Behavior Result in
Diminished Performance Ratings for Non-White and Female
Leaders?" *Academy of Management Journal* 60(2):771–797.

Hemmer, Nicole. 2017. "'Scientific Racism' Is on the
Rise on the Right. But It's Been Lurking There for
Years." Retrieved June 26, 2018. https://www.vox.com/

the-big-idea/2017/3/28/15078400/scientific-racism-murray-alt-right-black-muslim-culture-trump.

Herrnstein, Richard J., and Charles Murray. 1994. *The Bell Curve: Intelligence and Class Structure in American Life.* New York: Free Press Paperbacks.

Hetey, Rebecca C., and Jennifer L. Eberhardt. 2018. "The Numbers Don't Speak for Themselves: Racial Disparities and the Persistence of Inequality in the Criminal Justice System." *Current Directions in Psychological Science* 27(3):183–187.

Hobson, Jeremy. 2016. "After 9 High-Profile Police-Involved Deaths of African-Americans, What Happened to the Officers?" Retrieved December 18, 2018. https://www.wbur.org/hereandnow/2016/07/11/america-police-shooting-timeline.

Hofstadter, Richard. 2009. "Abraham Lincoln and the Self-Made Myth," pp. 3–40, in *The Best American History Essays on Lincoln*, edited by Sean Wilentz. New York: Palgrave Macmillan.

Holloway, Daniel. 2017. "New 2017–2018 TV Shows Are Mostly White and Male." Retrieved February 11, 2019. https://variety.com/2017/tv/news/new-2017-18-tv-shows-no-diversity-1202436493/.

Howard, Adam. 2017. "More New England Patriots Stars Say They Won't Go to Trump White House." Retrieved July 1, 2019. https://www.nbcnews.com/news/us-news/6-new-england-patriots-stars-want-no-part-trump-white-n719296.

H.R. Res. 40. 2017.

H.R. Res. 751. 2018.

H.R. Res. 3239. 2017.

Hunt, Darnell, Ana-Christina Ramón, Michael Tran, and Amberia Sargent. 2018. "Hollywood Diversity Report 2018: Five Years of Progress and Missed Opportunities."

Retrieved February 11, 2019. https://socialsciences.ucla
.edu/wp-content/uploads/2018/02/UCLA-Hollywood-
Diversity-Report-2018-2-27-18.pdf.

Japanese American Citizens League. 2008. "An Unnoticed
Struggle: A Concise History of Asian American Civil
Rights Issues." Retrieved March 17, 2019. https://jacl
.org/wordpress/wp-content/uploads/2015/01/Unnoticed-
Struggle.pdf.

Jasiri X. 2010. "What If the Tea Party Was Black?"
Retrieved June 27, 2019. https://www.youtube.com/
watch?v=ZtH7vH4yRcY.

Jawando, Michele L., and Allie Anderson. 2016. "Racial
and Gender Diversity Sorely Lacking in America's Courts."
Retrieved December 22, 2018. https://www.americanprogress
.org/issues/courts/news/2016/09/15/144287/racial-and-
gender-diversity-sorely-lacking-in-americas-courts/.

The JBHE Foundation, Inc. 1998. "A Convocation of Bigots:
The 1998 American Renaissance Conference." *The Journal
of Blacks in Higher Education* 21:120–124.

Jefferson, Thomas. 1820. "Extract from Thomas Jefferson to
John Wayles Eppes." Retrieved July 1, 2019. http://tjrs
.monticello.org/letter/380.

Jefferson, Thomas. 1853. *Notes on the State of Virginia*.
Richmond, VA: J. W. Randolph.

Jones, Robert P. 2017. "What Does the Confederate Flag
Symbolize? Seven in Ten Working-Class Whites Say
'Southern Pride.'" Retrieved June 4, 2018. https://
www.prri.org/spotlight/white-working-class-americans-
confederate-flag-southern-pride-racism/.

Kang, Sonia K., Katherine A. DeCelles, András Tilcsik,
and Sora Jun. 2016. "Whitened Résumés: Race and Self-
Presentation in the Labor Market." *Administrative Science
Quarterly* 61(3):469–502.

Kaufman, Robert L. 2002. "Assessing Alternative Perspectives on Race and Sex Employment Segregation." *American Sociological Review* 67(4):547–572.

Keith, Ross, and Matan Gilat. 2015. "Popular Music Hasn't Been This White since 1981." Retrieved February 11, 2019. https://www.vocativ.com/culture/music/pop-music-billboard/.

*Kelo v. City of New London*. 2005. 545 U.S. 469.

Kersten, Andrew Edmund. 2000. *Race, Jobs, and the War: The FEPC in the Midwest, 1941–1946*. Urbana: University of Illinois Press.

King, Jr., Martin Luther. 1960. "Interview on 'Meet the Press.'" Retrieved June 26, 2018. http://okra.stanford.edu/transcription/document_images/Vol05Scans/17Apr1960_InterviewonMeetthePress.pdf.

Kooistra, Paul, John S. Mahoney, and Lisha Bridges. 1993. "The Unequal Opportunity for Equal Ability Hypothesis: Racism in the National Football League?" *Sociology of Sport Journal* 10(3):241–255.

Korte, Gregory. 2016. "White House Wants to Add New Racial Category for Middle Eastern People." Retrieved July 21, 2018. https://www.usatoday.com/story/news/politics/2016/09/30/white-house-wants-add-new-racial-category-middle-eastern-people/91322064/.

Krieger, Nancy, and Stephen Sidney. 1996. "Racial Discrimination and Blood Pressure: The CARDIA Study of Young Black and White Adults." *American Journal of Public Health* 86(10):1370–1378.

Krogstad, Jens Manuel, and Mark Hugo Lopez. 2017. "Use of Spanish Declines among Latinos in Major U.S. Metros." Retrieved July 23, 2018. http://www.pewresearch.org/fact-tank/2017/10/31/use-of-spanish-declines-among-latinos-in-major-u-s-metros/.

Krysan, Maria, and Sarah Patton Moberg. 2016. "Trends in Racial Attitudes." Retrieved January 4, 2018. https://igpa .uillinois.edu/programs/racial-attitudes#section-8.

Kuppens, Toon, and Russell Spears. 2014. "You Don't Have to Be Well-Educated to Be an Aversive Racist, but It Helps." *Social Science Research* 45:211–223.

Kurtzleben, Danielle. 2018. "What the Latest Immigration Polls Do (and Don't) Say." Retrieved June 28, 2018. https://www.npr.org/2018/01/23/580037717/ what-the-latest-immigration-polls-do-and-dont-say.

Lancianese, Adelina. 2019. "Before Black Lung, The Hawks Nest Tunnel Disaster Killed Hundreds." Retrieved February 6, 2019. https://www.npr.org/2019/01/20/685 821214/before-black-lung-the-hawks-nest-tunnel-disaster- killed-hundreds.

Lapchick, Richard. 2017. "College Sport Racial & Gender Report Card." Retrieved February 14, 2019. http://nebula .wsimg.com/5665825afd75728dc0c45b52ae6c412d?Access KeyId=DAC3A56D8FB782449D2A&disposition=0&allow origin=1.

Lapchick, Richard. 2018a. "The 2018 Racial and Gender Report Card: Major League Baseball." Retrieved February 14, 2019. http://nebula.wsimg.com/2b20e1bb7ea3fad9f45263 b846342d04?AccessKeyId=DAC3A56D8FB782449D2A& disposition=0&alloworigin=1.

Lapchick, Richard. 2018b. "The 2018 Racial and Gender Report Card: National Basketball Association." Retrieved February 14, 2019. http://nebula.wsimg.com/b10c21a67a6 d1035091c4e5784c012f4?AccessKeyId=DAC3A56D8FB7 82449D2A&disposition=0&alloworigin=1.

Lapchick, Richard. 2018c. "The 2018 Racial and Gender Report Card: Women's National Basketball Association." Retrieved February 14, 2019. https://docs.wixstatic.com/ug d/71e0e0_40c980bc9dcd4a7e97d04fdb1e218c7c.pdf.

Lapchick, Richard. 2019a. "Once Again, Racist Acts in Sports Are on the Rise." Retrieved February 20, 2019. http://

www.espn.com/espn/story/_/id/25675586/racism-sports-continued-rear-ugly-head-2018.

Lapchick, Richard. 2019b. "The 2018 Racial and Gender Report Card: Major League Soccer." Retrieved February 14, 2019. https://docs.wixstatic.com/ugd/71e0e0_ f681280d5ea24ff3bf5c7730b1cf4869.pdf.

Lapchick, Richard. 2019c. "The 2018 Racial and Gender Report Card: National Football League." Retrieved February 14, 2019. https://docs.wixstatic.com/ugd/7d86e5_8a53e ea031f64ec48177a167c8f3479a.pdf.

Lardieri, Alexa. 2017. "Despite Diverse Demographics, Most Politicians Are Still White Men." Retrieved July 23, 2018. https://www.usnews.com/news/politics/articles/2017-10-24/ despite-diverse-demographics-most-politicians-are-still-white-men.

Laybourn, Wendy M. 2017. "The Cost of Being 'Real': Black Authenticity, Colourism, and Billboard Rap Chart Rankings." *Ethnic and Racial Studies* 41(11):2085–2103.

League of American Orchestras. 2016. "Racial/Ethnic and Gender Diversity in the Orchestra Field." Retrieved February 11, 2019. http://www.ppv.issuelab.org/resources/ 25840/25840.pdf.

Lincoln, Abraham. 1865. "The First Edition of Abraham Lincoln's Preliminary Emancipation Proclamation." Retrieved June 30, 2019. https://cdn.loc.gov/service/rbc/lprbscsm/ scsm1017/scsm1017.pdf.

Lind, Dara. 2015. "Black Lives Matter vs. Bernie Sanders, Explained." Retrieved January 25, 2019. https://www.vox .com/2015/8/11/9127653/bernie-sanders-black-lives-matter.

Liptak, Adam. 2013. "Supreme Court Invalidates Key Part of Voting Rights Act." Retrieved July 21, 2018. https://www .nytimes.com/2013/06/26/us/supreme-court-ruling.html.

Liptak, Adam. 2019. "Justices Dismiss Appeal in Virginia Racial Gerrymandering Case." Retrieved August 31, 2019. https://www.nytimes.com/2019/06/17/us/politics/virginia-racial-gerrymandering-supreme-court.html.

Little, Becky. 2019. "Why FDR Didn't Support Eleanor Roosevelt's Anti-Lynching Campaign." Retrieved June 30, 2019. https://www.history.com/news/fdr-eleanor-roosevelt-anti-lynching-bill.

Long, Heather. 2018. "Black Unemployment Falls to Lowest Level on Record." Retrieved November 7, 2018. https://www.denverpost.com/2018/01/06/black-unemployment-lowest-level-on-record/.

Lopez, German. 2018. "This Is One of the Most Racist Remarks a Contemporary Politician Has Made about Drug Policy." Retrieved June 26, 2018. https://www.vox.com/identities/2018/1/9/16866754/marijuana-legalization-racism-alford-kansas-republican.

López, Gustavo, and Jens Manuel Krogstad. 2017. "Key Facts about Unauthorized Immigrants Enrolled in DACA." Retrieved January 7, 2019. http://www.pewresearch.org/fact-tank/2017/09/25/key-facts-about-unauthorized-immigrants-enrolled-in-daca/.

Louis de Malave, Florita Z. 1999. "Sterilization of Puerto Rican Women: A Selected, Partially Annotated Bibliography." Retrieved June 22, 2018. https://www.library.wisc.edu/gwslibrarian/publications/bibliographies/sterilization/.

Lozada, Carlos. 2015. "How People Convince Themselves That the Confederate Flag Represents Freedom, Not Slavery." Retrieved June 5, 2018. https://www.washingtonpost.com/news/book-party/wp/2015/06/19/how-people-convince-themselves-that-the-confederate-flag-represents-freedom-not-slavery/.

Maki, Mitchell T., Harry H. Kitano, and S. Megan Berthold. 1999. *Achieving the Impossible Dream: How Japanese Americans Obtained Redress*. Urbana: University of Illinois Press.

Mangan, Dan. 2019. "Colin Kaepernick Reaches Settlement in National Anthem Kneeling Collusion Case against NFL." Retrieved March 24, 2019. https://www.cnbc

.com/2019/02/15/colin-kaepernick-reaches-settlement-in-collusion-case-against-nfl-lawyer-says.html.

Martin, Nathan D., Kenneth I. Spenner, and Sarah A. Mustillo. 2016. "A Test of Leading Explanations for the College Racial-Ethnic Achievement Gap: Evidence from a Longitudinal Case Study." Retrieved July 23, 2018. https://link.springer.com/article/10.1007%2Fs11162-016-9439-6.

Massey, Douglas S., and Nancy A. Denton. 1993. *American Apartheid: Segregation and the Making of the Underclass.* Cambridge, MA: Harvard University Press.

Massey, Douglas S., and Garvey Lundy. 2001. "Use of Black English and Racial Discrimination in Urban Housing Markets: New Methods and Findings." *Urban Affairs Review* 36(4):452–469.

Matsuda, Mari J. 1997. "We Will Not Be Used: Are Asian Americans the Racial Bourgeoisie?," pp. 149–160, in *Where Is Your Body? And Other Essays on Race, Gender, and the Law.* Boston, MA: Beacon Press.

Matthew, Danya Bowen, Edward Rodrigue, and Richard V. Reeves. 2016. "Time for Justice: Tackling Race Inequalities in Health and Housing." Retrieved January 4, 2019. https://www.brookings.edu/research/time-for-justice-tackling-race-inequalities-in-health-and-housing/.

Meyer, Robinson. 2017. "Oil Is Flowing through the Dakota Access Pipeline." Retrieved July 1, 2019. https://www.theatlantic.com/science/archive/2017/06/oil-is-flowing-through-the-dakota-access-pipeline/529707/.

Mikati, Ihab, Adam F. Benson, Thomas J. Luben, Jason D. Sacks, and Jennifer Richmond-Bryant. 2018. "Disparities in Distribution of Particulate Matter Emission Sources by Race and Poverty Status." *American Journal of Public Health* 108(4):480–485.

Milman, Oliver. 2017. "U.S. People of Color Still More Likely to Be Exposed to Pollution Than White People." Retrieved December 10, 2018. https://www.theguardian

.com/environment/2017/sep/14/us-people-of-color-still-more-likely-to-be-exposed-to-pollution-than-white-people.

Miranda, Carolina A. 2017. "You Might See More Women and Minorities on TV, but Hollywood Has a Ways to Go When It Comes to Diversity, Report Says." Retrieved February 11, 2019. https://www.latimes.com/entertainment/la-et-cam-ucla-hollywood-diversity-report-20170220-story.html.

Moore, Solomon. 2001. "Census' Multiracial Option Overturns Traditional Views." Retrieved July 21, 2018. http://articles.latimes.com/2001/mar/05/news/mn-33659.

Mora, Christina. 2014. *Making Hispanics: How Activists, Bureaucrats & Media Constructed a New American*. Chicago: The University of Chicago Press.

Morris, Edward W., and Brea L. Perry. 2016. "The Punishment Gap: School Suspension and Racial Disparities in Achievement." *Social Problems* 63(1):68–86.

Morrison, Toni. 2004. *Beloved*. New York: Vintage Books.

Mort, E. A., J. S. Weisman, and A. M. Epstein. 1994. "Physician Discretion and Racial Variation in the Use of Surgical Procedures." *Archives of Internal Medicine* 154:761–767.

Moss, Hilary. 2017. "'Dove VisibleCare' Ad Called Out for Being Racist." Retrieved February 20, 2019. https://www.huffpost.com/entry/dove-visiblecare-ad-racist_n_865911.

Museum Geographies. 2015. "Smartguide to the Exhibition 'Black Like Who? Exploring Race and Representation' at Birmingham Museum of Art (Alabama, USA)." Retrieved June 27, 2019. https://museumgeographies.wordpress.com/2015/07/17/smartguide-to-the-exhibition-black-like-who-exploring-race-and-representation-at-birmingham-museum-of-art-alabama-usa/.

Muwakkil, Salim. 2016. "Does Black Lives Matter Really Matter?" Retrieved January 25, 2019. https://www

.aljazeera.com/indepth/features/2016/03/black-lives-matter-matter-160318080936188.html.

Myre, Greg. 2018. "Deadly Connection: Neo-Nazi Group Linked to 3 Accused Killers." Retrieved March 6, 2018. https://www.npr.org/2018/03/06/590292705/5-killings-3-states-and-1-common-neo-nazi-link.

Nadeem, Shehzad, John D. Skrentny, Jennifer Lee, Zulema Valdez, and Donna R. Gabaccia. 2015. "Fifty Years of 'New' Immigration." Retrieved June 26, 2019. https://contexts.org/articles/fifty-years-of-new-immigration/#lee.

National Academies of Sciences, Engineering, and Medicine. 2016. "Immigration's Long-Term Impacts on Overall Wages and Employment of Native-Born U.S. Workers Very Small, Although Low-Skilled Workers May Be Affected, New Report Finds; Impacts on Economic Growth Positive, While Effects on Government Budgets Mixed." Retrieved July 2, 2018. http://www8.nationalacademies.org/onpinews/newsitem.aspx?RecordID =23550.

National Low Income Housing Coalition. 2018. "UPDATE: President Trump Calls for Drastic Cuts to Affordable Housing, February 12, 2018." Retrieved November 14, 2018. https://nlihc.org/news/update-president-trump-calls-drastic-cuts-affordable-housing-february-12-2018.

National Public Radio, Robert Wood Johnson Foundation, and Harvard University T. H. Chan School of Public Health. 2017. "Discrimination in America: Experiences and Views of Asian Americans." Retrieved December 10, 2018. https://www.npr.org/assets/news/2017/12/discriminationpoll-asian-americans.pdf.

Nelson, Alan. 2002. "Unequal Treatment: Confronting Racial and Ethnic Disparities in Health Care." Retrieved December 26, 2018. https://www.ncbi.nlm.nih.gov/pmc/articles/PMC2594273/pdf/jnma00325-0024.pdf.

Newkirk II, Vann R. 2017. "North Carolina's Voter ID Law Is Defeated, for Now." Retrieved July 21, 2018.

https://www.theatlantic.com/politics/archive/2017/05/north-carolinas-voter-id-law-supreme-court-cert/526713/.

Newkirk II, Vann R. 2018. "Trump's White-Nationalist Pipeline." Retrieved June 29, 2019. https://www.theatlantic.com/politics/archive/2018/08/trump-white-nationalism/568393/.

Newport, Frank. 2018. "The Harvard Affirmative Action Case and Public Opinion." Retrieved January 4, 2019. https://news.gallup.com/opinion/polling-matters/243965/harvard-affirmative-action-case-public-opinion.aspx.

Newport, Frank, Jack Ludwig, and Sheila Kearney. 2001. "Black-White Relations in the United States 2001 Update." Retrieved May 27, 2018. http://media.gallup.com/GPTB/specialReports/sr010711.PDF.

New York Civil Liberties Union. 2018. "Annual Stop-and-Frisk Numbers." Retrieved December 10, 2018. https://www.nyclu.org/en/stop-and-frisk-data.

Ng, Wendy L. 2002. *Japanese American Internment during World War II: A History and Reference Guide*. Westport, CT: Greenwood Press.

Nittle, Nadra. 2018. "Students Are Waging War on Sexist and Racist School Dress Codes—And They're Winning." Retrieved November 14, 2018. https://www.vox.com/the-goods/2018/9/13/17847542/students-waging-war-sexist-racist-school-dress-codes.

*North Carolina State Conference of the NAACP v. McCrory*. 2016. 831 F.3d 204.

Nova, Annie. 2018. "Congress Eases Rules against Racial Discrimination in the Auto Loan Market." Retrieved December 8, 2018. https://www.cnbc.com/2018/05/09/congress-eases-rules-against-racial-discrimination-in-the-auto-loan-market.html.

Office of the Press Secretary. 2014. "Presidential Memorandum—Creating and Expanding Ladders of Opportunity for Boys and Young Men of Color." Retrieved

January 8, 2019. https://obamawhitehouse.archives.gov/
the-press-office/2014/02/27/presidential-memorandum-
creating-and-expanding-ladders-opportunity-boys-.

Office of the Press Secretary. 2016. "Presidential
Memorandum—Promoting Diversity and Inclusion in
the National Security Workforce." Retrieved January 8,
2019. https://obamawhitehouse.archives.gov/the-press-
office/2016/10/05/presidential-memorandum-promoting-
diversity-and-inclusion-national.

Office of the Press Secretary. 2017. "Presidential
Memorandum—Promoting Diversity and Inclusion in
Our National Parks, National Forests, and Other Public
Lands and Waters." Retrieved January 8, 2019. https://
obamawhitehouse.archives.gov/the-press-office/2017/01/
12/presidential-memorandum-promoting-diversity-and-
inclusion-our-national.

Okeowo, Alexis. 2016. "Hate on the Rise after Trump's
Election." Retrieved June 29, 2019. https://www
.newyorker.com/news/news-desk/hate-on-the-rise-after-
trumps-election.

Oyez. 2019. "*Schuette v. Coalition to Defend Affirmative
Action.*" Retrieved January 8, 2019. https://www.oyez.org/
cases/2013/12-682.

Page, Scott E. 2007. *The Difference: How the Power of
Diversity Creates Better Groups, Firms, Schools, and Societies.*
Princeton, NJ: Princeton University Press.

Pager, Devah. 2003. "The Mark of a Criminal Record."
*American Journal of Sociology* 108(5):937–975.

Pager, Devah, and Hana Shepherd. 2008. "The Sociology of
Discrimination: Racial Discrimination in Employment,
Housing, Credit, and Consumer Markets." *Annual Review
of Sociology* 34:181–209.

Peffley, Mark, and Jon Hurwitz. 2007. "Persuasion and
Resistance: Race and the Death Penalty in America."
*American Journal of Political Science* 51(4):996–1012.

Petersen, William. 1966. "Success Story, Japanese-American Style." Retrieved June 26, 2019. http://inside.sfuhs.org/dept/history/US_History_reader/Chapter14/modelminority.pdf.

Pettigrew, Thomas F., and Linda R. Tropp. 2005. "Allport's Intergroup Contact Hypothesis: Its History and Influence," pp. 262–277, in *On the Nature of Prejudice: Fifty Years after Allport*, edited by John F. Dovidio, Peter Glick, and Laurie A. Budman. Malden, MA: Blackwell Publishing.

Pew Research Center. 2016. "On Views of Race and Inequality, Blacks and Whites Are Worlds Apart." Retrieved January 3, 2019. http://www.pewsocialtrends.org/2016/06/27/on-views-of-race-and-inequality-blacks-and-whites-are-worlds-apart/.

Pew Research Center. 2017a. "More Say Understating Discrimination Is the Bigger Problem Than Overstating It." Retrieved June 4, 2018. http://www.people-press.org/2017/10/05/4-race-immigration-and-discrimination/4_8-6/.

Pew Research Center. 2017b. "Demographic Portrait of Muslim Americans." Retrieved October 22, 2018. http://www.pewforum.org/2017/07/26/demographic-portrait-of-muslim-americans/.

Pew Research Center. 2018. "Conservatives: Religious Composition of Conservatives." Retrieved June 28, 2018. http://www.pewforum.org/religious-landscape-study/political-ideology/conservative/.

Pirani, Fiza. 2017. "Tenn. Teacher Suspended for Video of Student's Hijab Being Ripped Off: 'Lol All That Hair Covered Up.'" Retrieved October 22, 2018. https://www.ajc.com/news/national/tenn-teacher-suspended-for-video-student-hijab-being-ripped-off-lol-all-that-hair-covered/XFoUAkRIWk9LxF4dkttUNP/.

Pitt, Jenelle S., Mya Vaughn, Aisha Shamburger-Rousseau, and LaKeisha L. Harris. 2015. "Black Women in

Academia: The Invisible Life," pp. 209–224, in *Racial Battle Fatigue: Insights from the Front Lines of Social Justice Advocacy*, edited by Jennifer L. Martin. Santa Barbara, CA: Praeger.

Pittman, Chavella T. 2010. "Race and Gender Oppression in the Classroom: The Experiences of Women Faculty of Color with White Male Students." *Teaching Sociology* 38(3):183–196.

Pitts, Michael J. 2018. "What Has Twenty-Five Years of Racial Gerrymandering Doctrine Achieved?" *UC Irvine Law Review* 9(1):229–273.

Rapaport, Daniel. 2017. "LeBron James Responds to Donald Trump's Tweet Rescinding Stephen Curry's White House Invite." Retrieved July 2, 2019. https://www.si.com/ nba/2017/09/23/lebron-james-respond-donald-trump-stephen-curry-white-house.

Rasmussen Reports. 2017. "48% Favor Continuing 'Dreamers' Program to Shield Illegal Immigrants." Retrieved July 2, 2018. http://www.rasmussenreports.com/ public_content/politics/current_events/immigration/septe mber_2017/48_favor_continuing_dreamers_program_to_ shield_illegal_immigrants/.

Reed, Jr., Adolph. 2008. "Race and the New Deal Coalition." Retrieved July 1, 2019. https://www.thenation.com/article/ race-and-new-deal-coalition/.

Reich, Michael, David M. Gordon, and Richard C. Edwards. 1973. "A Theory of Labor Market Segmentation." *American Economic Review* 63(2):359–365.

Reid, T. R. 2005. "Spanish at School Translates to Suspension." Retrieved July 23, 2018. http://www.washingtonpost.com/ wp-dyn/content/article/2005/12/08/AR2005120802122 .html?noredirect=on.

Rice, Lisa, and Erich Schwartz Jr. 2018. "Discrimination When Buying a Car: How the Color of Your Skin Can Affect Your Car-Shopping Experience." Retrieved

December 8, 2018. https://nationalfairhousing.org/wp-content/uploads/2018/01/Discrimination-When-Buying-a-Car-FINAL-1-11-2018.pdf.

Rivas, Jorge. 2013. "California Prisons Caught Sterilizing Female Inmates without Approval." Retrieved June 20, 2018. https://abcnews.go.com/ABC_Univision/doctors-california-prisons-sterilized-female-inmates-authorizations/story?id=19610110.

Robinson, Otis. 2018. "Are Dreadlocks Cultural Appropriation? Who Gets to Wear Dreads, and Why?" Retrieved October 22, 2018. https://medium.com/@overtake/are-dreadlocks-cultural-appropriation-b2489a271601.

Roscigno, Vinnie J., Diana L. Karafin, and Griff Tester. 2009. "The Complexities and Processes of Racial Housing Discrimination." *Social Problems* 56(1):49–69.

Ross, Matthew B., James Fazzalaro, Ken Barone, and Jesse Kalinowski. 2017. "Traffic Stop Data Analysis and Findings, 2015–2016." Retrieved March 18, 2019. http://sue.apps-1and1.com/wp-content/uploads/2018/08/November-2017-Connecticut-Racial-Profiling-Report.pdf.

Saroglou, Vassilis, Vanessa Delpierre, and Rebecca Dernelle. 2004. "Values and Religiosity: A Meta-Analysis of Studies Using Schwartz's Model." *Personality and Individual Differences* 37(4):721–724.

Sawyer, Jeremy, and Anup Gampta. 2018. "Implicit and Explicit Racial Attitudes Changed during Black Lives Matter." Retrieved February 4, 2019. https://journals.sagepub.com/doi/abs/10.1177/0146167218757454?journalCode=pspc.

Seabury, Seth A., Sophie Terp, and Leslie I. Boden. 2017. "Racial and Ethnic Differences in the Frequency of Workplace Injuries and Prevalence of Work-Related Disability." *Health Affairs* 36(2):266–273.

The Sentencing Project. 2015. "Black Lives Matter: Eliminating Racial Inequality in the Criminal Justice System." Retrieved December 19, 2018. https://www.sentencingproject.org/wp-content/uploads/2015/11/Black-Lives-Matter.pdf.

Serwer, Adam. 2014. "Lyndon Johnson Was a Civil Rights Hero. But Also a Racist." Retrieved June 30, 2019. http://www.msnbc.com/msnbc/lyndon-johnson-civil-rights-racism.

S. 411-ERRPA. 2017.

Shockley, William. 1972. "Dysgenics, Geneticity, Raceology: A Challenge to the Intellectual Responsibility of Educators." *The Phi Delta Kappan* 53(5):297–307.

Shoichet, Catherine, Susannah Cullinane, and Tal Kopan. 2017. "U.S. Immigration: DACA and Dreamers Explained." Retrieved January 8, 2019. https://www.cnn.com/2017/09/04/politics/daca-dreamers-immigration-program/index.html.

S. J. Res. 57. 2018.

Smith, Aaron. 2017. "Kellogg's Gets Rid of Racially Insensitive Art on Corn Pops Box." Retrieved February 20, 2019. https://money.cnn.com/2017/10/26/news/companies/kelloggs-corn-pops-racism/index.html.

Smith, Daryl G. 1997. *Diversity Works: The Emerging Picture of How Students Benefit.* Washington, DC: Association of American Colleges & Universities.

Smith, Stacy L., Marc Choueiti, Katherine Pieper, Traci Gillig, Carmen Lee, and Dylan DeLuca. 2016. "Inequality in 700 Popular Films: Examining Portrayals of Gender, Race, and LGBT Status from 2007 to 2014." Retrieved February 9, 2019. https://annenberg.usc.edu/sites/default/files/MDSCI_Inequality_in-700_Popular.pdf.

Snider, Mike. 2018. "Heineken Pulls 'Lighter Is Better' Commercial after Some Call It Racist." Retrieved February 20, 2019. https://www.usatoday.com/story/money/

business/2018/03/27/heineken-pulls-lighter-better-commercial-after-some-call-racist/461395002/.

Soloski, Alexis. 2019. "White Noise Review—Suzan-Lori Parks Provokes and Disturbs." Retrieved June 27, 2019. https://www.theguardian.com/stage/2019/mar/20/white-noise-review-public-theater-new-york-suzan-lori-parks.

Somin, Ilya. 2011. "The Civil Rights Implications of Eminent Domain Abuse: Testimony before the United States Commission on Civil Rights." Retrieved June 11, 2018. https://www.law.gmu.edu/assets/files/faculty/Somin_USCCR-aug2011.pdf.

Sommers, Samuel R. 2006. "On Racial Diversity and Group Decision Making: Identifying Multiple Effects of Racial Composition on Jury Deliberations." Retrieved December 25, 2018. https://www.apa.org/pubs/journals/releases/psp-904597.pdf.

Sommers, Samuel R. 2007. "Race and the Decision Making of Juries." *Legal and Criminological Psychology* 12:171–187.

Sooke, Alastair. 2014. "Kerry James Marshall: Challenging Racism in Art History." Retrieved June 27, 2019. http://www.bbc.com/culture/story/20141023-i-show-black-is-beautiful.

Southern Poverty Law Center. 2018. "Pioneer Fund." Retrieved June 22, 2018. https://www.splcenter.org/fighting-hate/extremist-files/group/pioneer-fund.

Southern Poverty Law Center. 2019. "Nation of Islam." Retrieved June 24, 2019. https://www.splcenter.org/fighting-hate/extremist-files/group/nation-islam.

SPARQ. 2016. "Executive Summary: The Stanford Reports on Improving Policy-Community Relations in Oakland, CA." Retrieved December 11, 2018. https://stanford.app.box.com/v/OPD-Executive-Summary.

Spero, Sterling D., and Abram L. Harris. 1931. *The Black Worker: The Negro and the Labor Movement*. Port Washington, NY: Kennikat.

Staggenborg, Suzanne. 2016. *Social Movements*, 2nd ed. New York: Oxford University Press.

Steele, Claude M. 2011. *Whistling Vivaldi: How Stereotypes Affect Us and What We Can Do.* New York: W. W. Norton & Company, Inc.

Stewart, Lathonia Denise, and Richard Perlow. 2001. "Applicant Race, Job Status, and Racial Attitude as Predictors of Employment Discrimination." *Journal of Business and Psychology* 16(2):259–275.

Stinson, Philip M. 2017. "Police Shootings Data: What We Know and What We Don't Know." *Criminal Justice Faculty Publications* 78.

Stowe, Harriet Beecher. 2008. *Uncle Tom's Cabin.* Oxford, UK: Oxford University Press.

Struyk, Ryan. 2017. "Blacks and Whites See Racism in the United States Very, Very Differently." Retrieved June 4, 2018. https://www.cnn.com/2017/08/16/politics/blacks-white-racism-united-states-polls/index.html.

Taddonio, Patrice. 2018. "Inside a New-Nazi Group with Members Tied to the U.S. Military." Retrieved June 29, 2019. https://www.pbs.org/wgbh/frontline/article/inside-a-neo-nazi-group-with-members-tied-to-the-u-s-military/.

Tataki, Ronald. 1989. *Strangers from a Different Shore: A History of Asian-Americans.* New York: Penguin.

Taylor, Jon E. 2013. *Freedom to Serve: Truman, Civil Rights, and Executive Order 9981.* New York: Routledge.

Tenold, Vegas. 2018. *Everything You Love Will Burn: Inside the Rebirth of White Nationalism in America.* New York: Nation Books.

Thomas, Dexter. 2016. "This Chinese Laundry Ad Is Racist, But It's Hardly the First." Retrieved February 20, 2019. https://www.latimes.com/nation/la-na-racist-chinese-commercial-20160526-snap-story.html.

Thomas, Ian. 2018. "NHL Looks to Broaden Diversity Endeavors." Retrieved February 13, 2019. https://www.sportsbusinessdaily.com/Journal/Issues/2018/10/01/In-Depth/Diversity.aspx.

*Trump v. Hawaii.* 2017. No. 17-965.

Tucker, William H. 2002. *The Funding of Scientific Racism: Wickliffe Draper and the Pioneer Fund.* Urbana: University of Illinois Press.

Tyson, Karolyn. 2011. *Integration Interrupted: Tracking, Black Students, and Acting White after Brown.* New York: Oxford University Press.

United States Sentencing Commission. 2017. "Demographic Differences in Sentencing: An Update to the 2012 *Booker* Report." Retrieved December 26, 2018. https://www.ussc.gov/sites/default/files/pdf/research-and-publications/research-publications/2017/20171114_Demographics.pdf.

University of Texas at Austin College of Liberal Arts. 2005. "History of the Right to Vote in the United States." Retrieved July 21, 2018. https://www.laits.utexas.edu/lawdem/unit01/reading1/history_to_vote.html.

Urban, Jessica Leann. 2008. *Nation, Immigration, and Environmental Security.* New York: Palgrave Macmillan.

U.S. Census Bureau. 2017. "Quick Facts: United States." Retrieved December 12, 2018. https://www.census.gov/quickfacts/fact/table/US/PST045217.

U.S. Commission on Civil Rights. 2014. "The Civil Rights Implications for Eminent Domain Abuse." Retrieved June 11, 2018. https://www.usccr.gov/pubs/docs/FINAL_FY14_Eminent-Domain-Report.pdf.

U.S. Constitutional Amendment XIII.

U.S. Department of Housing and Urban Development. 2013. "Housing Discrimination against Racial and Ethnic

Minorities 2012." Retrieved December 10, 2018.
https://www.huduser.gov/portal/Publications/pdf/HUD-514_HDS2012_execsumm.pdf.

U.S. Department of Justice. 2017. "About Section 5 of the Voting Rights Act." Retrieved July 21, 2018. https://www.justice.gov/crt/about-section-5-voting-rights-act.

U.S. Department of State. 2019. "June 26 Supreme Court Decision on Presidential Proclamation 9645." Retrieved March 23, 2019. https://travel.state.gov/content/travel/en/us-visas/visa-information-resources/presidential-proclamation-archive/june_26_supreme_court_decision_on_presidential_proclamation9645.html.

U.S. Government Accountability Office. 2018. "K-12 Education: Discipline Disparities for Black Students, Boys, and Students with Disabilities." Retrieved October 22, 2018. https://www.gao.gov/assets/700/690828.pdf.

Voigt, Rob, Nicholas P. Camp, Vinodkumar Prabhakaran, William L. Hamilton, Rebecca C. Hetey, Camilla M. Griffiths, David Jurgens, Dan Jurafsky, and Jennifer L. Eberhardt. 2017. "Language from Police Body Camera Footage Shows Racial Disparities in Officer Respect." *Proceedings of the National Academy of Sciences* 114(25):6521–6526.

Volz, Brian D. 2015. "Race and Quarterback Survival in the National Football League." Retrieved February 20, 2019. https://journals.sagepub.com/doi/abs/10.1177/1527002515609659.

Waldstreicher, David. 2009. *Slavery's Constitution: From Revolution to Ratification*. New York: Hill and Wang.

Walker, Alice. 1982. *The Color Purple*. New York: Mariner Books.

Wamsley, Laurel. 2019. "Neo-Nazi Who Killed Charlottesville Protester Is Sentenced to Life in Prison." Retrieved

June 29, 2019. https://www.npr.org/2019/06/28/7369 15323/neo-nazi-who-killed-charlottesville-protester-is-sentenced-to-life-in-prison.

Wang, Hansi Lo. 2018. "No Middle Eastern or North African Category on 2020 Census, Bureau Says." Retrieved July 21, 2018. https://www.npr.org/2018/01/29/581541111/no-middle-eastern-or-north-african-category-on-2020-census-bureau-says.

Whatley, Warren C. 1993. "African-American Strikebreaking from the Civil War to the New Deal." *Social Science History* 17(4):525–558.

White, Abbey. 2017. "Why Halle Berry Says Her Historic 2002 Oscar Win Is Now Meaningless." Retrieved February 9, 2019. https://www.vox.com/culture/2017/7/3/15887198/halle-berry-oscars-win-meaningless.

Williams, David R., and Chiquita Collins. 2001. "Racial Residential Segregation: A Fundamental Cause of Racial Disparities in Health." Retrieved February 4, 2019. https://www.ncbi.nlm.nih.gov/pmc/articles/PMC1497358/pdf/12042604.pdf.

Williams, David R., and Selina A. Mohammed. 2009. "Discrimination and Racial Disparities in Health: Evidence and Needed Research." *Journal of Behavioral Medicine* 32:20–47.

Williams, David R., and Michelle Sternthal. 2010. "Understanding Racial/Ethnic Disparities in Health: Sociological Contributions." *Journal of Health and Social Behavior* 51(Suppl):S15–S27.

Wilson, Valerie, Janelle Jones, Kayla Blado, and Elise Gould. 2017. "Black Women Have to Work 7 Months into 2017 to Be Paid the Same as White Men in 2016." Retrieved November 7, 2018. https://www.epi.org/blog/black-women-have-to-work-7-months-into-2017-to-be-paid-the-same-as-white-men-in-2016/.

Wingfield, Adia Harvey. 2015. "Being Black—But Not Too Black—in the Workplace." Retrieved November 24, 2018. https://www.theatlantic.com/business/archive/2015/10/being-black-work/409990/.

Wise, Tim. 2008. *Speaking Treason Fluently: Anti-Racist Reflections from an Angry White Male.* Berkeley, CA: Soft Skull Press.

Wolfe, Patrick. 2006. "Settler Colonialism and the Elimination of the Native." *Journal of Genocide Research* 4:387–409.

Wren, Ian. 2018. "Congress Rolls Back Anti-Discrimination Auto Loan Rule." Retrieved January 8, 2019. https://www.npr.org/2018/05/08/609468562/congress-rolls-back-anti-discrimination-auto-loan-rule.

Wright, Dwayne Kwaysee, and Liliana M. Garces. 2018. "Understanding the Controversy around Race-Based Affirmative Action in American Higher Education," pp. 3–21, in *Controversies on Campus: Debating the Issues Confronting American Universities in the 21st Century*, edited by Joy Blanchard. Santa Barbara, CA: ABC-CLIO.

Xu, Huanan. 2018. "First Fired, First Hired? Business Cycles and Immigrant Labor Market Transitions." Retrieved December 7, 2018. https://link.springer.com/article/10.1186/s40176-018-0127-5.

Yancey-Bragg, N'dea. 2018. "Florida School Receiving Death Threats after Turning Away 6-Year-Old with Dreadlocks." Retrieved October 22, 2018. https://www.usatoday.com/story/news/nation-now/2018/08/16/florida-school-faces-backlash-rejecting-6-year-old-dreadlocks/1010132002/.

Yen, Rhoda J. 2000. "Racial Stereotyping of Asians and Asian Americans and Its Effect on Criminal Justice: A Reflection on the Wayne Lo Case." *Asian Law Journal* 7(1):1–28.

Yi, David. 2015. "Black Armor." Retrieved February 22, 2019. https://mashable.com/2015/08/08/black-men-dressing-up-police/#GN99I0E41GqQ.

Young, Abe Louise. 2010. "BP Hires Prison Labor to Clean Up Spill While Coastal Residents Struggle." Retrieved March 23, 2019. https://www.thenation.com/article/bp-hires-prison-labor-clean-spill-while-coastal-residents-struggle/.

Yuen, Nancy Wang. 2017. *Reel Inequality: Hollywood Actors and Racism.* New Brunswick, NJ: Rutgers University Press.

Zaru, Deena. 2017. "Joey Badass: How Hip-Hop Is Evolving in the Age of Trump." Retrieved June 27, 2019. https://www.cnn.com/2017/04/14/politics/joey-badass-album-all-amerikkan-badass-hip-hop/index.html.

*This chapter showcases the diverse voices of experts with a wealth of professional and personal knowledge regarding racism in America. The contributors to this chapter come from a variety of backgrounds from academia to law to journalism to grassroots activism. Their arguments are their own and are presented without censorship. Their viewpoints may or may not align with those of the author but are all worthy of careful consideration.*

*Dr. Victor Ray, a sociologist at the University of Tennessee, Knoxville, discusses the dangers of viewing history as a long arc toward progress. He notes that racial progress narratives obscure the ever-present potential of old manifestations of racism reemerging or new manifestations of racism developing. Assumptions of consistent racial progress also produce a "political cudgel" with which to blame the victims of racial inequality; the assumption is made that, given racial progress, if some racial minorities are not succeeding, then it must be the result of their own decisions or inadequacies.*

*Dr. Sahar D. Sattarzadeh, an assistant professor of multi-interdisciplinary studies at Champlain College, and Dr. Matthew W. Hughey, a sociologist at the University of Connecticut, discuss racism in the press, radio, film, television, and alternative and new media.*

---

A woman and child approach the U.S.–Mexico border on foot. In the last several years, the prevalence of deportations and the enforcement of draconian immigration policies have increased alongside rising xenophobic fears among Americans. (Maxironwas/Dreamstime.com)

*Efrén C. Olivares, Racial and Economic Justice Program direc-tor at Texas Civil Rights Project, shares his experiences working with immigrants who face continual threats from law enforcement and immigration enforcement and addresses how these threats have been magnified with the passage of Texas Senate Bill 4.*

*Louise Seamster, a sociologist at the University of Tennessee, Knoxville, addresses the process and consequences of gentrification and the ways in which it contributes to racial inequality. She also addresses how racial minorities may benefit from or participate in gentrification themselves, but those benefits may not necessarily be long-lasting ones.*

*Dwanna L. McKay reminds us that, even in an age in which overt racism has become less publicly acceptable, racist conceptual-izations of indigenous people frequently go unchallenged. She con-textualizes the treatment of indigenous people in historical events, pointing out that the "pervasiveness of overt racism never slowed for Native people—it just became unseen."*

*Catalina Adorno Castillo, a volunteer organizer with immi-grant rights movement Movimiento Cosecha, discusses the personal impact of the Trump administration's decision to rescind DACA (Deferred Action for Childhood Arrivals) protections.*

*Alison Ho, an interdisciplinary artist and designer, shares the trials and tribulations of navigating the social world at various intersections of race and gender.*

*A. Rochaun Meadows-Fernandez, a journalist and author, dis-cusses the emotional incapacitation and struggle to find racial em-pathy accompanying police brutality against black Americans and the age of Trump.*

## The Perils of Racial Progress Narratives
*Victor Ray*

Barack Obama's election had both scholars and pundits pro-claiming the end of racial history. Trump's election unleashed a wave of open white nationalism that many scholars argued was a thing of the past, casting doubt on this triumphalist linear narrative of racial progress. Buoyed by the so-called alt-right, a loose collection of men's rights activists, disaffected gamers, and open Nazis, Trump's campaign defied the political class who had long relied on covert racial appeals to mobilize white racism. This rising tide of anti-immigrant sentiment and racial violence points to the need for a more nuanced understanding of racial progress. Poor thinking about racial progress— typically framed as simple linear movement through time—is used to deny the political claims of full citizenship for people of color. Here, I briefly outline how the idea of racial progress has shaped American sociology and offer a better way to think about changes in the racial order.

Nearly every debate in the sociology of race and ethnicity revolves around a notion of racial progress. The assumptions underlying the idea of progress are themselves tainted with racism. Early social science ranked societies according to their relative level of "progress" from white civilization to racialized savagery. In American sociology, early sociological treatments of the notion of progress arose from social Darwinist, eugenic thinking. Social Darwinism and eugenics both claimed that people of color were naturally inferior to whites and advocated for sterilization, restrictions on immigration, and sometimes ethnic cleansing. Scholars saw progress in the idea that black people in the United States were physically dying out (Muhammad 2010). More recently, sociologists have claimed considerable racial progress following the civil rights movement, with some going so far as to claim that race had "declined in significance" (Wilson 1978) as class became more important in defining the lives of black Americans. Sociological notions of racial progress are rarely explicitly defined, but progress is nonetheless taken as prima facie good.

Sociology's focus on racial progress has always held an uneasy relationship with the empirical data on racial inequality. Since at least Du Bois's (2017) analyses in *Black Reconstruction*, sociologists have shown that racial inequality is structural. Du Bois demonstrated how white supremacists quickly regrouped following the Civil War, using the power of the state to institutionalize and legalize racial inequality. In *The Philadelphia Negro*, Du Bois (2014) argues that black Philadelphia's poverty was created and maintained by whites. Since Du Bois wrote these masterpieces in the early part of the twentieth century, many of the inequalities he chronicled have changed in form but not necessarily substance. For instance, hiring discrimination against black men has remained intractable since the 1980s (Quillian et al. 2017) despite antidiscrimination laws. Black and Latino Americans "make up about 30 percent of the U.S. population, but collectively they own about 7 percent of the nation's private wealth" (Federal Reserve Bank of St. Louis, Hamilton, and Darity 2017:60). Schools are more racially segregated than they were before the landmark *Brown v. Board* decision. And the criminal justice system is deeply implicated in reproducing racial inequality, with some going so far as to claim it is a "New Jim Crow" (Alexander 2012:312). Similar racial inequalities shape many aspects of American life.

Despite the strong historical continuity of racial inequality in the United States, many whites believe they experience more discrimination than people of color. For instance, Norton and Sommers (2011) reported that whites see decreasing racial animus against out-groups as *rising animus against themselves*. Although whites remain firmly at the top of America's racial hierarchy, the perception of increasing minority advantage feels like a loss. This view is especially pronounced among some white subgroups, with white Christians believing they are more persecuted than nonwhites (Wong 2018). Of course, whites' assertions about their social position are empirically disprovable, but this hardly matters. Whites' vested interest in racial inequality points to the inadequacy of mainstream narratives on racial progress. Ultimately, sociologists need a more complex and nuanced understanding of racial progress.

### Racism as a Fundamental Cause of Social Inequality

Rather than thinking of racism as an individual trait or a feature of society declining over time, we would be better served to think of racism as changing in relation to historical conditions (Hall 1986). I argue that racism is a "fundamental cause" of social inequality (Link and Phelan 1995; Ray and Seamster 2016). This means that basic relations of inequality—that is, gaps between racial groups on social indicators such as health, life expectancy, wealth, income, marriage, and outcomes—remain even while the proximate causes of that inequality may change. There is no reason to put up a "no blacks allowed" sign when one can simply decide to not hire. There is no reason to say that the laws are unequal when one can simply enforce drug laws unequally or one can simply refuse to prosecute or convict an officer who has shot and killed another unarmed black man. These changing mechanisms have ensured that whites have, on average, remained at the top of the social hierarchy, over the long sweep of American history.

Progress narratives are often used as a political cudgel to delegitimate the claims of people of color. These narratives typically begin by claiming that because past sins—slavery, eugenics, or Jim Crow—have been partially remedied, people of color should stop complaining. Relatedly, these narratives suggest that if only people of color would behave, pull up their pants, and act like white folks, more would happen. In practical terms, seeing racism as a fundamental cause should make us pause in the face of claims of racial progress. Often improvements in one area offset by setbacks in another—or organizational forms themselves transform in the face of changes in the racial order.

## References

Alexander, Michelle. 2012. *The New Jim Crow: Mass Incarceration in the Age of Colorblindness*. New York, NY: The New Press.

Du Bois, W.E.B. 2014. *The Philadelphia Negro*. New York, NY: Oxford University Press.

Du Bois, W.E.B. 2017. *Black Reconstruction in America*. New York, NY: Routledge.

Federal Reserve Bank of St. Louis, Darrick Hamilton, and William A. Darity. 2017. "The Political Economy of Education, Financial Literacy, and the Racial Wealth Gap." *Review* 99(1):59–76.

Hall, Stuart. 1986. "Gramsci's Relevance for the Study of Race and Ethnicity." *Journal of Communication Inquiry* 10(2):5–27.

Link, B. G., and J. Phelan. 1995. "Social Conditions as Fundamental Causes of Disease." *Journal of Health and Social Behavior* 35:80–94.

Muhammad, Khalil G. 2010. *The Condemnation of Blackness: Race, Crime, and the Making of Modern Urban America*. Cambridge, MA: Harvard University Press.

Norton, Michael I., and Samuel R. Sommers. 2011. "Whites See Racism as a Zero-Sum Game That They Are Now Losing." *Perspectives on Psychological Science* 6(3):215–218.

Quillian, Lincoln, Devah Pager, Ole Hexel, and Arnfinn H. Midtbøen. 2017. "Meta-Analysis of Field Experiments Shows No Change in Racial Discrimination in Hiring over Time." *Proceedings of the National Academy of Sciences* 114(41):10870–10875.

Ray, Victor, and Louise Seamster. 2016. "Rethinking Racial Progress: A Response to Wimmer." *Ethnic and Racial Studies* 39(8):1361–1369.

Wilson, William J. 1978. *The Declining Significance of Race: Blacks and Changing American Institutions*. Chicago, IL: The University of Chicago Press.

Wong, J. 2018. "The Evangelical Vote and Race in the 2016 Presidential Election." *The Journal of Race, Ethnicity, and Politics* 3(Special Issue 1):81–106.

*Victor Ray is an assistant professor of sociology at the University of Tennessee, Knoxville. His academic work examines race and gender discrimination in organizations and has been published in the* Sociology of Race and Ethnicity, Ethnic and Racial Studies, Annals of the American Academy of Political and Social Science, The Journal of Marriage and Family, *and* Contexts.

## Racism and the Media Landscape in the United States
*Sahar D. Sattarzadeh and*
*Matthew W. Hughey*

Alternative media, new media, and/or social media comprise countless technologies and activities impossible to singularly define. Such media is often (re)defined, interpreted, and used to both reproduce and resist racial stratification and dominant racial ideologies. Hence, racism—in both its "new" and traditional forms of categorizing arbitrary characteristics into hierarchies—traffics in media images, discourse, rituals, and systems. This essay presents a broad overview of various contemporaneous manifestations of the interplay between media and racism in the United States.

### The Press

Mainstream press (especially newspaper) coverage of explicit racism was nearly nonexistent prior to the 1954 *Brown v. Board of Education* Supreme Court decision (van Dijk 1991). Historically, racist reporting and biased news masqueraded as white normative worldviews. The mass media market was largely exclusive to and dominated by white men (ibid.). While there have been some changes, ethnic and racial stereotypes persist in political, pop culture, and sports coverage. For instance, significant double standards persist in coverage of white versus people of color in terms of their scrutinization, criminalization, and/or victimization (Budarick and Han 2017; Churchill 1998; Gilens 1999; Leonard and King 2011; Said 1981; Sanders 2015; Steuter and Wills 2008; van Dijk 1991).

Prior to the mid-1950s, media production was also hyper-segregated (Sanders 2015). In response, Asian, black, Hispanic, indigenous, Latinx, and varied ethnic groups established media outlets that focus on news by and about their respective communities (e.g., Colorlines, Essence, Indian Country Media Network, and The Latin Post). While political-economic changes have taken place, biased reporting still prevails (Lyle 1968; Martindale 1986; Said 1981; Sanders 2015; Steuter and Wills 2008). Furthermore, the employment of people of color in media production occupations is underrepresented compared to whites. When employed, people of color are often assigned journalistic positions in which they report on "minority issues" (Sanders 2015). However, the recent emergences of digitized press, via alternative and new media on the World Wide Web, provide more opportunities to not only broadcast but also challenge racist news narratives.

### Radio, Film, and Television

Before the rise of television, radio programs were popular entertainment venues. Racially stereotyped caricatures dominated programs. The first nationally syndicated show *Amos 'n' Andy* starred two white men portraying two black men in a clichéd and racist fashion. Indigenous peoples were often represented as savage enemies, such as the persona of "Tonto" in *The Lone Ranger* (1933), which was also replicated on television (1949–1957) and film (2013) (Wilson, Gutiérrez, and Chao 2013). Such stereotypes also related to whites. For instance, the "white savior" character is a television and film stable. Films such as *Glory* (1989), *Dangerous Minds* (1996), *Amistad* (1997), *Finding Forrester* (2000), *The Blind Side* (2009), *The Help* (2011), and *The Great Wall* (2016) reinforce depictions of whiteness as saviors of the nonwhite "victim" (Hughey 2009, 2013). Alternatively, characters of color can save whites if they are given racially fetishized and stereotypical powers, what filmmaker Spike Lee once called "magical negro" films, such as *The Green Mile* (1999), *Legend of Bagger Vance* (2000), or *Bruce Almighty* (2003) (Hughey 2009).

Television and film also feature white subversion of diversity through "blackface" or "yellowface" to "whitewash" diversity (Wilson, Gutiérrez, and Chao 2013), such as Laurence Olivier in *Othello* (1956), Mickey Rooney in *Breakfast at Tiffany's* (1961), Al Pacino in *Scarface* (1983), and Scarlett Johansson in *Ghost in the Shell* (2017). Some attempts to diversify the media industry, even if benevolent in intent, can perpetuate racial stereotypes. For instance, the ethnic miscasting of white actors for characters of color is an example, as seen in the casting of Antonio Banderas in *The 13th Warrior* (1999) and *Black Gold* (2011), Ben Kingsley in *House of Sand and Fog* (2003), Michelle Yeoh and Zhang Ziyi in *Memoirs of a Geisha* (2005), and Naomi Scott in *Aladdin* (2018).

The persistence of racial segregation, inequality, and misrepresentations has led to more actors, directors, producers, and writers of color taking the lead in establishing media production companies, projects, and programs both within and outside of Hollywood. Examples of some of their work are *The Birth of a Nation* (2017), *Moonlight* (2017), *Bamboozled* (2000), *Dear White People* (2014), and *Get Out* (2017), as well as *Stand and Deliver* (1988), *The Joy Luck Club* (1993), *Once Were Warriors* (1994), and *Smoke Signals* (1998). Television programs such as *The Cosby Show* (1984), *A Different World* (1987–1993), *George Lopez* (2002–2007), *Ugly Betty* (2006–2010), *The Mindy Project* (2012–present), *Orange Is the New Black* (2013–2019), *Master of None* (2015–2017), and *Queen Sugar* (2016) challenge stereotypes, feature intra-racial heterogeneity, and star nonwhite leading roles (Bodenheimer 2017; Davis 2017; Wilson, Gutiérrez, and Chao 2013).

## Alternative and New Media

The emergence of alternative and new media provides opportunities to counterbalance mainstream media racism. *Alternative media*—nonmainstream media—manifests from newspapers to online blogs and from street art to fanzines (Atton 2007). Some alternative media may be deemed *new media*, which is "a site of constant reinvention" (Green 2010:1) but can be understood as digital media capable of being compressed, manipulated, and networkable (Konieczny 2009). Social media platforms (e.g., Facebook, Instagram, Twitter, and YouTube), Netflix, websites, blogs, computer or video games, computer software, and so on are all examples of new media, because they require digital interaction. Because of this flexibility, alternative media and new media are prime spaces for both challenging and reproducing racism. For instance, in 2002, the Anti-Defamation League found that white racist groups use interactional computer games to promote racial hatred (Ramanan 2017). Moreover, the posting of audience comments and dialogue between audience members on digital media sites are common. Attempts to regulate or mitigate racist discourse on college sports and news sites are varied (Hughey 2010; Hughey and Daniels 2013) and are seen to both amply and dampen racist rhetoric.

## References

Anti-Defamation League. 2002. "Racist Groups Use Computer Gaming to Promote Hate." Retrieved June 6, 2017. https://www.adl.org/sites/default/files/documents/ assets/pdf/combating-hate/Racist-groups-use-computer-gaming.pdf.

Atton, Chris. 2007. "Current Issues in Alternative Media Research." *Sociology Compass* 1(1):17–27.

Bodenheimer, Rebecca. 2017. " 'Orange Is the New Black' and Ethnic and Racial Differences within the Latinx Community." *Popmatters.* March 7. www.popmatters.com/ feature/orange-is-the-new-black-and-ethnic-racial-differences-latinx/.

Budarick, John, and Gil-Soo Han, eds. 2017. *Minorities and Media: Producers, Industries, Audiences.* London: Palgrave Macmillan.

Churchill, Ward. 1998. *Fantasies of the Master Race: Literature, Cinema, and the Colonization of American Indians.* San Francisco: City Light Books.

Davis, Jonita. 2017. "How Queen Sugar Turns the Stereotype of the Drug-Addicted Black Mother on Its Head." *Paste.* July 11. Retrieved July 20, 2017. https://www.paste magazine.com/articles/2017/07/how-queen-sugar-turns-the-stereotype-of-the-drug-a.html.

Gilens, Martin. 1999. *Why Americans Hate Welfare: Race, Media, and the Politics of Antipoverty Policy.* Chicago, IL: The University of Chicago Press.

Green, Lelia. 2010. *The Internet: An Introduction to New Media.* Oxford: Berg.

Hughey, Matthew W. 2009. "Cinethetic Racism: White Redemption and Black Stereotypes in 'Magical Negro' Films." *Social Problems* 56(3):543–577.

Hughey, Matthew W. 2010. "The White Savior Film and Reviewers' Reception." *Symbolic Interaction* 33(3):475–496.

Hughey, Matthew W. 2013. "Film Review: Slavery, Emancipation, and the Great White Benefactor: A Review of Lincoln and Django Unchained." *Humanity and Society* 37(4):351–353.

Hughey, Matthew W., and Jessie Daniels. 2013. "Racist Comments at Online News Sites: A Methodological Dilemma for Discourse Analysis." *Media, Culture & Society* 35(3):332–347.

Konieczny, Piotr. 2009. "Governance, Organization, and Democracy on the Internet: The Iron Law and the Evolution of Wikipedia." *Sociological Forum* 24(1):162–192.

Leonard, David J., and C. Richard King. 2011. *Commodified and Criminalized: New Racism and African Americans in Contemporary Sports.* Lanham, MD: Rowman & Littlefield.

Lyle, Jack, ed. 1968. *The Black American and the Press.* Los Angeles: Ward Ritchie.

Martindale, Carolyn. 1986. *The White Press and Black America.* New York: Greenwood Press.

Ramanan, Chella. 2017. "The Video Game Industry Has a Diversity Problem—But It Can Be Fixed." *Guardian*. March 15. Accessed July 22, 2017. https://www.the guardian.com/technology/2017/mar/15/video-game-industry-diversity-problem-women-non-white-people.

Said, Edward W. 1981. *Covering Islam*. London: Routledge.

Sanders, Joshunda. 2015. *How Racism and Sexism Killed Traditional Media: Why the Future of Journalism Depends on Women and People of Color*. Santa Barbara: Praeger.

Steuter, Erin, and Deborah Wills. 2008. *At War with Metaphor: Media, Propaganda, and Racism in the War on Terror*. Lanham, MD: Lexington Books.

van Dijk, Teun A. 1991. *Racism and the Press*. London: Routledge.

Wilson II, Clint C., Félix Gutiérrez, and Lena M. Chao. 2013. *Racism, Sexism, and the Media: Multicultural Issues into the New Communications Age*. Thousand Oaks, CA: Sage.

*Sahar D. Sattarzadeh is assistant professor of multi-disciplinary studies at Champlain College and a research associate at the Chair for Critical Studies in Higher Education Transformation at Nelson Mandela University.*

*Matthew W. Hughey is associate professor of sociology at the University of Connecticut and a research associate for the Centre for Critical Studies in Higher Education Transformation at the Nelson Mandela University in Port Elizabeth, South Africa.*

## Law Enforcement and Immigration Enforcement in the Rio Grande Valley
*Efrén C. Olivares*

For people in the Rio Grande Valley of Texas, living with the permanent presence of Border Patrol and Immigration and Customs Enforcement (ICE) has become the norm. For many immigrants, it can be a constant source of intimidation. For undocumented immigrants, that presence, coupled with the immigration "checkpoints" lining every highway heading north, becomes the defining trait of their lives in this part of the country.

This section reviews some of the threats to civil rights experienced by immigrants and their families in the Rio Grande Valley of Texas, particularly in light of the increasing collusion between local and state law enforcement entities and federal immigration entities.

## Laura

The night of June 9, 2009, twenty-two-year-old Laura was on her way home from work with relatives and coworkers, when they were stopped by a Pharr police department officer for failing to maintain a single lane. When asked for ID, she could not present a document showing that she had authorization to be in the United States. The officer indicated that he would refer her to Border Patrol. She pled with him not to call Border Patrol: her ex-partner had been abusive to her, was reportedly working with the Zetas drug cartel across the border in Reynosa, and had threatened to kill her if he ever saw her again.

Despite her pleas, the police officer made the call. When the Border Patrol agent arrived, Laura pleaded with him too. Her friends and relatives in the car also pleaded with both officers not to take her. But she was taken nonetheless, and, a mere four hours later, she was escorted to the international bridge and sent back to Reynosa.

Five days later, her body was found. Her ex-partner had tied her to the steering wheel of her car and set the car on fire, burning her alive (*Maria v. Doe* 2017).

Laura had no criminal record. (There is often a misconception that simply being in the United States without authorization is a felony. It is not, although reentering the country after a person has been deported can be a felony under 8 U.S.C. §§ 1325 and 1326. Laura had never been charged under either section of the statute.) The traffic violation she and her friends were stopped for would have lead, in most instances, to no more than a warning. In her case, it led to her murder. She left behind three minor children, including two U.S. citizens.

This type of immigration enforcement by law enforcement officials has existed for years in the Rio Grande Valley, sometimes with deadly consequences. Law enforcement agencies are tasked with preventing and prosecuting crimes; immigration agencies are tasked with enforcing federal immigration laws. In this part of the state, unfortunately, the lines dividing those jurisdictions are often blurred, to the detriment of those caught in the middle.

In 2017, media outlets reported about Texas Department of Public Safety (DPS) (the state police) agents riding alongside Border Patrol agents in Border Patrol vehicles, and DPS formally instructed all its officers that they must refer anyone whom they suspect is in the country illegally—regardless of whether they may have committed or even be suspected of having committed a crime—to Border Patrol or ICE (Nathan 2017).

These practices and policies have increasingly turned law enforcement agencies into de facto immigration authorities. In some parts of the Valley, this has eroded the trust of undocumented immigrants and their families in police officers, for fear that any encounter with local or state police—however minor and for whatever purpose—might lead to them being referred to Border Patrol.

The chilling effect is real, and families are already turning away from police for this very reason. In the summer of 2017, a potential client visited the Texas Civil Rights Project's Alamo office to ask for assistance. She was involved in a car accident, and the other person involved refused to share his insurance information. She wanted to file a police report, but she was undocumented and hesitated to go to the police for fear that they might inquire into her immigration status.

In addition to the constant presence of immigration authorities, residents of the Rio Grande Valley have to live with the permanent immigration "checkpoints" that line every highway heading to and from the U.S.-Mexico border. These checkpoints are Border Patrol stations where passersby are stopped and are only allowed to go through after they confirm their immigration status. Despite not being backed by probable cause, the U.S. Supreme Court has since the 1970s allowed these immigration checkpoints to be set up along public highways (*United States v. Martinez-Fuerte* 1976). For undocumented people living south of the checkpoint, this means they cannot travel past the checkpoint, even in times of mandatory evacuations when a hurricane is approaching or to seek medical services that are not available south of the checkpoint (U.S. Customs and Border Protection 2017). In practice, undocumented residents—often including their U.S. citizen children—are effectively trapped between the U.S.-Mexico border and the checkpoint (Alvarado 2017).

## Texas Senate Bill 4

As if the de facto transformation of law enforcement officials into immigration officers was not sufficient, in May 2017 Texas governor Greb Abbott signed Senate Bill 4 "SB 4" into law (Svitek 2017). Among other things, SB 4 makes it unlawful for cities, counties, and university campuses to enact policies that prohibit or materially limit cooperation with immigration authorities. SB 4 is an attempt to complete the transformation de jure, and turn every police officer, Sheriff's deputy, and campus police officer into an immigration enforcement agent.

SB 4 contains significant penalties for individuals or localities that fail to comply. The first violation carries a civil penalty of $1,000 and the second $25,000. It may also lead to the official's removal from office and, in certain circumstances, to jail time. SB 4 also makes compliance with so-called ICE detainer requests mandatory, and the failure to comply with such requests is a Class A misdemeanor carrying a punishment of up to a year in jail. In light of these harsh penalties, it is reasonable to expect over-enforcement of immigration laws by police officers afraid of being accused of violating the statute and being subjected to these harsh penalties.

SB 4 raised significant constitutional questions and was promptly challenged legally. The cities of Austin, Dallas, El Paso, Houston, San Antonio, and El Cenizo, among other counties and organizations, sued the state of Texas in federal court alleging myriad constitutional violations, including of the First, Fourth, and Tenth Amendments, as well as the Supremacy Clause and the Texas Constitution. In August 2017, a federal district court in San Antonio enjoined (prevented from entering into force) major sections of SB 4, and a Court of Appeals allowed some of them to take effect in September (*City of El Cenizo, Texas v. Texas* 2017, 2018a). In May 2018, the Court of Appeals for the Fifth Circuit issued an opinion largely reversing the district court and allowing the majority of the provisions of SB 4 to go into effect. The only provision that remained suspended was the provision that prohibited government officials from supporting a policy of limited cooperation with immigration authorities (*City of El Cenizo, Texas v. Texas* 2018b). However, this provision was enjoined only with respect to *elected* officials.

### Civil Rights Consequences of Blurring the Lines between Immigration and Law Enforcement Authorities

Opponents of SB 4 raised concerns early on that the law would lead to racial profiling against people of Hispanic descent in Texas. In the debate surrounding the law, San Antonio police chief William McManus put it succinctly:

> How else do you determine to ask someone for their "papers," other than their skin color, or their accent, or their lack of ability to speak the language. What else do you base it on? That, ladies and gentlemen, is profiling in its pure form. (ABC 2017)

This type of racial profiling, despite being unconstitutional, is the reality that many of us living in the Rio Grande Valley have become accustomed to. And SB 4 is an attempt to make this kind of profiling the law of the land in Texas. In addition to the stops at the checkpoints, SB 4 is likely to lead to unreasonable stops and seizures of people simply for being suspected of being in the country illegally, in violation of the Fourth Amendment.

The immigration and criminal justice systems, along with their constitutional limits, have existed and developed separately over the course of more than a century. They are designed to accomplish different goals, through different means, and therefore are subject to different standards. Immigration is not a crime, and the immigration policies and laws in the United States have ebbed and flowed over time depending on the needs of the country. For instance, the Immigration and Nationality Act contains certain visa incentives to encourage certain types of skilled professionals to immigrate to the United States; it provides protections for immigrants who are victims of certain crimes and preferences to immigrants from certain countries, typically those undergoing civil wars or severe natural disasters.

Criminal law, by contrast, has for the most part developed consistently with public safety as a constant, guiding factor. In the criminal law context, individual rights are weighed against the government's obligation to ensure the safety of society, not to curtail or encourage the entry or exit of individuals from the country.

For these reasons, it is not only wise but also constitutionally mandated that immigration enforcement and law enforcement of criminal law be separate systems and handled by different agencies and agents, each with clearly defined jurisdictions and limitations. Doing otherwise is a disservice not only to immigrants and people caught up in the criminal justice system but also to society in general. Those of us who live in the Rio Grande Valley—including Laura's family— know this all too well.

## References

ABC. 2017. "Video: SAPD Chief McManus: SB4 'Is Profiling in Its Pure Form.'" Retrieved July 20, 2019. https://www
.ksat.com/news/video-sapd-chief-mcmanus-sb4-is-profiling-in-its-pure-form.

Alvarado, Beatriz. 2017. "Parents Face Deportation after Transferring Son to Driscoll Children's Hospital." Retrieved July 20, 2019. https://www.usatoday.com/story/news/local/2017/09/21/parents-face-deportation-after-transferring-son-driscoll-childrens-hospital/691005001/.

*City of El Cenizo, Texas v. Texas.* 2017. 5:17-CV-404-OLG.

*City of El Cenizo, Texas v. Texas.* 2018a. 5:17-CV-00404.

*City of El Cenizo, Texas v. Texas.* 2018b. 890 F.3d 164.

*Maria v. Doe.* 2017. 267 F.Supp.3d 923.

Nathan, Debbie. 2017. "DPS Director Steve McGraw Issues Immigration Marching Orders." Retrieved July 20, 2019. https://www.austinchronicle.com/news/2017-07-07/dps-director-steve-mccraw-issues-immigration-marching-orders/.

Svitek, Patrick. 2017. "Texas Gov. Greg Abbott Signs 'Sanctuary Cities' Bill into Law." Retrieved July 20, 2019. https://www.texastribune.org/2017/05/07/abbott-signs-sanctuary-cities-bill/.

*United States v. Martinez-Fuerte.* 1976. 428 U.S. 543.

U.S. Customs and Border Protection. 2017. "Border Patrol Checkpoint Operations during Hurricane Harvey." Retrieved July 20, 2019. https://www.cbp.gov/newsroom/speeches-and-statements/border-patrol-checkpoint-operations-during-hurricane-harvey.

*Efrén C. Olivares is racial and economic justice director at the Texas Civil Rights Project, www.texascivilrightsproject.org.*

## Reclaiming the City: Racial Gentrification as Urban Policy
*Louise Seamster*

Gentrification connects concerns of territory, money, policy, social control, and culture. Far from a neutral process, I argue gentrification is the result of top-down policies oriented around putting land and resources into the hands of the dominant group. As such, it is an important site to study racial inequality in the United States.

Traditionally, gentrification scholars have described the process as occurring in stages, where poor, minority neighborhoods are transformed into wealthy, white neighborhoods by replacing their inhabitants several times over. First come the "starving artists," displacing black and brown residents for low rent and "authentic" culture (Brown-Saracino 2009). In a second phase, the "pioneers" are then themselves displaced by middle-class and wealthy white people. However, in many locations the gentrification process has become streamlined by contemporary urban development. As cities become sites of consumption and investment rather than manufacturing, cities compete to draw the "creative class" (Florida 2002) of educated professionals to their doors. But these policies direct resources to some (usually transient, wealthy outsiders) at the expense of others.

Although gentrification can look like a natural result of shifting individual interests, concerted policy and dedicated resources are behind gentrification, just as government policy segregated cities, built the suburbs, and created the disaster of "urban renewal." The new model for urban development presumes cities must either privatize assets or sacrifice tax revenue to attract investment. Moreover, where cities are improving public amenities, from bike lanes to schools, public space and parks, and transit, these improvements have been found to speed gentrification (Chapple 2009; Hankins 2007; Stehlin 2015). Many of the upscale buildings sprouting up across the urban United States, seeming to represent cities' renaissance and success, in fact represent the upward redistribution of wealth as public funding goes to private luxury. The promise is that this giveaway of public money will eventually create increased returns, but the deck is stacked against cities.

Gentrification studies usually focus on value creation in the form of new businesses and jobs and rising rents, but value *destruction* is an important prerequisite before gentrification can occur. Without cheap square footage, there would be no basis for "discovery" of new, low-cost neighborhoods. Scholars noted a primary feature of gentrification was this cycle of urban disinvestment and reinvestment (Palen and London 1984)—once assets have been devalued, it becomes easy to come back and retake them. Some scholars suggest the term "ruination" (Mah 2012) to describe the policies that actively destroyed neighborhoods before they were ready for gentrification. (For instance, federal policy "redlined" black and brown neighborhoods as ineligible for federal mortgages for decades, depressing home prices and creating blight.)

In fact, much wealth in American cities has been created, paradoxically, from "creative destruction" (Schumpeter 1975) and "accumulation by dispossession" (Harvey 2004). Anti-gentrification activists are greatly concerned by the dynamic of *dispossession*, in which residents, often people of color, are pushed out of homes, schools, neighborhoods, and sometimes out of cities altogether. Urban renewal, from the 1950s to 1970s, was a federal policy of "slum clearance," creating a "blank slate" for developers to build public housing towers, as well as convention centers and stadiums. Known to many victims as "Negro removal," urban renewal led to destabilization or outright destruction of minority neighborhoods (Fullilove 2004) and overcrowding in new or remaining black neighborhoods. Government policies systematically devalued the spaces now rediscovered as valuable. The process of dispossession, sinking property value, poverty, and so on, is not an incidental outcome: it's an essential component of contemporary urban wealth.

The "culture" of gentrification, while dismissed by some who focus on its economics (Smith and Williams 1986), is essential to carry out the urban takeover, especially in a consumption-oriented economy focused on leisure and entertainment (Hannigan 1998). As Neil Smith (1996) has noted, the new residents often use "frontier discourse" and imagery—down to real estate listings advertising to "urban pioneers." Just like for Native Americans in the original frontier, existing city inhabitants must be made invisible to justify the takeover, to claim that nobody had been using the space. Further, white culture is often rendered as morally neutral or positive in gentrifying spaces: but art walks (Shaw and Sullivan 2011), parks, dog runs (Tissot 2011), and farmers' markets (Zukin 2008) can be wielded as top-down weapons for racial exclusion. Although the language of "revitalization" and "cleaning up" neighborhoods can sound innocuous, what we see as being "clean" or "disorderly" in a neighborhood is influenced by the race of the people we see there (Sampson and Raudenbush 2004). If you live in a swiftly changing city, look at what events your city sponsors or encourages (e.g., beer races or folk festivals) and who attends those events. Moreover, making this new group of residents feel "safe" in the city comes alongside increased punitive policing, targeting people of color (Laniyonu 2017; Sharp 2014).

Do people of color benefit from gentrification? Some say "yes," that they also benefit from rising home values and the better city services (Freeman 2006), and in some cases, middle-class people of color successfully engage in gentrification themselves (Pattillo), or that organizing can bring benefits (Saito 2012). While supporters of gentrification often focus on rising property values, cleaned-up neighborhoods, greater amenities, and a better set of social activities, critics usually ask, better for whom? That is, focusing on changes in *space* can hide the drastic changes in the *occupants* of that space. Others note that the people in these studies may be enjoying temporary benefits before they, too, are pushed out of the neighborhood. Researchers cannot expect "snapshot" studies to capture long-term outcomes in a multistage process. To truly understand the impact of gentrifications, investigations should foreground resource transfers, value destruction, and take a longitudinal approach that understands gentrification in proper historical context. Above all, we need to understand gentrification as a dominant modern-day urban policy, not a natural phenomenon.

## References

Brown-Saracino, Japonica. 2009. *A Neighborhood That Never Changes: Gentrification, Social Preservation, and the Search for Authenticity.* Chicago, IL: The University of Chicago Press.

Chapple, Karen. 2009. "Mapping Susceptibility to Gentrification: The Early Warning Toolkit." Retrieved November 14, 2019. https://www.reimaginerpe.org/files/Gentrification-Report%284%29.pdf.

Florida, Richard. 2002. *Rise of the Creative Class.* New York: Basic Books.

Freeman, Lance. 2006. *There Goes the 'Hood: Views of Gentrification from the Ground Up.* Philadelphia, PA: Temple University Press.

Fullilove, Mindy Thompson. 2004. *Root Shock: How Tearing Up City Neighborhoods Hurts America.* New York: One World/Ballantine Books.

Hankins, Katherine B. 2007. "The Final Frontier: Charter Schools as New Community Institutions of Gentrification." *Urban Geography* 28(2):113–128.

Hannigan, John. 1998. *Fantasy City: Pleasure and Profit in the Postmodern Metropolis.* London and New York: Routledge.

Harvey, David. 2004. "The New Imperialism: Accumulation by Dispossession." *Socialist Register* 40:63–87.

Laniyonu, Ayobami. 2017. "Coffee Shops and Street Stops: Policing Practices in Gentrifying Neighborhoods." *Urban Affairs Review* 54(5):898–930.

Mah, Alice. 2012. *Industrial Ruination, Community, and Place: Landscapes and Legacies of Urban Decline.* Toronto, Canada: University of Toronto Press.

Palen, John, and Bruce London, eds. 1984. *Gentrification, Displacement, and Neighborhood Revitalization.* Albany: State University of New York Press.

Saito, Leland. 2012. "How Low-Income Residents Can Benefit from Urban Development: The La Live Community Benefits Agreement." *City & Community* 11(2):129–150.

Sampson, Frank, and Stephen Raudenbush. 2004. "Seeing Disorder: Neighborhood Stigma and the Social Construction of 'Broken Windows.'" *Social Psychology Quarterly* 67(4):319–342.

Schumpeter, Joseph. 1975. *Capitalism, Socialism and Democracy.* New York: Harper.

Sharp, Elaine. 2014. "Politics, Economics, and Urban Policing: The Postindustrial City Thesis and Rival Explanations of Heightened Order Maintenance Policing." *Urban Affairs Review* 50(3):340–365.

Shaw, Samuel, and Daniel Sullivan. 2011. "'White Night': Gentrification, Racial Exclusion, and Perceptions and Participation in the Arts." *City & Community* 10(3):241–264.

Smith, Neil. 1996. *The New Urban Frontier: Gentrification and the Revanchist City.* London: Routledge.

Smith, Neil, and Peter Williams, eds. 1986. *Gentrification of the City.* Winchester, MA: Allen & Unwin.

Stehlin, John. 2015. "Cycles of Investment: Bicycle Infrastructure, Gentrification, and the Restructuring of the San Francisco Bay Area." *Environment and Planning A* 47(1):121–137.

Tissot, Sylvie. 2011. "Of Dogs and Men: The Making of Spatial Boundaries in a Gentrifying Neighborhood." *City & Community* 10(3):265–284.

Zukin, Sharon. 2008. "Consuming Authenticity: From Outposts of Difference to Means of Exclusion." *Cultural Studies* 22(5):724–748.

*Louise Seamster is a Center for the Study of Social Justice fellow at the University of Tennessee, Knoxville. Her research centers on the interactive financial and symbolic factors reproducing racial inequality, focusing on urban development, space, and political arrangements, and has been published in such ven-ues as* Critical Sociology, Racial and Ethnic Studies, Sociol-ogy Compass, Humanity & Society, *and* Political Power and Social Theory.

## The Normalcy of Legitimized Racism against Indigenous Peoples
*Dwanna L. McKay*[1]

Legitimized racism against Indigenous Peoples exists in its nor-malcy as part of the social character of the United States. Na-tive people cope daily with overtly racist language, images, and behaviors without social recourse. Overt racism includes racial epithets, stereotypical representations, and blatant cultural ap-propriation. For example, words like "redskin" and "squaw" and stereotypical depictions of Natives as sports mascots con-tinue to enjoy social acceptance. Informal communication per-petuates racist meaning against Natives with phrases like "don't be an Indian giver" or "they're going off the reservation." The myth of "cowboys versus Indians" is alive and well in contem-porary movies, songs, and literature.

---

[1]Author's note: Passionate debate persists in academia over the most useful term(s) to describe Indigenous Peoples of the United States. I use the term "American Indian" because of its usage at the U.S. Census Bureau. I use the term "Indian" because it is the legal term used within Federal Indian Policy and "Native" and "Indigenous" interchangeably as my preferences.

Anti-Indian terminology, imagery, and behavior have become legitimized to such a degree that even other marginalized people accept overt racism against Natives as nonracist and readily maintain and participate in it. Dressing up to play Indian seems harmless to the public school educator. High school sports teams with Indian mascots are reputed to be honoring Native people. Culturally appropriating sacred objects like war bonnets for a fashion statement is considered innocent. Another important characteristic of legitimized racism is the resistance to recognizing these terms, images, and behaviors as racist at all. White people deny it. Empathy is not easily forthcoming from other marginalized groups, because they also participate in it. Individuals who protest are accused of being too sensitive or simply silly. Groups who protest are charged with being subversive and acting in their own interests and not for the good of society.

But these are the homelands of Indigenous Peoples. Contrary to the myth of the Doctrine of Discovery, the entirety of the North American continent was not a vast wilderness without civilization when white colonizers arrived. Around the end of the fifteenth century, an estimated twenty to one hundred million citizens of over one thousand sovereign Indigenous Nations occupied the geographic area currently known as the United States (Thornton 1990). For perspective, Europe had less than fifty million people at this same time (Dunbar-Ortiz 2014). When Europeans invaded this continent, they found advanced civilizations with extensive trade networks and economic centers; superior agricultural cultivation; well-developed metalwork, pottery, and weaving; and little disease due to the practices of herbal medicines, dentistry, surgery, and daily hygienic bathing (Dunbar-Ortiz 2014). Indigenous polities emphasized equity and community over the individual.

Racism began with contact. Europeans mislabeled all Native people they encountered as "Indians" and thus distorted the autonomy of independent Indigenous Nations by redefining them as a homogenized, uniform, oversimplified racial group. Through this process of racialization, citizens of hundreds of different governance systems, cultural traditions, and language groups were reduced to one singular racial identity of "Indian." Indigenous Peoples are not a race, of course. Indigenous Peoples are distinct, sovereign nations. Muscogees are very different from Tulalips. Racializing all peoples from the same continent as one race makes little sense. Political systems, geographic location, shared histories, and common languages matter. People from Germany are quite different than people from Italy on the continent of Europe.

Presently, 567 federally recognized tribal nations exist—326 on federal Indian reservations for a total of 56.2 million acres. At just 1.8 percent of the current U.S. land base of 2.3 billion acres, Indian reservations are also severely fragmented due to federal land sales, seizures, and allotments. Out of 308.7 million Americans, 2.9 million (0.9 percent) self-identify as fully indigenous and 5.2 million (1.7 percent) identify as American Indian and some other race (Norris, Vines, and Hoeffel 2012). On one hand, the devastation of Indigenous Peoples seems overwhelming. Since contact, the number of sovereign tribal cultures has decreased by at least 43 percent; the land base controlled by tribal governments by 98.2 percent; and population numbers of tribal citizens, at the very least, by 98.3 percent but as high as 99.1 percent. On the other hand, to be present at all after more than 500 years of settler colonialism shows the resilience and strength of the original inhabitants of North America. Both European and American governments used genocidal policies, religious dominance, economic dependence, and corporate violence against Indigenous Nations. As this land was invaded by colonial powers on every side, Native Peoples resisted and survived and maintained and adapted their cultural and ceremonial ways.

Covert (color-blind) racism began as a result of the post–civil rights era. Color-blind racism takes form through ideologies of individualism without historical context, which frames the political and economic inequality of people of color as their own fault (Bonilla-Silva 2006). For example, research shows that most Americans believe that all Native people get free college tuition, pay no taxes, and receive inordinate amounts of casino monies (Robertson 2012). In reality, Natives disproportionately experience high rates of poverty (27 percent), unemployment (9.3 percent), and sexual assault (80 percent). Only 67 percent of Native students graduated high school compared to the national average of 80 percent. Less than 13 percent of Natives hold a college degree compared to 28 percent of Americans. Color-blind racism means that non-Native people justify dismal statistics like these as the consequences of personal laziness of individuals and generalized cultural tendencies rather than the result of hundreds of years of public policies and social norms benefiting white people while constraining life opportunities for Natives.

The pervasiveness of overt racism never slowed for Native people—it just became unseen. Overt racism becomes invisible when racist social discourse becomes legitimized. That is, discourse functions to structure society by providing the framework to manage interactions between institutions, individuals, and groups. Racist social discourse becomes legitimized through the normalization of it created within social institutions—like education, media, legislation, and family. In other words, institutions that shape social norms make it seem appropriate for society to enact racial violence against Indigenous Peoples through the commonness of stereotypes, national myths, and revisionist history—all in service to the master narrative of white supremacy. Through racial discourse, myth becomes accepted as fact within the social imagination.

Federal Indian policy has systematically racialized Indians as inferior, incapable, and uncivilized (e.g., see Hoxie 1989; Prucha 1990; Wilford 1991). With the establishment of the Office of Indian Affairs in 1824, the U.S. government began to wage genocidal campaigns against Native nations through the system of law. The U.S. justice system facilitated the forced removal of Native nations to Indian reservations, taking Native children from their parents to live in boarding schools, outlawing Indigenous religions and languages, and abolishing tribal governments. It also facilitated the theft of Indigenous land and resources (Robertson 2013). Public education continues to teach mythical narratives of naive or savage Indians with pilgrims, settlers, cowboys, and soldiers. Children play Indian and participate in school activities with Indian mascots with Indigenous students in attendance. National holidays like Columbus Day, the Fourth of July, and Thanksgiving symbolize genocide, suffering, and a loss of culture and homelands for Indigenous Peoples; yet Native people are Americans too. This is like asking Jewish people to celebrate the Holocaust. Adults drive cars named for different Indigenous Peoples without their approval—Cherokee, Dakota, Winnebago. Products utilize stereotyped logos and names, like the Land O'Lakes Indian maiden, Indian Head Cornmeal, and Eskimo Pie. The federal government continues to appropriate "Indian" names for its military weapons and machines and code words for its military combat operations—the Apache, Chinook, and Blackhawk helicopters and "Geronimo" as the code name for Osama Bin Laden.

To legitimize is to make legitimate—that is, to justify, reason, or rationalize as in accordance with established or accepted patterns and standards (*Merriam-Webster's Collegiate Dictionary* 2003). In other words, the institutions that shape social norms—those seen as social authorities—reproduce symbolic racial violence through legal structures, public education locations, consumer products, sports associations, and so on. Power achieves racialization, just as racialization achieves racist discourse. Racial discourse then legitimates the racial order, reinforcing the social structures in place (e.g., hegemonic racial ideologies). It organizes what is to be known and understood and what is to be ignored about the racial other. Both covert and overt racism are made invisible through legitimization. Invisibility does not indicate absence; rather, it indicates presence not easily perceptible—like the blowing wind is evidenced by the movement of the tree branches. People know the wind exists because of its effect upon our persons and our environments. Indigenous people know that legitimized racism is real because we experience it every single day in every space that we occupy.

## References

Bonilla-Silva, Eduardo. 2006. *Racism without Racists: Colorblind Racism and the Persistence of Racial Inequality in the United States*, 2nd ed. Lanham, MD: Rowman & Littlefield.

Dunbar-Ortiz, Roxanne. 2014. *An Indigenous Peoples' History of the United States*. Boston, MA: Beacon Press.

Hoxie, Frederick E. 1989. *A Final Promise: The Campaign to Assimilate the Indians, 1880–1920*. Cambridge: Cambridge University Press.

*Merriam-Webster's Collegiate Dictionary*. 2003. Springfield, MA: Merriam-Webster, Inc.

Norris, Tina, Paula L. Vines, and Elizabeth M. Hoeffel. 2012. "The American Indian and Alaska Native Population: 2010." U.S. Census Bureau: Census Briefs. Retrieved March 8, 2018. https://www.census.gov/prod/cen2010/briefs/c2010br-10.pdf.

Prucha, Francis Paul. 1984. *The Great Father: The United States Government and the American Indians*. Lincoln: University of Nebraska Press.

Robertson, Dwanna L. 2012. "The Myth of Indian Casino Riches." Indian Country Today Media Network. June 23. Retrieved March 9, 2018. https://newsmaven.io/indian countrytoday/archive/the-myth-of-indian-casino-riches-3H8eP-wHX0Wz0H4WnQjwjA/.

Robertson, Dwanna L. 2013. "A Necessary Evil: Framing an American Indian Legal Identity." *American Indian Culture and Research Journal* 37(4):115–139.

Thornton, Russell. 1990. *American Indian Holocaust and Survival: A Population History since 1492.* Norman: University of Oklahoma Press.

Wilford, John Noble. 1991. *The Mysterious History of Columbus: An Exploration of the Man, the Myth, the Legacy.* New York: Alfred Knopf.

*Dwanna L. McKay is a citizen of the Muscogee (Creek) Nation and assistant professor in the Race, Ethnicity, and Migration Studies program at Colorado College. McKay's research focuses on the reproduction of social inequality through institutionalized race, ethnicity, and gender processes, particularly for indigenous peoples. Her work has been published in numerous scholarly journals, including* Sociology of Race and Ethnicity Journal, American Indian Quarterly, American Indian Culture and Research Journal, *and the* European Sociological Review.

## Beyond DACA: Why the Immigration Battle Must Be Fought for the 11 Million
*Catalina Adorno Castillo*

On September 5, 2017, I found myself on the intersection of 5th Avenue and 56th street in New York City, right outside the Trump Tower, blocking traffic as part of a civil disobedience in response to the rescission of the Deferred Action for Childhood Arrivals (DACA) program. It had been leaked that Jeff Sessions, then attorney general of the United States, was going to make the announcement that the program that had provided temporary protection to undocumented youth was ending.

I woke up feeling angry. I was angry at knowing that a program that had come about from such sacrifice was being taken away so easily. DACA was a program that was won through the resilience of so many undocumented youth who risked deportation when participating in civil disobediences, when occupying Capitol offices, when heckling then President Obama.

I felt angry thinking of the undocumented youth who were looking forward to their fifteenth birthday just so they could apply for this program and finally have a sense of relief. I felt angry at how this administration was playing with the lives of undocumented youth; we were being used as pawns in a dirty political game. DACA was not ended because it was temporary or because it was not a successful program—it was ended to teach the immigrant community a lesson. It was ended because we are refusing to buy into the demands of the new administration, particularly the ask for more enforcement and for the infamous wall. It was ended because we will no longer be silent about the inhumane way immigrants are treated in this country.

I made it out of bed. I don't remember getting to New York City, nor the taste of the blueberry scone I ate that morning. I made my way to meet the other DACA recipients who were also going to be getting arrested with me in this civil disobedience action. At 11 A.M. that morning, all the arrestees made a circle around a phone to watch the livestream of the announcement. Jeff Sessions stood behind a podium announcing that the DACA program was ending. There was no time for tears. No time to vent. We listened. We stayed quiet for a minute after the announcement, and then we started walking toward the intersection. Once we got to the intersection, we sat down in the middle of the street blocking all the traffic on 5th Avenue of New York City. As soon as I sat down. I could feel all the emotions inside me trying to escape my body.

As I sat down on that street I thought of the complexity of the issue of immigration. We can't have a conversation about immigration without also discussing mass incarceration, racism, class, and other nuances of what it means to be brown in the United States. As a college student I volunteered with a group that made visits to immigrants and refugees in detention centers. I had never visited people in detention, let alone people I didn't know. I remembered my first visit. I remembered getting to the detention center, signing in and giving my information (a process scary in itself as I also don't have a legal status) and entering the visitation room. As I sat down and waited for the person I was visiting, I made a dark realization— all the people who were incarcerated were all either black or brown. It became clear to me that there are immigrants who are welcome and there are immigrants who are not. I belong to the group of immigrants who are not welcome. I am brown. I have indigenous features. I am from Mexico. My father is labeled a "bad hombre." My brother is labeled an "anchor baby." People in my community are labeled "criminals, thugs, rapists, gangsters."

I sat on that intersection because we have been robbed of our humanity. Detention centers make profits off our incarceration. Immigration and Customs Enforcement has quotas to meet, and so they visit courts, schools, and hospitals waiting to pick us up. Employers take advantage of us. They pay us "under the table" with cash so as to not leave a paper trail. They pay us below the minimum wage because we are not "legal in this country." They overwork us, making us work twelve to fifteen hours a day knowing they can get away with it. And, when we call out the injustices at the workplace, employers threaten us saying they'll call immigration. The public, especially those who fall under the more conservative/hateful spectrum, hate us. They say we're drug dealers. They beat us up because we have an accent. They call us terrorists. They want to ban us from this country. They want a wall and more enforcement. But we will no longer be dehumanized. The saying "No human being is illegal" is not just a slogan. We deserve to be seen and recognized as human beings.

I wasn't participating in this civil disobedience and risking deportation for myself. I am a DACA recipient. I am what the American public calls "a Dreamer," but the fight for immigrants' rights goes beyond DACA and the DREAM Act. The fight is for all of us who find ourselves without a legal status in this country. The fight is for all of us who regardless of the hate we encounter every day still manage to laugh, to care for our families, and to love our communities. The fight is for all of us who are not recognized as worthy. The fight is so that someday all the eleven million and more people who are undocumented in this country can finally have protection and the dignity and respect that we all deserve.

*Catalina Adorno Castillo was born in Puebla, Mexico, and came to the United States when she was nine years old. She is currently a volunteer organizer with Movimiento Cosecha, where she organizes with undocumented immigrant communities to fight for permanent protection, dignity, and respect.*

## White Dog, Yellow Mother
*Alison Ho*

"You have the Chris Hemsworth of dogs," she exclaimed. "The what?" I thought to myself. My friend took a tidy bite of her samosa. "And I am his biggest fan," she concluded, wiping the crumbs off her face. This comment was a first. But more pressingly, who is Chris Hemsworth? Sitting in a crowded restaurant in San Francisco eating doshas and samosas, I pulled out my phone and googled C-h-r-i-s H-e-m-s-w-o-r-t-h. He's white, real white—blond hair, blue eyes, little bit of scruff, and a smoldering smile on a perfectly chiseled bod. Every Oscar-winning actor type of white. He's so white that he's confused with Chris Pratt, Chris Pine, and Chris Evans. How am I supposed to keep up with that?

"He is a very handsome boy," Andrew, my now fiancé, responded. Andrew is as white as they come. Andrew is so white that he refers to himself as an "American Mutt" with familial ties to the Civil War via a Southern father.

This past year, we took a leap of faith and adopted a dog. We figured that we were probably never going to be able to afford to buy a house in the Bay Area and we might as well move on with our lives. After all, a puppy is really just a practice baby.

We did the millennial thing and set up an Instagram account for our Australian Labradoodle (whom we named "Archie"), because we wanted him to be a part of the A-team of Alison and Andrew. Now, when people ask, we just say that his name is "Archie" because of his red coloring and the famous comic character. Even before we brought Archie home, his Instagram account was set up. We had only the slightest twinkle of a thought that he could be insta-famous. We quickly realized we did not have time for this. All we wanted to do was share the best photos of Archie with our family and friends. Archie has an extraordinarily loyal cult following. He is the first thing our friends mention when we see them—not our recent engagement— but how cute and muppet-like Archie is. They cannot believe he is, in fact, a real dog.

Our social lives are now irreversibly changed. We have been involuntarily accepted into the community of professional couples with dogs but no kids in our apartment building. Now random people notice us. It is like we have giant sign on us at all times that invites people to come and talk to us about Archie. Everyone is excited to see Archie, and he is immediately accepted.

I catch myself wondering, "Is this what it's like to be a white man in American society?" After all, Archie is the Chris Hemsworth of dogs.

Who am I to argue? Archie has a beautiful silky wavy red coat with white patches on his paws, belly, and face. He has hazel eyes that change color with his surroundings much like Andrew's.

In this day and age, Andrew and I have assigned a race to our dog. We concluded he is a white, male dog because he has received all the privileges that come with that role in society. Archie charms with his ever-so-happy demeanor and magnetizes the attention of the room toward him. People automatically engage him first, much like how they engage Andrew when he and I go to the Apple store or really any store. It has become so common that Andrew has to say, "It's not me you have to impress, it's her. She has the money." It always throws the salesperson. It feels like this is such a dramatic change in their thinking that they cannot or will not adapt. They stumble on their words and struggle to face me as they attempt to sell their product. They try to laugh it off, but deep down I know Andrew and I have subverted their expectations rather than just going along with the story they have started. I have come to expect this response and learned to use these expectations to my advantage. I may as well game the system I was born disadvantaged into. I will say, "Andrew go use your white white face to get what we want," knowing he has been successful most of the time especially in places like Oregon, which is also known as the last white state. On the flip side, he also knows full well there are places where I am accepted, and he feels that he is on the outside, the classic example being Ranch 99, an Asian food supermarket, or the Chinese takeout place that refused to take his order because he did not speak Mandarin.

I am jealous of the privileges that Archie has because he is a white dog, a Hemsworth. No one questions if he belongs because he already belongs. When I am with Archie and Andrew, my mind drifts to my own situation of being an Asian American woman with a white man. I am fully aware that I inhabit the stereotype of being an Asian woman with a white man and the weirdness that comes with that. Andrew will be the first white person to marry into my family, and I will be the first Chinese person to marry into his. Belonging. The word reverberates through my head, shaking my skull and striking the scars accumulated on my Asian body.

If Andrew and I decide to have a child biologically, this child will be multiracial, and this is not an experience that either one of us can relate to. Will this child be perceived as one race? As another? As both? Will this child be accepted by society? How will we face these challenges when our lives become once again irreversibly changed?

*Alison Ho is an interdisciplinary artist and designer. Originally from Campbell, California, Alison is currently based in San Mateo, California. In 2013, she graduated from the University of California Santa Barbara as a Regents Special Fellow and holds an MFA in art. In 2010, she graduated magna cum laude from the University of Oregon and holds a BFA in digital arts. As an artist, Alison works with narrative, language, and identity, crafting pieces based on personal experience. She believes the construction of cultural identities is an ongoing process, which cannot be merely picked and chosen.*

## The Cost of Silence
*A. Rochaun Meadows-Fernandez*

I can vividly remember the moment my college best friend and I stood in a dormmate's room watching the news explain the unjust murder of seventeen-year-old Trayvon Martin.

It wasn't our first-time hearing of the story. News travels much faster than one would expect on a college campus—several of our instructors even found ways to make the circumstance a part of class lectures. It was the first of many polarizing discussions that would occur during my college years. The black students, as well as a handful of other students of color, seemed emotionally impacted. We weren't as talkative as we usually were. And when we did talk, it was about the frustration and fear we felt. His murder was the most public event of many of our lifetimes that put a spotlight on the ways implicit bias and stereotyping left black and brown folks at risk.

In a matter of days, the campus clubs that focused on multiculturalism were discussing the best time and place to organize visuals and walkouts. But a large percentage of the campus seemed unconcerned. There was a clear line of demarcation that showed who did and didn't care about the impact. While I sat in class too distracted to focus and thinking of how my brother could easily be the next casualty, many of my white peers had the same smiles and joke-filled exchanges, as usual, requiring a reminder of why the classroom had a more somber feel than normal. When the specifications of our sadness came up, their puzzled expressions said what their mouths wouldn't.

Why were we so impacted by someone none of us knew personally? For them, this was an unfortunate isolated event; for me, it was a reminder of the hesitancy toward law enforcement I'd been taught since birth.

At the time, I was involved in a student-led bible study group that was connected to a nearby campus. Its background story was somewhat nonconventional. Two separate bible study groups, one that was exclusively black and one that was almost exclusively white, had been combined shortly before I attended. The goal was to exist as a model for removing the racial divide that profoundly exists in virtually every area of the church. In some ways, it was successful. Jokes were made in mixed company, and relationships developed that wouldn't have otherwise. In others, it wasn't.

To quote the late Dr. Martin Luther King Jr, "In the end we will remember not the words of our enemies . . . but the silence of our friends" (Perez 2019). I went into those first meetings hoping for a place of empathy and understanding from my brothers and sisters in Christ. However, as with many mixed-race interactions in the past, I was let down.

Sadly, a forced merging of bible studies wasn't enough to teach racial empathy. But it was enough to make me leave mainstream Christianity.

The meetings in the weeks shortly after Martin's death easily reflected the classroom environment: the white members functioning normally and the black members showing signs and words of preoccupation among themselves.

During group chats, there was no room for black members to discuss the pain we were feeling. After the meetings, the social media pages of those we fellowshipped walked a line of "neutrality."

White members blamed hatred, and therefore sin, as the singular cause for what we were witnessing. To say the least, I was hurt that individuals who claimed to care so much about "my eternal soul" showed so little concern for the everyday experiences underwent in my earthly body. To say the most, I was angry and disgusted that white privilege had once again proved itself to be a blindfold.

As a black woman, I'd been raised to believe that the God I served was against racial injustice. The tales of my ancestors covered brave women and men who experienced the worst manifestations of racism. But they kept going because their faith taught that God would deliver them through any trial or tribulation. The God they served stood firmly on the side of justice—a justice that wasn't possible without speaking out firmly against racial injustice.

I started having questions.

If the murder of a seventeen-year-old unarmed and innocent black youth wasn't injustice, what was? And why wasn't calling out the legacy of racism in the United States as crucial to being vocal about the horrendous life choice of choosing not to commit your life to our Lord and Savior Jesus Christ?

I wish I could say that the bible study group members came to their senses, and this was the last time my white Christians friends let me down. It wasn't.

After Martin's killer George Zimmerman got off with virtually no consequences, the black community suffered travesty after travesty.

I cut ties with the individuals from the group. By that point, my relationship to religion as a whole had been forever changed. I just couldn't understand how someone could claim to love God and humankind but be so insensitive to the continued victimization of black Americans.

The pain was recycled with each headline. As we saw more deaths, the arguments got progressively worse. My original set of white Christian friends were long gone. But any new connections with white Americans, who are overwhelmingly Christian, were eerily similar.

After 2012, the police incidents started to feel like a weekly occurrence. They were so frequent that the original wounds never healed, and I felt like one of many black Americans thrown into a whirlwind of racial trauma due to the constant portrayal of black death on the news.

All of the pain from 2012 forward came to a head during the 2016 presidential election. Again, my timeline was divided. I wasn't friends with anyone who directly advocated for Donald Trump, but the apathy I witnessed from my white friend toward his hateful rhetoric and divisive policies was enough to make my stomach turn.

I was one of the millions who falsely believed there was no way in hell that someone like this could ever be the face of the United States. I firmly thought that a mutual disdain for his hate mongering would build a bridge between myself and my white Christian peers. I was wrong.

Those who did support him said he was the candidate for Christians based on his opposition to marriage equality and women's reproductive right like abortion and his embrace of the Nixon-channeling self-characterization as the "law and order candidate."

And the majority was silent about the wrongness of messages filled with undeniable racism. Even those who disliked him as a candidate responded with minimal "Regardless of who lives in the Oval Office, I get my directions from God" statuses.

Some of the women responded differently. For many white Christian women, a candidate like Trump, who fully embraced the patriarchy and the accompanying sexism, was too much.

Seeing them speak out taught me something. White evangelicals did have a voice. My issues just weren't worth speaking up over.

That was the last straw. The selective rejection of oppression I saw from my white evangelical peers was more than I was willing to tolerate. I answered the questions on my own and chose to move on.

I felt lost and alone, but I couldn't accept a belief system that claimed to stand for all while leaving its historically marginalized members most vulnerable.

In a way, their silence cost my faith. I haven't stopped believing in God. But I have put a healthy distance between myself and many of the critical tenets of the Christian church.

It wasn't enough to hear someone preach come as you are, while they hope you would leave changed. It didn't sit well for me to have someone say they have my best interests in mind but turn a blind eye to my community's struggles. Any theology I follow from here forward is going to have love, not salvation, as the cornerstone.

And since stepping off, I haven't looked back.

## Reference

Perez, Maria. 2019. "Martin Luther King Jr. Day: 17 Quotes to Honor the American Civil Rights Activist." Retrieved November 14, 2019. https://www.newsweek.com/martin-luther-king-jr-powerful-quotes-honor-american-civil-rights-activist-1296354.

*A. Rochaun Meadows-Fernandez is an award-winning journalist, a diversity content specialist, and the author of* Investigating Institutional Racism *in the* Racial Literacy Series.

# 4 Profiles

Racism and anti-racism, though impacted more dramatically by some individuals than by others, are structural, group-level, institutional processes. Thus, rather than focus each profile on a particular individual, this chapter emphasizes the groups in which notable individuals were and are embedded. For example, this chapter discusses Malcolm X, but it discusses him in the context of the Nation of Islam, which was fundamentally important to his life and his approach to civil rights. Though this chapter profiles protagonists and antagonists of racism in the United States, it retains this book's characteristic focus on how racism transcends individual prejudice.

## American Civil Liberties Union

Roger Baldwin, Crystal Eastman, Arthur Garfield Hays, and others who objected to the suppression of free speech under President Woodrow Wilson formed the National Civil Liberties Bureau and, subsequently, its successor, the American Civil Liberties Union (ACLU), in 1920 (American Civil Liberties Union 2019b). The ACLU has played an active role in contesting racial abuses in a variety of institutions. Regarding criminal justice, ACLU attorneys successfully appealed the

---

Stokely Carmichael, a leader in the Student Nonviolent Coordinating Committee (SNCC), eventually advocated for progress by more militant means as a member of the Black Panthers. (Library of Congress)

false conviction of eight African American men (known as the "Scottsboro Boys") for rape before the Supreme Court in *Powell v. Alabama* (1932). The verdict extended Sixth Amendment protections to defendants against inadequate counsel. In *Patterson v. Alabama* (1935), another case stemming from the prosecution of the Scottsboro Boys, ACLU attorneys secured a Supreme Court decision that black defendants could not be given a fair trial if there were no black people in the jury pool. The ACLU would go on to push back against the exclusion of black jurors in *Whitus v. Georgia* (1967) after the Supreme Court reversed the conviction of a black man on trial for murder in a county where no juries ever included a black person despite black people comprising 45 percent of the local population. More recently, in 1999, the ACLU successfully opposed an anti-loitering law that disproportionately targeted black and Latino youths in an ostensible effort to crack down on gangs (*Chicago v. Morales* 1999). The American Civil Liberties Union (2019c) also filed a number of lawsuits against police officers who engaged in brutality toward racial minorities and released a community action manual for use in pushing back against police abuses.

Aside from opposing racism in the criminal justice process, the ACLU has also worked to defend Americans' rights against racial discrimination in a variety of other venues. Regarding voting rights, the ACLU pushed back against Texas's allowance of the Democratic Party restricting primary voting to whites alone in *Smith v. Allwright* (1944). More recently, the American Civil Liberties Union (2019a) opposed voter ID laws and voting restrictions that disproportionately impacted the ability of people of color to vote in Pennsylvania, Arkansas, and North Carolina. The ACLU also worked to end the unconstitutional imposition of curfews against and internment of Japanese Americans in *Hirabayashi v. United States* (1943) and *Korematsu v. United States* (1944). Further, the organization has opposed the use of covenants and homeowner agreements designed to prohibit white homeowners from selling their homes to racial minorities in *Shelley v. Kraemer* (1948). The ACLU has also made headlines in recent years for assisting those in opposition to President Trump's immigration policies (e.g., his attempts to restrict asylum claims and his bans on immigration from primarily Middle Eastern and predominantly Muslim countries) in court (American Civil Liberties Union 2019d). Its arguably most high-profile contribution involved assisting attorneys in supporting Oliver Brown against Topeka, Kansas's Board of Education, leading to the end of school segregation (*Brown v. Board of Education of Topeka* 1954).

On the one hand, in the aforementioned instances, the ACLU acted in ways designed to reduce racism in the United States. On the other hand, in its rigid defense of freedom of speech and assembly, the ACLU has also helped protect displays of racism on numerous occasions. Among other groups, the ACLU has backed the Ku Klux Klan, neo-Nazi groups, and "Unite the Right" white supremacist demonstrators in court cases concerning alleged violations of their civil rights (Lopez 2017).

## Black Lives Matter

In 2012, George Zimmerman shot an unarmed teenager (Trayvon Martin) whom he deemed suspicious. Zimmerman was charged with murder but acquitted in a controversial case in which he claimed that he had acted in self-defense. In response, Alicia Garza, Patrisse Cullors, and Opal Tometi began using the hashtag #BlackLivesMatter on social media (Khan-Cullors and Bandele 2018). While it did not achieve widespread recognition initially, a large number of people began using it in 2014 in response to Ferguson, Missouri, police officer Darren Wilson's shooting of Michael Brown. Before long, the hashtag emerged throughout social media whenever police killed black people under suspicious circumstances, such as Eric Garner and Freddie Gray (McLaughlin 2016). During the 2016 election season, Black Lives Matter (BLM) activists challenged Hillary Clinton over her involvement with the war on drugs, given its consequences for the mass incarceration of black people during Bill Clinton's presidency. They also interrupted Bernie Sanders and Martin O'Malley's campaign rallies with tangible effects. After facing BLM protests, both Sanders and O'Malley more explicitly incorporated racial justice and criminal justice reform plans into their campaigns (Merica and Bradner 2015). As more people began to identify with the BLM movement, there were protests against police brutality in New York City, in Washington, and in numerous other places both domestic and international. Unionized BLM activists even engaged in strikes, refusing to load millions of dollars in goods onto cargo ships in Oakland, California (Taylor 2016).

In more recent years, BLM activists have expanded to new methods by which to critique American racism and focused on new areas in which racism is rampant beyond institutional violence. Part of this effort has involved the expansion of educational media; for example, when the National Rifle Association (NRA) released an ad that suggested Americans should respond to those protesting against racism "with a clenched fist," BLM responded with a scathing ad of its own to critique the violence against black people and the NRA's implicit encouragement of that violence (Holley 2017; Morrison 2017). More recently, BLM activists have begun rallying for educational reform to incorporate more black history into curricula, diversify the faculty, and address economic disparities between schools that have negatively impacted people of color (Katinas 2019). Along the way, BLM activists have taken intersectionality into account, affirming people across the spectrums of "actual or perceived sexual identity, gender identity, gender expression, economic status, ability, disability, religious beliefs or disbeliefs, immigration status [and] location" (Black Lives Matter 2019).

## Black Panther Party for Self-Defense

In 1966, Bobby Seale saw Huey Newton debating at Merritt College about civil rights. Inspired, he joined Newton in the

Afro-American Association, where there were a number of book discussions. Newton became interested in the work of Malcolm X and considered joining the Nation of Islam but ultimately found religion insufficient to answer his questions and address his concerns. Instead, he and Seale founded the Black Panther Party for Self-Defense (whose name would soon change to the Black Panther Party). The name came from a voter registration pamphlet that described how the Lowndes County Freedom Organization represented itself with a black panther symbol (Abu-Jamal 2004).

From the beginning, the Black Panther Party represented something different from what whites had come to expect from the civil rights movement. It was Maoist and secularist (Self 2006). It was the first national black organization in the United States to advocate for gay rights and ally with gay rights groups (Ongiri 2010). It was also notably more willing to use force when necessary; as Mumia Abu-Jamal (2004:7, emphasis in original) described it, "The Party was *not* a civil rights group. It did not believe in turning the other cheek. . . . It did not preach nonviolence, but practiced the human right of self-defense. . . . The Black Panther Party made (white) Americans feel many things, but safe wasn't one of them." The Party saw its initial mission as the defense of Oakland, California, in the face of a police force that committed acts of brutality against blacks in the community. Its members would drive around with rifles to keep an eye on police activities (Self 2006). When Bobby Seale wrote his own version of the Black Panther Party's history, it included a dedication to Huey Newton that referenced these words from Newton to the police: "I'm not going to allow you to brutalize me. I'm going to stop you from brutalizing my people. You got your gun, pig, I got mine. If you shoot at me, I'm shooting back" (Seale 1996).

Despite its willingness to meet violence with violence if necessary, the Black Panther Party was also committed to aiding the community in more traditional and normative ways. The Party provided free breakfast for schoolchildren and established free health clinics that ran screening programs for sickle cell anemia alongside the Sickle-Cell Anemia Research Foundation and provided laboratory testing in partnership with nearby hospitals (Bassett 2016; The Dr. Huey P. Newton Foundation 2008). The Party also operated a free ambulance service and created plans for the People's Shoe Factory—an all-volunteer shoe provider for those in need (The Dr. Huey P. Newton Foundation 2008).

The Black Panther Party developed a ten-point program to clarify and publicize its goals. The program called for black people to (1) be free to determine their own destinies, (2) have access to full employment (with the means of production wrested away from white businessmen and given to the community if they refused to provide said employment), (3) receive reparations from the federal government, (4) have access to decent housing, (5) have access to education that would "give to our people a knowledge of self," and (6) be exempted from military service. The Black Panther Party also called for (7) the end of police brutality, (8) the release of all black men held in prisons or jails (due to their inability to receive fair trials), and (9) the right for black people to be tried by a jury of their peer, with these peers being from "similar economic, social, religious, geographical, environmental, historical, and racial background[s]." The final point (10) called for "land, bread, housing, education, clothing, justice, and peace" and quoted the opening portion of the Declaration of Independence, suggesting that separation might be necessary if access to basic human rights proved impossible (Marxist History Archive 2001). Later, they would call for a UN-supervised black state (Self 2006).

By the late 1960s, Black Panther Party chapters had emerged in cities across the country and inspired the formation of other groups, such as the Young Lords, a Puerto Rican organization (Self 2006). However, as it grew, it faced challenges both from within and from without. Internally, its identity became more contentious as Newton wanted to continue to focus the Party's efforts on policing the police and getting involved with local politics to effect change, while Eldridge Cleaver wanted to involve the Party in black freedom struggles in Africa and Asia (Ongiri 2010). Externally, the Black Panther Party faced intense scrutiny by the police, who successfully cultivated informants within their ranks and targeted high-level members for arrest. At one point, twenty-one prominent members from the Party's New York chapter were arrested, but, after two years, all were exonerated, and the charges were found to be unwarranted. The police also assassinated some of the Black Panther Party's chapter leaders in night raids and shot the windows out of the Party's headquarters after Newton received what they considered to be light sentencing on a manslaughter charge (Self 2006). The Black Panther Party eventually disbanded in 1982 but not without leaving behind an important legacy of resistance against white supremacy (Abu-Jamal 2004).

## Ku Klux Klan

While there have been advances toward greater racial equality in America, the continued existence (and recent reawakening) of organized, public white supremacist organizations indicates that progress is by no means certain or immediate. The first major white supremacist group in America—the Ku Klux Klan (KKK)—maintains a presence to this day. The KKK emerged after the Civil War as a secret society for Confederate veterans formed by six young men in Pulaski, Tennessee. Its tactics were not initially violent, but its members would ride armed through the countryside at night in a manner reminiscent of the slave patrols of earlier years with their faces covered with grotesque masks to inspire fear. As time progressed, the federal government proceeded with Reconstruction policies that abolished Southern governments and established new constitutional conventions with military supervision. Angry and emboldened former Confederates met in Nashville, Tennessee, to plan the next steps for the KKK. This was when they officially adopted a platform of white supremacy and began engaging in widespread beatings and lynchings (Southern Poverty Law Center 1997).

The KKK's turn toward more pervasive violence brought the scrutiny of the federal government. With the passage of the 1871 Ku Klux Klan Act, President Ulysses S. Grant was able to send federal troops to crack down on KKK activity, arresting numerous members with the suspension of due process. However, the use of the military in this manner damaged support for Reconstruction and allowed ex-Confederate Democrat leaders to gain traction in their reassertion of power. Having regained control over former Confederate state governments, Democrats proceeded to pass draconian antiblack laws (Quarles 1999). Between the federal crackdown and the subsequent Democrat reassertion of white supremacy, the KKK lost its viability, but it would not remain sidelined for long.

Inspired by *Birth of a Nation*, a racist propaganda film that glorified the KKK, William Joseph Simmons began recruiting for a new KKK in 1915. The new KKK shared the racism of the previous version but differed in a few important respects. First, it broadened its targets of hatred beyond blacks to include immigrants, tapping into broad nativist sentiment in the United States, Catholics (by claiming that Catholics were following the Pope over their own country), and Jews. Second, the new KKK partnered with and recruited through fraternal organizations where similar prejudices already existed (such as with the Masons who also tended to be anti-Catholic). Resting its arguments on the pseudoscience of eugenics, the KKK became more comfortable acting out in the open, and its members included a number of public figures (Gordon 2017). While the organization only has an estimated 3,000 members now, a number of other white supremacist groups with similar aims have emerged over the years.

## Nation of Islam

Wallace D. Fard (later known as Wallace Fard Muhammad) founded the Nation of Islam, an Islamic and black nationalist movement, in Detroit in 1930 (Mintz 2015). Elijah Poole, having become convinced that Fard represented the prophesied second coming of Christ, changed his name to Elijah Muhammad and began spreading the Nation of Islam's teachings (Muhammad 1993; U.S. National Archives and Records Administration 2016).

Elijah Muhammad's *Message to the Blackman in America* (1973) laid out his theological interpretations and goals for the Nation of Islam. He suggests that Allah made black people first, whereas the white race was created by a scientist named Yakub through eugenics. In the Jewish Old Testament account of the Garden of Eden, Adam and Eve are expelled from the garden for the sin of eating from the tree of the knowledge of good and evil (from which they had been expressly forbidden to eat). In Muhammad's interpretation, the cherubim with flaming swords whom God placed at the east entrance of the garden to keep Adam and Eve out were Muslim guards. The "sword of Islam" kept Adam and Eve from returning to Asia from their exile in Europe (Muhammad 1973:133). He argued that whites (whom he frames as descendants of Adam) were the enemies of God and black Muslims and the chosen people of the devil (Muhammad 1973). Given this, Muhammad called for blacks to take pride in themselves, pursue economic self-determination, and segregate themselves from whites (including the avoidance of using European names). The emphasis on racial segregation brought support from the American Nazi Party (which referred to Muhammad as the "Hitler of blacks") and from the Ku Klux Klan (whose representatives met with members of the Nation of Islam in 1964) (Southern Poverty Law Center 2019).

Elijah Muhammad's teachings would go on to inspire a number of prominent individuals, including Malcolm X. Malcolm X is often presented as a foil to Martin Luther King Jr. Whereas King was a Baptist minister with the namesake of a widely known Protestant reformer (Moldovan 2019), Malcolm (1964:253) saw Islam as a remedy to the way that "the white man . . . brainwashed us black people to fasten our gaze upon a blond-haired, blue-eyed Jesus . . . that doesn't even *look* like us!" He suggested that Christianity told blacks to wait until death for an eternal reward "while this white man has his milk and honey in the streets paved with golden dollars right here on *this* earth!" (Malcolm X 1964:253, emphasis in original). Whereas King was perceived as more measured in tone and nonviolent, Malcolm argued that demonstrations, if they were to be effective, must imply that reciprocal bloodshed was possible—not simply violent repression of the demonstration by whites (Goldman 1973). When Malcolm was accused in a debate of being overly emotional, he replied, "When a man is hanging on a tree and he cries out, should he cry out unemotionally?" (Goldman 1973:228). This is perhaps unsurprising given not only the influence that the Nation of Islam had on him but also as a result of his family background. White men killed his father and three of his uncles. He stated in his autobiography, "It has always been my belief that I, too, will die by violence" (Malcolm X 1964:2).

Given the significant differences between Malcolm and King, there were moments of tension between the two civil rights leaders. When Malcolm's invitation to King to join him at a rally in Harlem went unanswered, he suggested that King and other moderates were afraid of upsetting or embarrassing whites (Baldwin 1986). When he was denied the opportunity to speak to the protesters gathered in Birmingham, Alabama, during the riots of 1963, he was infuriated (Baldwin 1986). Malcolm found the manner in which King approached negotiations with white leaders "degrading" and critiqued his receipt of the Nobel Peace Prize in 1964, explaining, "If I'm following a general . . . and the enemy tends to give him rewards, or awards, I get suspicious" (Goldman 1973:17). He characterized the event where King gave the "I Have a Dream" speech as a "circus" led by "clowns" (Baldwin 1986:397). He called King everything from a "fool" to a "traitor," a "false shepherd," and an "Uncle Tom" (Baldwin 1986:397). He suggested that white people should thank King for keeping blacks in check (Marable 2011). Although King did not typically refer to Malcolm by name, he did, at times, refer to him as "crazy," "tragic," and "demagogic" and suggested that there were more riots in the North at least partially because of him (Baldwin 1986:403). He also blamed Malcolm for an incident in which blacks in Harlem threw eggs at his car, although Malcolm denied involvement (Baldwin 1986).

On the other hand, until 1960, when King more clearly rejected black Muslims, Malcolm X often acknowledged King as an important fellow leader of the civil rights movement, and the two men admired each other's courage and dedication (Baldwin 1986). In addition, although he felt that other civil rights leaders had frequently attacked Muslims, Malcolm reasoned that "I would be most foolish to let the white man manoeuver me against the civil rights movement" (Malcolm X 1964:269). Malcolm supported civil rights actions where King was organizing demonstrations in Selma and even, after a speech to supporters of the Southern Christian Leadership Conference and the Student Nonviolent Coordinating Committee, told Coretta Scott King that he thought he could help Martin Luther King Jr.'s message resonate better with whites by making them "realize what the alternative is" (Baldwin 1986:398). When Malcolm was assassinated in 1965, King noted that, despite their disagreements, he still felt deep affection for him (Baldwin 1986).

Toward the end of his life, Malcolm X found himself at odds with Elijah Muhammad (who grew threatened by his rising influence and outspokenness and suspended him from the Nation of Islam). When Malcolm left the organization less than a year later, he went on a pilgrimage to Mecca, converted to orthodox Islam, and returned to the United States to found the more moderate Organization of Afro-American Unity. In that capacity, he became more influential in the mainstream civil rights movement (particularly with the Student Nonviolent Coordinating Committee) until his death. Yet that influence came at a price, as members of the Nation of Islam assassinated him on February 21, 1965 (History.com Editors 2019). Theories as to why vary, but there has been speculation that the assassination occurred because Malcolm X was aware that Elijah Muhammad fathered eight children with four teenagers, because his popularity sowed seeds of jealousy within the Nation of Islam, or because his conversion to orthodox Islam and pilgrimage to Mecca led to international connections that threatened Muhammad (Begum 2011).

When Elijah Muhammad died, his son, Wallace Muhammad (later Warith Deen Mohammed) made major changes to the Nation of Islam. He reversed the organization's labeling of whites as inherently evil, ended calls for a separate state for blacks, and made a number of other organizational changes (such as renaming the organization the World Community of Islam and emphasizing Orthodox Islam). Unhappy with the change in direction, Louis Farrakhan disassociated from the group and worked to reconstitute the Nation of Islam according to its historical focus on racial separatism (Lee 1996). Under Farrakhan, the Nation of Islam returned to a denunciation of whites as devils and was classified as a hate group by the Southern Poverty Law Center based on the "deeply racist, anti-Semitic, and anti-gay rhetoric of its leaders, including top minister Louis Farrakhan" (Southern Poverty Law Center 2019). In the process, Farrakhan strangely found support from white supremacists who supported his vision of racial separatism and had long wanted blacks to leave America. Richard Spencer, Jared Taylor, and others associated with alt-right/white nationalist groups reached out to Farrakhan for further discussion (Southern Poverty Law Center 2019).

## National Association for the Advancement of Colored People

William Edward Burghardt Du Bois (W.E.B. Du Bois) was a pioneer in many respects. He was the first African American to earn a doctorate from Harvard, arguably the first to conduct a detailed and rigorous sociological study of an American community using statistics (*The Philadelphia Negro*), and one of the founders of the National Association for the Advancement of Colored People (NAACP) (Appiah 2014). His *The Souls of Black Folk*—a seminal work in the social sciences—had an impact on a number of people, not the least of whom was Oswald Garrison Villard, heir to a railroad fortune and grandson of William Lloyd Garrison. Villard owned both the *New York Evening Post* and the *Nation*, both of which acknowledged the value of Du Bois's contributions. The *Evening Post* would later report on Du Bois's 1905 meeting in Harper's Ferry with a group of black men who became known as the Niagara Movement and sought to secure equal rights for blacks in America. After the 1906 white riots in Atlanta that killed dozens of black and destroyed a number of black homes and businesses, Villard became convinced that there was a need for a "Committee for the Advancement of the Negro Race" that would include research, publicity, legal, and other divisions to further black rights. Following race riots in Springfield, Illinois, in which whites burned black homes and businesses and lynched two older adults, that could only be quelled by 4,000 troops, William English Walling, Mary White Ovington, Charles Edward Russell, and others began planning a conference in New York to prevent future violence. The conference would involve Villard, Du Bois, and a variety of important figures in activism efforts in New York (Sullivan 2010).

The conference featured speeches undercutting pseudoscientific arguments of racial differences in ability, and Ida B. Wells-Barnett spoke of the continued problem of lynchings. She advised those gathered to bring the dangers of mob rule to the attention of more people to influence public opinion. Those gathered approved of resolutions condemning racial discrimination and calling for greater enforcement of existing provisions regarding equal rights as well as the expansion of equal rights into the realm of education. They planned for the future creation of a more permanent organization, establishing the roots of the National Negro Committee, which would become the NAACP in 1910 (Sullivan 2010).

From the start, the NAACP faced enormous challenges. Even aside from the fact that it was an organization pushing for black rights at a time when blacks were literally being lynched and having their homes burned, the organization also faced financial troubles. Moreover, its assertive stance (including, for example, the argument that blacks were entitled to equal treatment in all areas of society, including economics) brought criticism from Booker T. Washington, who had long pursued a slow, compromising approach to civil rights. Washington undermined the NAACP repeatedly, attempting to convince its members to end their involvement (Rudwick 1960).

Despite all of these difficulties, the organization would go on to make important contributions to the expansion and defense of black rights. Probably the most widely recognized success occurred in *Brown v. Board of Education of Topeka* (1954) with the desegregation of schools, but there were many other successes as well. In the 1923 case *Moore v. Dempsey*, the NAACP secured the freedom of black men convicted of murder who were tortured until they confessed and whose trials took place in courthouses with all-white juries surrounded by a mob threatening to lynch them if they were not convicted. In 1944, the NAACP convinced the Supreme Court to strike down a Texas law that allowed parties to exclude blacks from participating in primary elections in *Smith v. Allwright*. In 1946, the Supreme Court struck down a law that segregated interstate buses in Virginia thanks to the efforts of the NAACP. Cases in the 1950s, 1960s, and 1970s created precedents for the desegregation of city buses (*Browder v. Gayle* 1956), prohibitions against racial discrimination in restaurants (*Boynton v. Virginia* 1960), protections against colleges rescinding admission offers on the basis of race (*Meredith v. Fair* 1962), and fairer pay for black workers (*Griggs v. Duke Power Co.* 1971). In more recent years, the NAACP also fought to preserve affirmative action in university admissions, arguing that we need not only equal opportunity but also diversity (e.g., in *Fisher v. University of Texas at Austin* 2016).

## The Sentencing Project

The Sentencing Project was formed in 1986 with the goal of reducing racial disparities in the criminal justice system. In 2018, The Sentencing Project submitted a report addressing these disparities to the United Nations Special Rapporteur on Contemporary Forms of Racism, Racial Discrimination, Xenophobia, and Related Intolerance. The report noted that, although the United States theoretically offers a number of constitutional protections for suspects, the prison population remains disproportionately black, suggesting that these protections are not universally accessible. This being the case, The Sentencing Project accused the United States of violating Article 2 and Article 26 of the International Covenant on Civil and Political Rights, which require equal treatment under the law across racial groups. It then requested that the UN special rapporteur call on the United States to draw down the war on drugs, end mandatory minimum sentencing, reduce the use of cash bail, and increase support for indigent defense. The Sentencing Project also asked the special rapporteur to have the United States require racial impact statements at the state and federal levels for any sentencing policies (as had already been implemented in Iowa, Connecticut, Oregon, and New Jersey); create and implement implicit racial bias training for police officers, attorneys, judges, juries, and parole boards; and work toward the elimination of employment, education, housing, voting, and other restrictions impacting people with previous criminal histories (The Sentencing Project 2018).

## Southern Christian Leadership Conference

Among civil rights organizations, the Southern Christian Leadership Conference (SCLC) was unique. Some accounts suggested that its organizational structure was ill-defined and its finances were not always meticulously maintained, but the SCLC produced a faith in its members usually only catalyzed by churches, and it was effective in a way that influenced policy at the highest levels of government (Fairclough 1987).

The faith of those who participated in the SCLC and its mission is perhaps unsurprising given that the organization emerged from the leadership of black preachers—not the least of whom was Reverend Dr. Martin Luther King Jr., who would emerge as the organization's principal spokesperson and leader. The ministers—including King—had the benefit of being both trusted in their communities and capable of engaging in political action on behalf of the civil rights movement without worrying about retaliation in the form of losing their employment to an unsympathetic boss. They were accountable to their congregations, but those congregations were experiencing the same racial inequities that they were poised to fight (Fairclough 1987).

The SCLC's origins were in the Montgomery Bus Boycott that began in 1955 after Rosa Parks accepted arrest over giving up her seat to a white man simply to comply with an unjust law. She was not the first to test segregation laws on buses (e.g., a number of black women also sat where the law did not permit and were fined, and teenager Claudette Colvin actively resisted and was arrested). In fact, Colvin was even a plaintiff in *Browder v. Gayle*, the Supreme Court case that would end bus segregation in Alabama. However, the NAACP and other civil rights organizations believed that Parks would be better to rally around. Unlike Colvin, she was an adult whom they viewed as more reliable, she was the secretary of the NAACP, she was respected and liked, and she had a middle-class look (Adler 2019).

When Parks was arrested, the leaders of the local chapter of the NAACP and the Women's Political Council started a boycott of Montgomery buses (Fairclough 1987). The Montgomery Improvement Association (MIA) sought to extend boycott and chose Martin Luther King Jr. as its president. Just as Parks was carefully chosen to be the symbol to rally around, King was carefully chosen to convince the community to continue boycotting the bus system. He had the respect that came with being a minister and was relatively unknown having arrived in Montgomery and begun civil rights work recently enough that he did not have any strong enemies (Parks 1992). He also had a unique ability to connect to everyday people and inspire them (Fairclough 1987).

The Montgomery Bus Boycott was a success, and the MIA wanted to sustain the momentum and increase the scale to facilitate social action throughout the South. Leaders from the MIA and other groups furthered these ambitions with the creation of the SCLC (Southern Christian Leadership Conference 2019). While there had been a great deal of initial momentum, the early days of the SCLC were less than inspiring. While the Student Nonviolent Coordinating Committee (SNCC) was engaging in sit-ins, the SCLC was not engaged in very much direct action and primarily directed its attention to voter registration drives. Students from Atlanta University confronted King about his unwillingness to participate in a sit-in himself and shamed him into involvement (Fairclough 1987). When the SCLC did engage in its first major campaign—supporting SNCC's actions in the Albany Movement—a number of people were arrested pushing for racial equality, but there were few tangible gains. King would later admit to errors in the campaign, explaining, "The mistake I made there was to protest against segregation generally rather than against a single and distinct facet of it. . . . It would have been much better to have concentrated upon integrating the buses or the lunch counters" ("Martin Luther King: A Candid Conversation with the Nobel Prize-Winning Leader of the Civil Rights Movement" 1965).

Despite the early difficulties, the SCLC's members and its leader learned important lessons that benefited them in later, more successful campaigns. In Birmingham, Alabama, the SCLC focused on specific goals like desegregating the lunch counters and appointing a racially diverse commission to establish the schedule for school desegregation and targeted only merchants for boycotts, reasoning that they would in turn pressure lawmakers if sufficiently motivated. The Birmingham campaign was also different for another important reason—whereas King complied with an injunction prohibiting demonstrations in Albany (deflating efforts there), he determined to resist a similar injunction imposed in Birmingham. Thousands marched, and business leaders experienced noticeable hits to their profits. As a result, they capitulated to most of the movement leaders' demands (Morris 1993).

While nonviolence was a defining feature of the SCLC, that did not keep the organization from using others' violence to their advantage. The SCLC's campaigns in Birmingham, Alabama, St. Augustine, Florida, and Selma, Alabama, invited white violence that was anticipated (Fairclough 1987). King had faith in "redemptive suffering," believing that images of black protesters being subjected to fire hoses, billy clubs, and vicious dogs would humanize them to everyday Americans and transform their thinking about the racial hierarchy (Bates 2014). He was correct; the images from Birmingham of brutal attacks on protestors engendered sympathy nationally and even internationally for the civil rights movement and helped bring about the passage of the Civil Rights Act of 1964 (Garrow 1963; Morris 1993). Similarly, the images from Selma on Bloody Sunday, when people protesting for the right to vote were met with teargas, clubs, and bull whips, helped bring about passage of the Voting Rights Act of 1965 (Garrow 1978).

One of the most notable events of the SCLC was the 1963 March on Washington. More than 200,000 people surrounded the Lincoln Memorial to call for civil rights, and Martin Luther King Jr. gave the now-famous "I Have a Dream" speech. The march contributed to the ratification of the Twenty-Fourth Amendment to the Constitution, which ended poll taxes and the passage of the Civil Rights Act of 1964 (DuBrin 2016).

## Student Nonviolent Coordinating Committee

In response to concerns that young blacks were disheartened at the lack of speed of the civil rights movement's progress, Southern Christian Leadership Conference (SCLC) director Ella Jo Baker organized a meeting that drew 120 student activists and would lead to the formation of the Student Nonviolent Coordinating Committee (SNCC) in 1960 (Carson 1981; Zinn 2013). The students who attended included a number of people who remain influential to this day, such as U.S. representative John Lewis. The organization's purpose was initially informational in nature—SNCC helped organize and coordinate student sit-ins, boycotts, and demonstrations throughout the South via student newspapers (Murphree 2006). Many of the early members of SNCC were inspired by the actions of the four A&T College students, who staged a sit-in at a lunch counter in downtown Greensboro, North Carolina, to protest racial segregation and wanted to engage in direct action themselves. Marion Barry, who would later become the first chairperson of SNCC, saw what happened in Greensboro and played a significant role in similar sit-ins in Nashville, Tennessee. Although he was putting his scholarship and his place in graduate school on the line to do so, Barry reasoned, "If I had received my scholarship and Master's degree, and still was not a free man, I was not a man at all" (Zinn 2013).

The early activities of SNCC were relatively small in scale and strictly nonviolent (consistent with the message of Martin Luther King Jr. who was also a featured speaker at the initial conference from which SNCC was formed). However, as time went on, the organization would expand its scope to national action and adjust its standards regarding a universal commitment to nonviolence. Regarding the expansion of scope, in addition to coordinating demonstrations, SNCC participated in voter registration drives and addressed members of the Republican and Democratic convention platform committees (Carson 1981). Some of the members of SNCC would participate in the Congress of Racial Equality's (CORE) freedom rides in which black and white volunteers sat together on public buses to determine whether the Supreme Court's 1960 decision in *Boynton v. Virginia* would be followed (Congress of Racial Equality 2014). Alongside CORE and the SCLC, SNCC would continue to send volunteers on freedom ride through the Freedom Riders Coordinating Committee (Carson 1981).

Two major campaigns that elevated the profile of SNCC were the "Freedom Vote" campaign of 1963 and the "Freedom Summer" campaign of 1964. The former was a mock election for governor and lieutenant governor launched to demonstrate that Mississippi blacks who had been denied the vote were ready and willing to exercise their right to enfranchisement. The latter led to the creation of the Mississippi Freedom Democratic Party and twenty-eight "Freedom Schools" designed to facilitate black student activism and involvement in the democratic process (Bond 2000; Hale 2018). By 1965, SNCC had a larger staff than any other civil rights organization in the South and had engaged in sit-ins, protests, and voter registration drives in twelve states.

The organization's shift in thinking about nonviolence came when Stokely Carmichael (who became chair of SNCC in 1966) used his leadership role to publicly argue that people in the civil rights struggle should be able to use force if necessary to defend themselves against racist violence (Murphree 2006). However, the rationale for this shift had been in the making long before. There was no question that SNCC volunteers had been in dangerous situations and found themselves undefended before. For example, in 1960, SNCC executive secretary James Forman and a group of freedom riders came to North Carolina to support Robert F. Williams (the head of a local NAACP chapter) in his desegregation efforts. Williams advocated for self-defense, but the SNCC representatives wanted to demonstrate the effectiveness of nonviolence and picketed outside a courthouse in support of demands that local activists had put before the Board of Aldermen. When a mob of thousands of white people came to the courthouse and threatened the nonviolent protesters, they ran to a police station for safety only to be targeted by the police themselves. The supposed law enforcers they ran to when set upon by a mob charged many of them with incitement to riot and sent them before courts that found them guilty and made them agree not to engage in demonstrations in North Carolina for two years as a condition of receiving suspended sentences instead of going to jail (Carson 1981).

Stokely Carmichael also moved SNCC toward an embrace of "Black Power," which emphasized black self-determination. As Student Nonviolent Coordinating Committee (1966) framed it in a position paper, "Negroes in this country have never been allowed to organize themselves because of white interference. . . . Blacks, in fact, feel intimidated by the presence of whites, because of their knowledge of the power that whites have over their lives." Black Power was about ensuring that blacks were in the driver's seat of their own liberation. SNCC, in this later phase, was not attempting to eschew white allies but, rather, to direct them to where their work would be more likely to avoid falling into old, familiar patterns of paternalism. SNCC called on whites to go into their own communities and call out the problems that their own people created and continued to perpetuate (Student Nonviolent Coordinating Committee 1966).

## United Farm Workers' Movement

Since the 1800s, southwestern agricultural production has relied substantially on the labor of Mexican workers. This reliance intensified when World War II led to labor shortages that prompted the United States to create the Bracero program

(Bruns 2011). Under the Bracero program, Mexican men were granted entry into the United States to work in the fields for limited periods of time. However, the program was ended in the 1960s when the United States found that more Mexicans were entering than were necessary to meet labor shortages and that some who crossed over were not returning to Mexico once they had completed their work assignments (Bruns 2011; Cohen 2011). Despite the formal end of the Bracero program, U.S. businesses (and, particularly, U.S. growers) continued to recruit Mexican workers in substantial numbers (Cohen 2011).

That Mexican workers were vital to meet labor demands in the United States and that they were actively recruited by American businesses did not imply that they would be treated with fairness. In 1965, a grape picker, for example, could expect to make about $0.90 an hour in addition to $0.10 per jug of grapes picked. Workers did not always have ready access to water and, in some cases, had to pay for it out of their wages. They also had to pay for temporary shelter in metal shacks without access to plumbing or cooking facilities. Injuries were frequent, and the average farmworker lived to be only forty-nine years old (Kim 2017). Ironically, the very Bracero program that brought a number of Mexican workers to American fields also enabled American businesses to develop a population of strikebreakers to replace them when they protested for better treatment (Bruns 2011). However, with the end of the program, effective organization against problematic work conditions became increasingly possible.

A watershed moment occurred when Cesar Chávez, Dolores Huerta, and their National Farm Workers Association (NFWA) joined forces with the Filipino workers of the Agricultural Workers Organizing Committee (AWOC) to engage in a massive grape strike that lasted five years and impacted Schenley Vineyards Corporation, DiGiorgio Fruit Corporation, S&W Fine Foods, and TreeSweet Corporation (Gutiérrez 2019). Chávez sent workers to cities nationwide to build support for the strike and a nationwide boycott of California grapes from nonunionized sources (Pao 2016). The NFWA and the AWOC would go on to participate in a 340-mile march to the California State capitol together and eventually merge into the United Farm Workers Organizing Committee (UFWOC) in 1966 (Bruns 2011).

Over time, the UFWOC grew with the addition of Eugene Nelson's Independent Workers Association, which had been advocating for workers' rights in the Rio Grande Valley in Texas (Gutiérrez 2019). By 1972, the UFWOC had become the United Farm Workers, AFL-CIO—full members of the American Federation of Labor and Congress of Industrial Organizations, the largest labor federation in America (United Farm Workers 2019). Its legacy includes successfully securing better working conditions, better pay, unionization and collective bargaining rights, and the right to vote in secret-ballot California elections for farmworkers (Pao 2016). The union continues to make strides for agricultural workers, pushing for overtime pay, protection against wage theft, and access to masks while working in areas with bad air from fires, among other things.

The path was not always easy or straightforward. The United Farm Workers at one point targeted Japanese American–owned farms for strikes, and they responded with ads in leading newspapers talking about how they had faced internment, lost everything, and were now being targeted as they tried to rebuild. Among Japanese Americans, older Nisei tended to oppose the UFW. However, younger Sansei tended to support the UFW's boycott of nonunion products, and there were other moments of interracial cooperation as well. For example, the Student Nonviolent Coordinating Committee joined UFW's march from Delano to Sacramento, California, in support of agricultural workers. Later, the UFW also received support for strikes and boycotts from the NAACP, the Southern Christian Leadership Conference, the National Urban League, and the Black Panther Party (Araiza 2013).

Whatever factionalism may have broken out at times among workers of different racial and ethnic backgrounds, members of the UFW recognized that the bigger problem was the racism of the growers toward the workers. In more recent years, UFW cofounder Dolores Huerta has discussed how the biggest challenge for agricultural workers was the racism of growers who had no problem subjecting workers to inhuman conditions. She noted that, although the UFW achieved a number of successes, racism never really changed, commenting, "Because I am Latina, and I am a person of color, every week I get these micro-aggressions. Because I am indigenous, they think you are coming to work somewhere" (Bratt 2017).

## References

Abu-Jamal, Mumia. 2004. *We Want Freedom: A Life in the Black Panther Party.* Cambridge, MA: South End Press.

Adler, Margot. 2009. "Before Rosa Parks, There Was Claudette Colvin." Retrieved July 1, 2019. https://www.npr.org/2009/03/15/101719889/before-rosa-parks-there-was-claudette-colvin.

American Civil Liberties Union. 2019a. "ACLU Accomplishments." Retrieved August 5, 2019. https://www.aclu.org/aclu-accomplishments.

American Civil Liberties Union. 2019b. "ACLU History: Advocating for Justice at the Supreme Court." Retrieved August 5, 2019. https://www.aclu.org/other/aclu-history-advocating-justice-supreme-court.

American Civil Liberties Union. 2019c. "Fighting Police Abuse: A Community Action Manual." Retrieved June 26, 2019. https://www.aclu.org/other/fighting-police-abuse-community-action-manual.

American Civil Liberties Union. 2019d. "Immigrants' Rights and Detention." Retrieved August 7, 2019. https://www.aclu.org/issues/immigrants-rights/immigrants-rights-and-detention.

Appiah, Kwame Anthony. 2014. *Lines of Descent: W.E.B. Du Bois and the Emergence of Identity* (The W.E.B. Du Bois Lectures). Cambridge, MA: Harvard University Press.

Araiza, Lauren. 2013. *To March for Others: The Black Freedom Struggle and the United Farm Workers.* Philadelphia: University of Pennsylvania Press.

Baldwin, Lewis V. 1986. "Malcolm X and Martin Luther King, Jr.: What They Thought about Each Other." *Islamic Studies* 25(4):395–416.

Bassett, Mary T. 2016. "Beyond Berets: The Black Panthers as Health Activists." *American Journal of Public Health* 106(10):1741–1743.

Bates, Karen Grigsby. 2014. "Stokely Carmichael, a Philosopher behind the Black Power Movement." Retrieved July 1, 2019. https://www.npr.org/sections/codeswitch/2014/03/10/287320160/stokely-carmichael-a-philosopher-behind-the-black-power-movement.

Begum, Fatima. 2011. "Who Killed Malcolm X? And Why?" Retrieved June 22, 2019. https://historynewsnetwork.org/article/142725.

Black Lives Matter. 2019. "What We Believe." Retrieved August 8, 2019. https://blacklivesmatter.com/about/what-we-believe/.

Bond, Julian. 2000. "SNCC: What We Did." Retrieved July 1, 2019. https://monthlyreview.org/2000/10/01/sncc-what-we-did/.

*Boynton v. Virginia.* 1960. 364 U.S. 454.

Bratt, Peter. 2017. *Dolores* [DVD]. Boston, MA: PBS Distribution.

*Browder v. Gayle.* 1956. 142 F. Supp. 707.

*Brown v. Board of Education of Topeka.* 1954. 347 U.S. 483.

Bruns, Roger. 2011. *Cesar Chavez and the United Farm Workers' Movement.* Santa Barbara, CA: ABC-CLIO.

Carson, Clayborne. 1981. *In Struggle: SNCC and the Black Awakening of the 1960s*. Cambridge, MA: Harvard University Press.

*Chicago v. Morales*. 1999. 527 U.S. 41.

Cohen, Deborah. 2011. *Braceros: Migrant Citizens and Transnational Subjects in the Postwar United States and Mexico*. Chapel Hill: The University of North Carolina Press.

Congress of Racial Equality. 2014. "CORE Volunteers Put Their Lives on the Road." Retrieved July 1, 2019. http://www.core-online.org/History/freedom%20rides.htm.

The Dr. Huey P. Newton Foundation. 2008. *The Black Panther Party: Service to the People Programs*. Albuquerque: University of New Mexico Press.

DuBrin, Doug. 2016. "The March on Washington and Its Impact—Lesson Plan." Retrieved July 2, 2019. https://www.pbs.org/newshour/extra/lessons-plans/the-march-on-washington-and-its-impact/.

Fairclough, Adam. 1987. *To Redeem the Soul of America: The Southern Christian Leadership Conference*. Athens: University of Georgia Press.

*Fisher v. University of Texas at Austin*. 2016. 579 U.S.

Garrow, David J. 1963. *Bearing the Cross: Martin Luther King, Jr. and the Southern Christian Leadership Conference*. New York: HarperCollins.

Garrow, David J. 1978. *Protest at Selma: Martin Luther King, Jr. and the Voting Rights Act of 1965*. New Haven, CT: Yale University Press.

Goldman, Peter. 1973. *The Death and Life of Malcolm X*. New York: Harper & Row.

Gordon, Linda. 2017. *The Second Coming of the KKK: The Ku Klux Klan of the 1920s and the American Political Tradition*. New York: Liveright Publishing.

*Griggs v. Duke Power Co*. 1971. 401 U.S. 424.

Gutiérrez, José Angel. 2019. *The Eagle Has Eyes: The FBI Surveillance of César Estrada Chávez of the United Farm Workers' Union of America, 1965–1975.* East Lansing: Michigan State University.

Hale, Jon N. 2018. *The Freedom Schools: Student Activists in the Mississippi Civil Rights Movement.* New York: Columbia University Press.

*Hirabayashi v. United States.* 1943. 320 U.S. 81.

History.com Editors. 2019. "Malcolm X Assassinated." Retrieved June 22, 2019. https://www.history.com/this-day-in-history/malcolm-x-assassinated.

Holley, Peter. 2017. "The NRA Recruitment Video That Is Even Upsetting Gun Owners." Retrieved August 8, 2019. https://www.washingtonpost.com/news/post-nation/wp/2017/06/29/the-nra-recruitment-video-that-is-even-upsetting-gun-owners/.

Katinas, Paula. 2019. "Black Lives Matter Rally to Focus on Racial Inequity in Schools." Retrieved August 8, 2019. https://brooklyneagle.com/articles/2019/02/06/black-lives-matter-rally-to-focus-on-racial-inequity-in-schools/.

Khan-Cullors, Patrisse, and Asha Bandele. 2018. *When They Call You a Terrorist: A Black Lives Matter Memoir.* New York: St. Martin's Press.

Kim, Inga. 2017. "The Rise of the UFW." Retrieved June 29, 2019. https://ufw.org/the-rise-of-the-ufw/.

*Korematsu v. United States.* 1944. 323 U.S. 214.

Lee, Martha F. 1996. *The Nation of Islam: An American Millenarian Movement.* Syracuse, NY: Syracuse University Press.

Lopez, German. 2017. "Why the ACLU Defends White Nationalists' Right to Protest—Including in Charlottesville." Retrieved August 7, 2019. https://www.vox.com/policy-and-politics/2017/8/12/16138326/aclu-charlottesville-protests-racism.

Malcolm X. 1964. *The Autobiography of Malcolm X.* New York: One World Books.

Marable, Manning. 2011. *Malcolm X: A Life of Reinvention.* New York: Viking.

"Martin Luther King: A Candid Conversation with the Nobel Prize-Winning Leader of the Civil Rights Movement." 1965. Retrieved July 1, 2019. https://playboysfw.kinja .com/martin-luther-king-jr-a-candid-conversation-with-the-n-1502354861.

Marxist History Archive. 2001. "The Ten-Point Program." Retrieved June 30, 2019. https://www.marxists.org/history/ usa/workers/black-panthers/1966/10/15.htm.

McLaughlin, Michael. 2016. "The Dynamic History of #BlackLivesMatter Explained." Retrieved June 26, 2019. https://www.huffpost.com/entry/history-black-lives-mat ter_n_56d0a3b0e4b0871f60eb4af5.

*Meredith v. Fair.* 1962. 305 F.2d 341.

Merica, Dan, and Eric Bradner. 2015. "Clinton Meets with #BlackLivesMatter Protesters after They Were Barred from Her Event." Retrieved June 26, 2019. https://www.cnn .com/2015/08/11/politics/hillary-clinton-new-hampshire-black-lives-matter-2016/index.html.

Mintz, Zoe. 2015. "What Is the Nation of Islam? History, Beliefs, and Practices of the Religious Movement." Retrieved June 21, 2019. https://www.ibtimes.com/what-nation-islam-history-beliefs-practices-religious-movement-1829370.

Moldovan, Russel. 2019. "Martin Luther King, Jr." Retrieved June 20, 2019. https://www.christianitytoday.com/history/ issues/issue-65/martin-luther-king-jr.html.

Morris, Aldon D. 1993. "Birmingham Confrontation Reconsidered: An Analysis of the Dynamics and Tactics of Mobilization." *American Sociological Review* 58(5):621–636.

Morrison, Aaron. 2017. "This Black Lives Matter Chapter Just Clapped Back at the NRA with a Biting Ad of Its Own." Retrieved August 8, 2019. https://www.mic.com/articles/181658/this-black-lives-matter-chapter-just-clapped-back-at-the-nra-with-a-biting-ad-of-its-own#.AQUROALim.

Muhammad, Elijah. 1973. *Message to the Blackman in America*. Maryland Heights, MO: Secretarius MEMPS Ministries.

Muhammad, Elijah. 1993. *History of the Nation of Islam*. Maryland Heights, MO: Secretarius MEMPS Ministries.

Murphree, Vanessa. 2006. *The Selling of Civil Rights: The Student Nonviolent Coordinating Committee and the Use of Public Relations*. New York: Routledge.

Ongiri, Amy Abugo. 2010. *Spectacular Blackness: The Cultural Politics of the Black Power Movement and the Search for a Black Aesthetic*. Charlottesville: University of Virginia Press.

Pao, Maureen. 2016. "César Chavez: The Life behind a Legacy of Farm Labor Rights." Retrieved June 29, 2019. https://www.npr.org/2016/08/02/488428577/cesar-chavez-the-life-behind-a-legacy-of-farm-labor-rights.

Parks, Rosa. 1992. *Rosa Parks: My Story*. New York: Puffin Books.

*Patterson v. Alabama*. 1935. 294 U.S. 600.

*Powell v. Alabama*. 1932. 287 U.S. 45.

Quarles, Chester L. 1999. *The Ku Klux Klan and Related American Racialist and Antisemitic Organizations: A History and Analysis*. Jefferson, NC: McFarland & Company.

Rudwick, Elliott M. 1960. "Booker T. Washington's Relations with the National Association for the Advancement of Colored People." *The Journal of Negro Education* 29(2):134–144.

Seale, Bobby. 1996. *Seize the Time: The Story of the Black Panther Party and Huey P. Newton*. Baltimore, MD: Black Classic Press.

Self, Robert O. 2006. "The Black Panther Party and the Long Civil Rights Era," pp. 15–55, in *In Search of the Black Panther Party: New Perspectives on a Revolutionary Movement*, edited by Jane Lazerow and Yohuru Williams. Durham, NC: Duke University Press.

The Sentencing Project. 2018. "Report of The Sentencing Project to the United Nations Special Rapporteur on Contemporary Forms of Racism, Racial Discrimination, Xenophobia, and Related Intolerance: Regarding Racial Disparities in the United States Criminal Justice System." Retrieved June 26, 2019. https://www.sentencingproject.org/publications/un-report-on-racial-disparities/.

*Shelley v. Kraemer*. 1948. 334 U.S. 1.

*Smith v. Allwright*. 1944. 321 U.S. 649.

Southern Christian Leadership Conference. 2019. "SCLC History." Retrieved July 1, 2019. https://nationalsclc.org/about/history/.

Southern Poverty Law Center. 1997. *Ku Klux Klan: A History of Racism and Violence*, 5th ed. Montgomery, AL: The Southern Poverty Law Center.

Southern Poverty Law Center. 2019. "Nation of Islam." Retrieved June 24, 2019. https://www.splcenter.org/fighting-hate/extremist-files/group/nation-islam.

Student Nonviolent Coordinating Committee. 1966. "The Basis of Black Power." Retrieved July 1, 2019. http://www2.iath.virginia.edu/sixties/HTML_docs/Resources/Primary/Manifestos/SNCC_black_power.html.

Sullivan, Patricia. 2010. *Lift Every Voice: The NAACP and the Making of the Civil Rights Movement*. New York: The New Press.

Taylor, Keeanga-Yamahtta. 2016. *From #BlackLivesMatter to Black Liberation*. Chicago, IL: Haymarket Books.

United Farm Workers. 2019. "UFW History." Retrieved June 29, 2019. https://ufw.org/research/history/ufw-history/.

U.S. National Archives and Records Administration. 2016. "Elijah Muhammad." Retrieved June 21, 2019. https://www.archives.gov/research/african-americans/individuals/elijah-muhammad.

*Whitus v. Georgia.* 1967. 385 U.S. 545.

Zinn, Howard. 2013. *SNCC: The New Abolitionists.* Cambridge, MA: South End Press.

# 5  Data and Documents

## Introduction

This chapter provides data and documents relevant to understanding racism in America. The data covers discrimination complaints, socioeconomic disparities, health inequality, and differential treatment within the criminal justice system. Specifically, the chapter provides and contextualizes statistics on U.S. Equal Employment Opportunity Commission complaints about unfair treatment based on race and skin tone, median income, wealth, assets, debt by race, age-adjusted death rates by race/ethnicity, arrests by race, and distribution of arrests by race/ethnicity compared with the racial distribution across the U.S. population.

Documents in this chapter address a wide range of topics, including the inhumanity of slavery, the judicial means by which the American government managed to get away with violating treaties with indigenous people, the unfair treatment of Chinese Americans immigrating to California, and the need to reassert the humanity of black people. The documents also explore the need for a constitutional end of slavery (even after the issuance of the Emancipation Proclamation), black class mobility, anti-miscegenation policy, and the extent to which the presumed threat of Japanese Americans during the period of

---

The Tape family in 1884. Mamie Tape successfully enrolled in a formerly segregated San Francisco school after the California State Supreme Court agreed that public education was open to children of all racial groups under state law. (Gado Images/Alamy Stock Photo)

internment was overstated. Other topics include the need to strengthen civil rights after the passage of the Civil Rights Act of 1964 and the Voting Rights Act of 1965 in response to continued threats and the judicial process by which anti-miscegenation laws were deemed unconstitutional via the Fourteenth Amendment. Specifically, the documents include a sermon from noted theologian Jonathan Edwards on the injustice of slavery, the text from the Supreme Court's decision in *Cherokee Nation v. Georgia*, a speech by renowned social reformer Frederick Douglass, the Thirteenth Amendment to the U.S. Constitution, an article from Howard University professor Kelly Miller on black class mobility, the text of a registration card in compliance with Virginia's 1924 "Act to Preserve Racial Integrity," the text from the Ringle Report, text from President Lyndon B. Johnson's 1996 "Special Message to the Congress Proposing Further Legislation to Strengthen Civil Rights," and the text from the Supreme Court's decision in *Loving v. Virginia*.

## Data

The U.S. Equal Employment Opportunity Commission (EEOC) accepts complaints from job applicants and employees who have been treated unfairly based on race or skin tone (among many other sociodemographic factors). Statistics about the number and nature of these complaints cannot give the whole picture of race or skin tone–based workplace discrimination (as a number of people who have faced such discrimination may never file with the EEOC, and it is possible that all complaints are valid). However, they do give a sense of the difference over time in how comfortable people feel about sharing their concerns in this arena with the federal government. From 1997 to 2017, there was a slight decline in the number of complaints about discrimination based on race, but it is a bit misleading as the number of race-based discrimination complaints fluctuated back and forth between a high of 37.3 percent in fiscal year (FY) 1997 and a low of 33.7 percent in FY 2012. In terms of an overall pattern, race-based complaints have consistently comprised more than a third of all complaints to the EEOC from 1997 to 2017.

Color-based discrimination complaints are far less common, but they have been consistently on the rise for the past few decades. While such complaints represented less than 1 percent of all employment discrimination complaints in FY 1997, they represented more than 1 percent from FY 1998 to FY 2006, more than 2 percent from FY 2007 to FY 2012, and more than 3 percent from FY 2013 to FY 2017. The 3,240 complaints in FY 2017 were the most ever received in a fiscal year by the EEOC (Table 5.1).

Income provides a concrete example of the extent to which America is racially stratified. Unsurprisingly, non-Hispanic, white-headed households enjoy some degree of advantage on this indicator, making almost $7,000 more per year than the median income across all households. Table 5.2 shows that Asian-headed households benefit substantially more, making nearly $20,000 more per year than the average household overall. Strikingly, the average Hispanic-headed household makes almost $18,000 less than the yearly average, while the average black-headed household makes almost $28,000 less. Asian-headed households make, on average, more than twice what black-headed households make.

Even if income inequality based on race lessens, stratification can continue via differences in other economic measures, such as

Table 5.1   Changes in EEOC Complaints for Race and Color (1997 and 2017)

| | Fiscal Year 1997 | Fiscal Year 2017 |
|---|---|---|
| Race | 29,199 | 28,528 |
| | 36.2% | 33.9% |
| Color | 762 | 3,240 |
| | 0.9% | 3.8% |

*Source:* U.S. Equal Employment Opportunity Commission. "Charge Statistics (Charges Filed with EEOC) FY 1997–FY 2017." Available at https://www.eeoc.gov/eeoc/statistics/enforcement/charges.cfm.

wealth. Thus, it is important to consider more than just income to assess differences in economic viability. In Table 5.3, census data shows differences in net worth, retirement accounts, and total debt by race. Overall, trends are similar to those of income. Although Asian-headed households have the most debt, they still have the highest net worth and the largest retirement accounts. Similarly, non-Hispanic white-headed households have the second-highest amount of debt but still have the second-highest net worth and retirement accounts. This conveys two important findings. First, Asian-headed households (and, to a lesser degree,

**Table 5.2  Median Income by Race (2017)**

| Race and Hispanic Origin of Householder | Median Income ($) in 2017 |
| --- | --- |
| All households | 61,372 |
| White | 65,273 |
| White, not Hispanic | 68,145 |
| Black | 40,258 |
| Asian | 81,331 |
| Hispanic (any race) | 50,486 |

*Source*: U.S. Census Bureau. "Income and Poverty in the United States: 2017." Available at https://www.census.gov/content/dam/Census/library/publications/2018/demo/p60-263.pdf.

**Table 5.3  Wealth, Assets, and Debt by Race (2014)**

| Race and Hispanic Origin of Householder | Net Worth ($) | Retirement Accounts ($) | Total Debt ($) |
| --- | --- | --- | --- |
| All households | 81,850 | 65,000 | 63,000 |
| White alone | 102,000 | 70,000 | 70,000 |
| White, not Hispanic | 130,800 | 77,000 | 75,130 |
| Black alone | 9,590 | 32,000 | 29,590 |
| Asian alone | 156,500 | 83,400 | 119,000 |
| Other (residual) | 25,520 | 30,000 | 42,000 |
| Hispanic origin (any race) | 17,530 | 28,600 | 35,300 |
| Not of Hispanic origin | 99,180 | 70,000 | 67,200 |

*Source:* U.S. Census Bureau. "Wealth, Asset Ownership, and Debt of Households Detailed Tables: 2014." Available at https://www.census.gov/data/tables/2014/demo/wealth/wealth-asset-ownership.html.

white-headed households) can carry a larger amount of debt while maintaining a relatively high net worth and savings for retirement, because of their larger salaries and inherited wealth. Second, to carry debt, in general, requires a lender or creditor to provide the money up front. Access to loans or a high credit limit requires a demonstration of the ability to repay (involving evidence of income and/or wealth sufficient to allay fears of default), and, on average, Asians and whites have more resources with which to secure credit. Hispanic and black-headed households have less debt, but their debt is more consequential given their lower average incomes and wealth, resulting in lower net worth and retirement savings.

Adjusting for age, racial and ethnic minorities face notable health disadvantages. Blacks die more frequently than any other group from diseases of the heart, cerebrovascular disease (e.g., strokes), malignant neoplasms (i.e., tumors), influenza/pneumonia, diabetes, HIV/AIDS, and homicides (by a substantial margin). American Indians/Alaskan Natives die more frequently than any other group from chronic liver disease/cirrhosis and motor vehicle-related injuries. However, there are three important exceptions; whites do die more frequently than other groups from Alzheimer's disease, drug overdoses, and suicide (Table 5.4).

In raw numbers, whites are arrested for more crimes than any other racial group. Specifically, more whites are arrested than any other racial group for rape, assault, burglary, larceny-theft, motor vehicle theft, arson, forgery/counterfeiting, fraud, embezzlement,

Table 5.4   Age-Adjusted Death Rates by Race/Ethnicity per 100,000 Population (2016)

| Cause of Death | White | Black or African American | American Indian or Alaskan Native | Asian or Pacific Islander | Hispanic or Latino |
|---|---|---|---|---|---|
| Diseases of heart | 164.5 | 205.3 | 115.4 | 85.2 | 115.8 |
| Cerebrovascular disease | 36.1 | 50.5 | 23.8 | 30.7 | 32.1 |

*(Continued)*

Table 5.4    (Continued)

| Cause of Death | White | Black or African American | American Indian or Alaskan Native | Asian or Pacific Islander | Hispanic or Latino |
|---|---|---|---|---|---|
| Malignant neoplasms | 156.6 | 177.9 | 103.4 | 97.1 | 110 |
| Chronic lower respiratory diseases | 43.3 | 29.3 | 29.7 | 11.7 | 17.1 |
| Influenza and pneumonia | 13.4 | 15 | 12.7 | 12.9 | 11.1 |
| Chronic liver disease and cirrhosis | 11.6 | 7.1 | 26.7 | 3.4 | 14.7 |
| Diabetes mellitus | 19.3 | 36.8 | 34.3 | 15.5 | 24.7 |
| Alzheimer's disease | 31.4 | 27.5 | 17.3 | 15 | 24.3 |
| HIV | 1 | 7.2 | 1 | 0.4 | 1.7 |
| Motor vehicle-related injuries | 12.4 | 13.5 | 17.8 | 5.2 | 11 |
| Drug overdose | 20.3 | 15.4 | 18.1 | 2.9 | 9.5 |
| Suicide | 15.2 | 6.1 | 13.5 | 6.7 | 6.7 |
| Homicide | 3.5 | 21.4 | 6.7 | 1.8 | 5.3 |

*Source*: National Center for Health Statistics. "Health, United States, 2017." Table 17. Available at https://www.cdc.gov/nchs/hus/contents2017.htm#Table.

buying/receiving/possessing stolen property, vandalism, carrying/possessing weapons illegally, prostitution and commercialized vice, sex offenses, drug abuse violations, offenses against the family and children, driving under the influence, liquor laws, drunkenness, disorderly conduct, vagrancy, and curfew and loitering violations. Blacks are only arrested more frequently for murder/nonnegligent manslaughter, robbery, and gambling, and no other racial group is arrested most frequently than whites and blacks for any major offense. Yet raw numbers in this case are deceiving, because they do not account for the differing sizes of each racial group within the American population (Table 5.5).

Table 5.5  Arrests by Race (2017)

| Offense Charged | Total | White | Black or African American | American Indian or Alaskan Native | Asian | Native Hawaiian or Other Pacific Islander |
|---|---|---|---|---|---|---|
| Total | 8,162,849 | 5,626,140 | 2,221,697 | 196,908 | 97,049 | 21,055 |
| Murder and nonnegligent manslaughter | 9,468 | 4,188 | 5,025 | 108 | 127 | 20 |
| Rape | 18,063 | 12,187 | 5,182 | 322 | 307 | 65 |
| Robbery | 73,764 | 32,128 | 40,024 | 679 | 664 | 269 |
| Aggravated assault | 302,941 | 188,087 | 101,513 | 7,531 | 4,881 | 929 |
| Burglary | 154,970 | 104,671 | 46,227 | 1,968 | 1,710 | 394 |
| Larceny-theft | 740,546 | 501,231 | 215,650 | 13,242 | 8,770 | 1,653 |
| Motor vehicle theft | 70,617 | 46,621 | 21,415 | 1,308 | 980 | 293 |
| Arson | 7,086 | 5,051 | 1,788 | 112 | 116 | 19 |
| Other assaults | 822,671 | 534,188 | 258,542 | 17,062 | 10,371 | 2,508 |
| Forgery and counterfeiting | 43,203 | 28,130 | 13,980 | 386 | 619 | 88 |
| Fraud | 95,997 | 63,908 | 29,556 | 1,256 | 1,174 | 103 |
| Embezzlement | 12,437 | 7,441 | 4,683 | 96 | 190 | 27 |
| Stolen property; buying, receiving, possessing | 76,477 | 48,607 | 25,585 | 1,034 | 940 | 311 |
| Vandalism | 145,934 | 99,818 | 40,861 | 3,265 | 1,681 | 309 |

(Continued)

Table 5.5 (Continued)

| Offense Charged | Total | White | Black or African American | American Indian or Alaskan Native | Asian | Native Hawaiian or Other Pacific Islander |
|---|---|---|---|---|---|---|
| Weapons; carrying, possessing, etc. | 128,009 | 68,787 | 56,143 | 1,357 | 1,400 | 322 |
| Prostitution and commercialized vice | 28,229 | 15,812 | 10,605 | 116 | 1,610 | 86 |
| Sex offenses (except rape and prostitution) | 37,518 | 26,615 | 9,355 | 691 | 741 | 116 |
| Drug abuse violations | 1,262,660 | 889,030 | 342,513 | 15,038 | 13,691 | 2,388 |
| Gambling | 2,493 | 955 | 1,294 | 20 | 183 | 41 |
| Offenses against the family and children | 71,656 | 46,926 | 20,106 | 4,067 | 534 | 23 |
| Driving under the influence | 755,726 | 617,443 | 105,585 | 15,950 | 14,294 | 2,454 |
| Liquor laws | 157,285 | 122,929 | 22,095 | 9,705 | 2,347 | 209 |
| Drunkenness | 287,985 | 212,908 | 41,073 | 30,632 | 2,931 | 441 |
| Disorderly conduct | 273,664 | 172,098 | 87,094 | 11,832 | 2,232 | 408 |
| Vagrancy | 18,453 | 12,609 | 5,148 | 473 | 209 | 14 |
| All other offenses (except traffic) | 2,540,842 | 1,750,366 | 700,984 | 57,979 | 24,046 | 7,467 |
| Suspicion | 669 | 250 | 148 | 258 | 7 | 6 |
| Curfew and loitering law violations | 23,486 | 13,156 | 9,523 | 421 | 294 | 92 |

*Source:* FBI. "2017 Crime in the United States." Table 43. Available at https://ucr.fbi.gov/crime-in-the-u.s/2017/crime-in-the-u.s.-2017/topic-pages/tables/table-43.

While raw numbers indicate that whites are most often arrested (followed by blacks, American Indian/Alaskan Natives, Asians, and Hawaiian or Other Pacific Islanders), it's entirely possible that this can be explained by the fact that whites comprise the largest racial group in America. Comparing the distribution of arrests by race to the population distribution by race gives us a more nuanced picture. Although whites are arrested more frequently for a number of crimes, they only account for more arrests than would be expected given their representation in the population in the case of driving under the influence. Blacks are arrested more frequently than would be expected based on their representation in the population for murder and nonnegligent manslaughter, rape, robbery, assault, burglary, larceny-theft, motor vehicle theft, arson, forgery and counterfeiting, fraud, embezzlement, buying/receiving/possessing stolen property, vandalism, carrying/possessing weapons, prostitution/commercialized vice, sex offenses other than rape and prostitution, drug abuse violations, gambling, offenses against the family and children, driving under the influence (although not by much), liquor laws (although not by much), disorderly conduct, vagrancy, and curfew/loitering law violations. American Indians/Alaskan Natives are arrested more frequently than would be expected for rape, assault, larceny-theft, motor vehicle theft, arson, buying/receiving/possessing stolen property, vandalism, sex offenses other than rape and prostitution, offenses against the family and children, driving under the influence, liquor laws, drunkenness, disorderly conduct, vagrancy, and curfew/loitering law violations. Asians are only arrested more frequently than would be expected for gambling, while Native Hawaiians/Pacific Islanders are arrested more frequently than would be expected for rape, robbery, assault, burglary, motor vehicle theft, arson, buying/receiving/possessing stolen property, carrying/possessing weapons, prostitution, sex offenses (other than rape and prostitution), gambling, driving under the influence, and curfew/loitering law violations.

These data might seem to suggest that whites and Asians commit less crime than blacks/African Americans, American Indians/Alaskan Natives, and Native Hawaiians/Pacific Islanders, but it is also possible that crime rates are more similar than arrest records indicate due to over-policing of some groups relative to others. This possibility is highlighted by the percentage of each racial group arrested on a suspicion charge. People included in the suspicion category are arrested for no specific crime and then let go without formal charges. Blacks account for 22.1 percent of suspicion arrests despite representing only 13.4 percent of the population, American Indians/Alaskan Natives account for 38.6 percent of suspicion charges despite representing only 1.3 percent of the population, and Native Hawaiians/Pacific Islanders account for 0.9 percent of suspicion arrests despite representing only 0.2 percent of the population. In short, police are arresting non-Asian racial minorities much more frequently than would be expected based on population demographics in cases where they cannot come up with any formal charge to file. This evidence suggests that racial minorities may not necessarily be committing more crime than expected given their representation in the population. They could simply appear to be committing more crimes because they are searched and surveilled more frequently, making their violations of law more visible and accessible for use to justify arrests (Table 5.6).

Table 5.6  Percentage Distribution of Arrests by Race Compared with Population Distribution (2017)

| | White (%) | Black or African American (%) | American Indian or Alaskan Native (%) | Asian (%) | Native Hawaiian or Other Pacific Islander (%) |
|---|---|---|---|---|---|
| Percentage of the population | 76.6 | 13.4 | 1.3 | 5.8 | 0.2 |
| **Offense charged** | | | | | |
| Total | 68.9 | 27.2 | 2.4 | 1.2 | 0.3 |
| Murder and nonnegligent manslaughter | 44.2 | 53.1 | 1.1 | 1.3 | 0.2 |
| Rape | 67.5 | 28.7 | 1.8 | 1.7 | 0.4 |
| Robbery | 43.6 | 54.3 | 0.9 | 0.9 | 0.4 |
| Aggravated assault | 62.1 | 33.5 | 2.5 | 1.6 | 0.3 |

| | White (%) | Black or African American (%) | American Indian or Alaskan Native (%) | Asian (%) | Native Hawaiian or Other Pacific Islander (%) |
|---|---|---|---|---|---|
| Burglary | 67.5 | 29.8 | 1.3 | 1.1 | 0.3 |
| Larceny-theft | 67.7 | 29.1 | 1.8 | 1.2 | 0.2 |
| Motor vehicle theft | 66.0 | 30.3 | 1.9 | 1.4 | 0.4 |
| Arson | 71.3 | 25.2 | 1.6 | 1.6 | 0.3 |
| Other assaults | 64.9 | 31.4 | 2.1 | 1.3 | 0.3 |
| Forgery and counterfeiting | 65.1 | 32.4 | 0.9 | 1.4 | 0.2 |
| Fraud | 66.6 | 30.8 | 1.3 | 1.2 | 0.1 |
| Embezzlement | 59.8 | 37.7 | 0.8 | 1.5 | 0.2 |
| Stolen property; buying, receiving, possessing | 63.6 | 33.5 | 1.4 | 1.2 | 0.4 |
| Vandalism | 68.4 | 28.0 | 2.2 | 1.2 | 0.2 |
| Weapons; carrying, possessing, etc. | 53.7 | 43.9 | 1.1 | 1.1 | 0.3 |
| Prostitution and commercialized vice | 56.0 | 37.6 | 0.4 | 5.7 | 0.3 |
| Sex offenses (except rape and prostitution) | 70.9 | 24.9 | 1.8 | 2.0 | 0.3 |
| Drug abuse violations | 70.4 | 27.1 | 1.2 | 1.1 | 0.2 |
| Gambling | 38.3 | 51.9 | 0.8 | 7.3 | 1.6 |
| Offenses against the family and children | 65.5 | 28.1 | 5.7 | 0.7 | <0.1 |
| Driving under the influence | 81.7 | 14.0 | 2.1 | 1.9 | 0.3 |
| Liquor laws | 78.2 | 14.0 | 6.2 | 1.5 | 0.1 |
| Drunkenness | 73.9 | 14.3 | 10.6 | 1.0 | 0.2 |
| Disorderly conduct | 62.9 | 31.8 | 4.3 | 0.8 | 0.1 |
| Vagrancy | 68.3 | 27.9 | 2.6 | 1.1 | 0.1 |
| All other offenses (except traffic) | 68.9 | 27.6 | 2.3 | 0.9 | 0.3 |

*(Continued)*

Table 5.6    (Continued)

| | White (%) | Black or African American (%) | American Indian or Alaskan Native (%) | Asian (%) | Native Hawaiian or Other Pacific Islander (%) |
|---|---|---|---|---|---|
| Suspicion | 37.4 | 22.1 | 38.6 | 1.0 | 0.9 |
| Curfew and loitering law violations | 56.0 | 40.5 | 1.8 | 1.3 | 0.4 |

*Source for arrest data*: FBI. "2017 Crime in the United States." Table 43. Available at https://ucr.fbi.gov/crime-in-the-u.s/2017/crime-in-the-u.s.-2017/topic-pages/tables/table-43.

*Source for population distribution by race*: U.S. Census Bureau. "Population Estimates, July 1, 2017 (V2017)." Available at https://www.census.gov/quickfacts/fact/table/US/PST045217.

## Documents

### Jonathan Edwards, "The Injustice and Impolity of the Slave Trade, and of Slavery" (September 15, 1791)

*In this sermon, renowned Congregationalist theologian Jonathan Edwards speaks out against slavery as both inherently immoral and particularly immoral in the manner in which it has operated in America. Although Christianity was often used to defend slavery, Edwards uses the Christian pulpit to condemn this tendency. First, he pushes back against the argument that Africans bear the curse of Ham (which Christian slave owners had used as justification for owning them). Second, he rejects the notion that Abraham owning slaves set a precedent for others to do so. Similarly, he argues that examples of the Israelites buying servants from surrounding nations also did not present an adequate precedent for slavery. Fourth, he affirms the immorality of slavery despite the fact that the apostles did not directly tell people that they could not own slaves and despite the fact that servants were told to obey their masters. Finally, he contends that, although some Africans brought to the United States were captives of war, this did not inherently justify their sale or purchase.*

Besides, this argument from the slavery prevailing in the days of the apostles, if it proves anything, proves too much, and so confutes itself. It proves, that we may enslave all captives taken in war, of any nation, and in any the most unjust war, such as the wars of the Romans, which were generally undertaken from the motives of ambition or avarice. On the ground of this argument we had a right to enslave the prisoners, whom we, during the late war, took from the British army; and they had the same right to enslave those whom they took from us; and so with respect to all other nations. . . .

It is said, that some men are intended by nature to be slaves. If this mean, that the author of nature has given some men a license, to enslave others; this is denied and proof is demanded. If it mean, that God hath made some of capacities inferior to others, and that the last have a right to enslave the first; this argument will prove, that some of the citizens of every country, have a right to enslave other citizens of the same country; nay, that some have a right to enslave their own brothers and sisters. But if this argument mean, that God in his providence suffers some men to be enslaved, and that this proves, that from the beginning he intended they should be enslaved, and made them with this intention; the answer is, that in like manner he suffers some men to be murdered, and in this sense, he intended and made them to be murdered. Yet no man in his senses will hence argue the lawfulness of murder. . . .

You may plead that you use your slave well; you are not cruel to him, but feed and clothe him comfortably, etc. Still every day you rob him of a most valuable and important right. And a highwayman, who robs a man of his money in the most easy and complaisant manner, is still a robber; and murder may be effected in a manner the least cruel and tormenting; still it is murder.

**Source:** Tryon Edwards. 1854. *The Works of Jonathan Edwards, D.D., Late President of Union College with a Memoir of His Life and Character.* Boston, MA: John P. Jewett & Co.

### *Cherokee Nation v. Georgia* (1831)

*Cherokee Nation v. Georgia is ostensibly a case about the consti-tutionality of Georgia state laws that took away Cherokee rights and land. More important, however, it set a broader precedent whereby the United States could fail to honor the treaties it signed with indigenous people without judicial repercussions at the high-est level. In this decision, the Supreme Court expresses sympathy for the plight of the Cherokee people, even going so far as to argue that a more sympathetic case could "scarcely be imagined." De-spite this, the Court still ruled that, although the Cherokee were clearly mistreated, they did not have standing to sue Georgia and, by extension, nor did any other indigenous group. Specifically, the Court characterized their relationship with the United States as one of a ward to a guardian rather than as a sovereign power to another sovereign power. Thus, the Supreme Court effectively washed its hands of the responsibility to hold the United States and its constituent state governments to the assurances they made to indigenous people.*

Mr. Chief Justice Marshall delivered the opinion of the Court.

This bill is brought by the Cherokee Nation, praying an in-junction to restrain the State of Georgia from the execution of certain laws of that State which, as is alleged, go directly to annihilate the Cherokees as a political society and to seize, for the use of Georgia, the lands of the Nation which have been assured to them by the United States in solemn treaties repeat-edly made and still in force.

If Courts were permitted to indulge their sympathies, a case better calculated to excite them can scarcely be imag-ined. A people once numerous, powerful, and truly indepen-dent, found by our ancestors in the quiet and uncontrolled possession of an ample domain, gradually sinking beneath our superior policy, our arts and our arms, have yielded their lands by successive treaties, each of which contains a solemn guarantee of the residue, until they retain no more of their formerly extensive territory than is deemed necessary to their comfortable subsistence. To preserve this remnant, the present application is made.

Before we can look into the merits of the case, a preliminary inquiry presents itself. Has this Court jurisdiction of the cause?

The third article of the Constitution describes the extent of the judicial power. The second section closes an enumeration of the cases to which it is extended, with "controversies" "between a State or the citizens thereof, and foreign states, citizens, or subjects." A subsequent clause of the same section gives the supreme Court original jurisdiction in all cases in which a State shall be a party. The party defendant may then unquestionably be sued in this Court. May the plaintiff sue in it? Is the Cherokee Nation a foreign state in the sense in which that term is used in the Constitution?

The counsel for the plaintiffs have maintained the affirmative of this proposition with great earnestness and ability. So much of the argument as was intended to prove the character of the Cherokees as a State as a distinct political society, separated from others, capable of managing its own affairs and governing itself, has, in the opinion of a majority of the judges, been completely successful. They have been uniformly treated as a State from the settlement of our country. The numerous treaties made with them by the United States recognize them as a people capable of maintaining the relations of peace and war, of being responsible in their political character for any violation of their engagements, or for any aggression committed on the citizens of the United States by any individual of their community. Laws have been enacted in the spirit of these treaties. The acts of our Government plainly recognize the Cherokee Nation as a State, and the Courts are bound by those acts.

A question of much more difficulty remains. Do the Cherokees constitute a foreign state in the sense of the Constitution?

The counsel have shown conclusively that they are not a State of the union, and have insisted that, individually, they are aliens, not owing allegiance to the United States. An aggregate of aliens composing a State must, they say, be a foreign state. Each individual being foreign, the whole must be foreign.

This argument is imposing, but we must examine it more closely before we yield to it. The condition of the Indians in relation to the United States is perhaps unlike that of any other two people in existence. In the general, nations not owing a common allegiance are foreign to each other. The term foreign nation is, with strict propriety, applicable by either to the other. But the relation of the Indians to the United States is marked by peculiar and cardinal distinctions which exist nowhere else.

The Indian Territory is admitted to compose a part of the United States. In all our maps, geographical treatises, histories, and laws, it is so considered. In all our intercourse with foreign nations, in our commercial regulations, in any attempt at intercourse between Indians and foreign nations, they are considered as within the jurisdictional limits of the United States, subject to many of those restraints which are imposed upon our own citizens. They acknowledge themselves in their treaties to be under the protection of the United States; they admit that the United States shall have the sole and exclusive right of regulating the trade with them, and managing all their affairs as they think proper; and the Cherokees, in particular, were allowed by the treaty of Hopewell, which preceded the Constitution, "to send a deputy of their choice, whenever they think fit, to Congress." . . .

. . . They may, more correctly, perhaps, be denominated domestic dependent nations. They occupy a territory to which we assert a title independent of their will, which must take effect in point of possession when their right of possession ceases. Meanwhile they are in a state of pupilage. Their relation to the United States resembles that of a ward to his guardian. . . .

The Court has bestowed its best attention on this question, and, after mature deliberation, the majority is of opinion that an Indian tribe or Nation within the United States is not a foreign state in the sense of the Constitution, and cannot maintain an action in the Courts of the United States. . . .

. . . But the Court is asked to do more than decide on the title. The bill requires us to control the Legislature of Georgia, and to restrain the exertion of its physical force. The propriety of such an interposition by the Court may be well questioned. It savours too much of the exercise of political power to be within the proper province of the judicial department. But the opinion on the point respecting parties makes it unnecessary to decide this question.

If it be true that the Cherokee Nation have rights, this is not the tribunal in which those rights are to be asserted. If it be true that wrongs have been inflicted, and that still greater are to be apprehended, this is not the tribunal which can redress the past or prevent the future.

**Source:** *The Cherokee Nation v. The State of Georgia*, 30 U.S. 1 (1831).

### A Protest against Prejudice (May 5, 1852)

*With the onset of the California gold rush, white Californians increasingly began to see Chinese immigrants as unwanted competition. John Bigler, the third governor of California, expressed his sentiment that Chinese Americans were coming to America in increasing numbers not to settle and contribute to the American economy but rather to plunder American gold and bring it back to their country of origin. Becoming aware of these arguments, San Franciscan restaurant owner and Chinese immigrant Norman Asing raised a spirited defense in an open letter to the* Daily Alta California *in 1852. Asing notes that China had the presumed markers of civilization (e.g., language, literature, art, and commerce) before Europe and certainly before the European colonies in North America developed the same. Further, he suggests that, if gold motivated Chinese immigration to California, this made*

*Chinese immigrants no different from European immigrants to North America who sought their own fortunes.*

Sir:

I am a Chinaman, a republican, and a lover of free institutions; am much attached to the principles of the government of the United States, and therefore take the liberty of addressing you as the chief of the government of this State.

Your official position gives you a great opportunity of good and evil. Your opinions through a message to a legislative body have weight, and perhaps none more so with the people, for the effect of your late message has been thus far to prejudice the public mind against my people, to enable those who wait the opportunity to hunt them down, and rob them of the rewards of their toil. You may not have meant that this should be the case, but you can see what will be the result of your propositions.

I am not much acquainted with your logic, that by excluding population from this State you enhance its wealth. I have always considered that population was wealth; particularly a population of producers, of men who by the labor of their hands or intellect, enrich the warehouses or the granaries of the country with the products of nature and art.

You are deeply convinced you say "that to enhance the prosperity and preserve the tranquility of this State, Asiatic immigration must be checked." This, your Excellency, is but one step towards a retrograde movement of the government, which, on reflection, you will discover; and which the citizens of this country ought never to tolerate. It was one of the principal causes of quarrel between you (when colonies) and England; when the latter pressed laws against emigration, you looked for immigration; it came, and immigration made you what you are—your nation what it is. It transferred you at once from childhood to manhood and made you great and respectable throughout the nations of the earth.

I am sure your Excellency cannot, if you would, prevent your being called the descendant of an immigrant, for I am sure you do not boast of being a descendant of the red man. But your further logic is more reprehensible. You argue that this is a republic of a particular race—that the Constitution of the United States admits of no asylum to any other than the pale face. This proposition is false in the extreme, and you know it. The declaration of your independence, and all the acts of your government, your people, and your history are all against you.

It is true, you have degraded the Negro because of your holding him in involuntary servitude, and because for the sake of union in some of your states such was tolerated, and amongst this class you would endeavor to place us; and no doubt it would be pleasing to some would-be freemen to mark the brand of servitude upon us. But we would beg to remind you that when your nation was a wilderness, and the nation from which you sprung barbarous, we exercised most of the arts and virtues of civilized life; that we are possessed of a language and a literature, and that men skilled in science and the arts are numerous among us; that the productions of our manufactories, our sail, and workshops, form no small share of the commerce of the world; and that for centuries, colleges, schools, charitable institutions, asylums, and hospitals, have been as common as in your own land.

That our people cannot be reproved for their idleness, and that your historians have given them due credit for the variety and richness of their works of art, and for their simplicity of manners, and particularly their industry. And we beg to remark, that so far as the history of our race in California goes, it stamps with the test of truth the fact that we are not the degraded race you would make us. We came amongst you as mechanics or traders, and following every honorable business of life. You do not find us pursuing occupations of degrading character, except you consider labor degrading, which I am sure you do not; and if our countrymen save the proceeds of their industry from the tavern and the gambling house to spend it on farms or town lots or on their families, surely you will admit that even these are virtues.

You say "you desire to see no change in the generous policy of this government as far as regards Europeans." It is out of your power to say, however, in what way or to whom the doctrines of the Constitution shall apply. You have no more right to propose a measure for checking immigration, than you have the right of sending a message to the Legislature on the subject. As far as regards the color and complexion of our race, we are perfectly aware that our population have been a little more tan than yours.

Your Excellency will discover, however, that we are as much allied to the African race and the red man as you are yourself, and that as far as the aristocracy of skin is concerned, ours might compare with many of the European races; nor do we consider that your Excellency, as a Democrat, will make us believe that the framers of your declaration of rights ever suggested the propriety of establishing an aristocracy of skin.

I am a naturalized citizen, your Excellency, of Charleston, South Carolina, and a Christian, too; and so hope you will stand corrected in your assertion "that none of the Asiatic class" as you are pleased to term them, have applied for benefits under our naturalization act. I could point out to you numbers of citizens, all over the whole continent, who have taken advantage of your hospitality and citizenship, and I defy you to say that our race have ever abused that hospitality or forfeited their claim on this or any of the governments of South America, by an infringement on the laws of the countries into which they pass. You find us peculiarly peaceable and orderly. It does not cost your state much for our criminal prosecution. We apply less to your courts for redress, and so far as I know, there are none who are a charge upon the state, as paupers.

You say that "gold, with its talismanic power, has overcome those natural habits of non-intercourse we have exhibited." I ask you, has not gold had the same effect upon your people, and the people of other countries, who have migrated hither? Why, it was gold that filled your country (formerly a desert) with people, filled your harbours with ships and opened our much-coveted trade to the enterprise of your merchants.

**Source:** Norman Asing. "To His Excellency Gov. Bigler." *Daily Alta California*, San Francisco, May 5, 1852.

### Frederick Douglass, "The Claims of the Negro" (July 12, 1854)

*It is remarkable to consider that one would feel the need to establish that black people were just as human as white people for the audience of a college graduation. Yet that is exactly what former slave and acclaimed orator Frederick Douglass found himself doing as part of a commencement address at Western Reserve College in 1854. His speech—set to print in this pamphlet—establishes the characteristics of what separates humans from animals and then, using that criteria, defends the personhood of blacks.*

A respectable public journal, published in Richmond, Va, bases its whole defense of the slave system upon a denial of the negro's manhood. "The white peasant is free, and if he is a man of will and intellect, can rise in the scale of society; or at least his offspring may. He is not deprived by law of those 'inalienable rights, liberty and the pursuit of happiness,' by the use of it. But here is the essence of slavery—that we do declare the negro destitute of these powers. We bind him by law to the condition of the laboring peasant for ever, without his consent, and we bind his posterity after him. Now, the true question is, have we a right to do this? If we have not, all discussions about his comfortable situation, and the actual condition of free laborers elsewhere are quite beside the point. If the negro has the same right to his liberty and the pursuit of happiness of his own happiness that the white man has, then we commit the greatest wrong and robbery to hold him as a slave—an act at which the sentiment of justice must revolt in every heart—and negro slavery is an institution which that sentiment must sooner or later blot from the face of the earth. . . . "—*Richmond Examiner.*

After stating the question thus, the *Examiner* boldly asserts that the negro has no such right—BECAUSE HE IS NOT A MAN! . . .

Tried by all the usual, and all the unusual tests, whether mental, moral, physical, or psychological, the negro is a MAN—considering him as possessing knowledge, or needing knowledge, his elevation or his degradation, his virtues, or his vices—whichever road you take, you reach the same conclusion, the negro is a MAN. His good and his bad, his innocence and his guilt, his joys and his sorrows, proclaim his manhood in speech that all mankind practically and readily understands.

*Strikingly, on the second page of the same pamphlet in which this speech appears—establishing the humanity of blacks to demonstrate the unjust nature of slavery in America—is the following legend which attempts to justify the subjugation of blacks and negative stereotypes about Native Americans:*

The Origin of the White, the Red, and the Black Man—In Washington Irving's new work "Woolfert Roost," we find the following pleasant legend:

"When the Great Spirit had made the three men, he called them together and showed them three boxes. The first was filled with books, and maps, and papers; the second with bows and arrows, and knives and tomahawks; the third with spades, axes, hoes, and hammers. 'These, my sons,' said he, 'are the means by which you are to live; choose among them according to your fancy.' "

"The white man, being the favorite, had the first choice. He passed by the box of working tools without notice; but when he came to the weapons of war and hunting, he stopped and looked hard at them. The red man trembled, for he had set his heart upon that box. The white man, however, after looking upon it for a moment, passed on, and chose the box of books and papers. The red man's turn came next; and you may be sure he seized with joy upon the bows and arrows and tomahawks. As to the black man, he had no choice left but to put up with the box of tools."

"From this it is clear that the Great Spirit intended that the white man should learn to read and write; to understand all about the moon and stars, and to make everything, even rum and whisky. That the red man should be a first-rate hunter, and a mighty warrior, but he was not to learn anything from books, as the Great Spirit had not given him any; nor was he to make rum and whisky, lest he should kill himself with drinking. As to the black man, as he had nothing but working tools, it was clear he was to work for the white and red men, which he has continued to do."

**Source:** "The Claims of the Negro, Ethnologically Considered: An Address before the Literary Societies of Western Reserve College, at Commencement. July 12, 1854." Available at https://www.loc.gov/resource/rbaapc.07900/?sp=1.

### Thirteenth Amendment to the Constitution (January 31, 1865)

*A number of individual states had outlawed slavery prior to the passage of the Thirteenth Amendment. In addition, President Abraham Lincoln's Emancipation Proclamation offered slaves in areas of the country in rebellion against the Union freedom if they escaped to the North or were present in rebel territory upon the arrival of Union troops. Yet neither addressed the plight of all slaves, and neither carried the weight of constitutional authority. Therefore, the Thirteenth Amendment was an important milestone in furthering racial equality, although it actually left open the possibility of holding people in prisons against their will provided they received due process. The end of formal slavery would give way to the continued revocation of freedom for a number of racial minorities through the rise of the prison industrial complex and the rise of mass incarceration in furtherance of the "war on drugs."*

Neither slavery nor involuntary servitude, except as a punishment for crime whereof the party shall have been duly convicted, shall exist within the United States, or any place subject to their jurisdiction.

**Source:** Charters of Freedom, National Archives.


### Kelly Miller, "Eugenics of the Negro Race" (1917)

*In this article, Kelly Miller, a professor of mathematics and sociology at Howard University, examines the concern that, although a post–Civil War, black upper class is beginning to develop in America, it is unstable due to its members' low fertility rates. Drawing from his study of other Howard University professors, he notes that these members of the new black upper class came from families with an average of 6.5 children but have an average of 0.7 children themselves. He attributes this to a combination of concern about bringing children into a prejudicially hostile environment and a desire to pursue education and secure a sufficiently high standard of living before raising children. Ultimately, he suggests that the growth of the black upper class will rely on the future progress of blacks with currently lower-class statuses.*

The problem of eugenics is receiving much attention from students of sociology at the present time. The future welfare of society depends very largely upon perpetuating and carrying forward the best characteristics derivable from physical heredity and social environment. The application of eugenics to the colored race of the United States suggests several new and interesting lines of inquiry.

A study of the number of children, contributed by the fifty-five colored teachers in Howard University, Washington, D. C., throws an interesting sidelight on the question of eugenics as it affects the negro race. Howard University is an institution for the higher education of the negro, comprising a student body of over fifteen hundred. The negro members of the faculty maintain, on the whole, perhaps, a status as high as any other group of colored people to be found in the United States. The present study is limited to the teachers of the academic faculties, as they constitute a coherent social entity, whose life focuses about the institution.

As outgrowth of sudden change of condition due to the Civil War, the negro has developed a small upper class with a wide fissure between it and the great mass life of the race. There are about fifty thousand negroes belonging to the professional class, who earn a livelihood by some form of intellectual endeavor; while the great bulk of the race lives mainly by manual exertion. All social stratification rests ultimately upon occupation. The negro has no considerable middle class, such as is found in well-regulated societies, which shades imperceptibly in both directions. According to the occupational test, the demarcation between the professional and laboring classes of the negro is as sharp as a knife-cut line.

It becomes a matter of sociological interest to know how far this upper class is self-sustaining through its own reproductivity. I have therefore undertaken to make a study of race eugenics in so far as this particular group is concerned. In the fifty-five families from which these teachers were derived, there were 363 children, or an average of 6.5 for each family. On the other hand, these fifty-five teachers who have passed from the lower to the upper section of negro life, have, so far, contributed only 37 children, or an average of .7 for each potential family involved. Of this number there are 41 males, 14 females; 22 are married, and 83 are single; the number of children for each family so far formed is 1.6; the largest number of children in any family is 6; four of the families are barren and four have one child each. The average age of the single members is over 32 years. This strongly indicates that the upward struggle defers the age of marriage to a time when only limited progeny might be expected. Considering all the probabilities in the case, it seems to me entirely likely that these fifty-five potential families, when the whole record is in, will not produce more than an average of two children to each family, while the fifty-five parent families, under the old regime, gave rise to 363 children. The new issue will scarcely produce sufficient progeny to perpetuate its own numbers.

There is always a certain sort of social restraint, in the case of an individual advancing from a lower to a higher level of life. The first descendants of foreigners in this country have a lower birth rate than any other element of our population. The intolerant social environment created by the white race may also produce a strong deterrent influence. Animals, in captivity or under restrained environment, do not breed as freely as when placed under free- and normal surroundings. The educated negro, especially when submerged in a white environment, is under a sort of social captivity. The effect of this psychophysical factor upon reproductivity awaits further and fuller study, both in its biological and psychological aspects.

From a wide acquaintance with the upper life of the negro race, under wide variety of conditions and circumstances, I am fully persuaded that this Howard University group is typical of like element throughout the race so far as fecundity is concerned. The upper class is headed towards extinction, unless reinforced from the fruitful mass below. It is doubtless true that the same restraining influence is exerted upon the corresponding element of the white race. But as there is not the same sharpness of separation between the social levels, nor such severe transitional struggle, the contributing causes do not perhaps operate with the same degree of intensity.

The prolonged period of education delays the age of marriage. The negro during the first generation of freedom acquired his education at a later period than the white children and by reason of the hard struggle he has had to undergo, his scholastic training was completed at a somewhat advanced age. The high standard of living, which the professional negro feels he must maintain, still further delays the age of marriage. A single illustration will serve to clarify this point. I half-jocularly asked one of our bachelor instructors, who has passed beyond his fortieth birthday, why he did not take unto himself a companion and help-mate. His reply was that his salary was not sufficient to allow him to support a family in the style and manner which he deemed appropriate. My reply was: "If your parents had been constrained by like consideration, you would probably not be in existence." His father was a laboring man with a family of eight children. It was the opinion of Grant Allen, the eminent English literary and scientific authority, that the human race would become extinct if all females deferred marriage beyond the age of twenty-six.

The conscious purpose of race suicide doubtless contributes somewhat to the low birth rate. There are some of sensitive and timid spirit who shirk the responsibility of parenthood, because they do not wish to bring into the world children to be subjected to the proscription and obloquy of the negro's social status.

Will this tendency, which threatens the extinction of the higher element of the negro race, continue to operate in the future with the same degree of intensity as at the present time? Probably not. The first generation after slavery was subjected to the severe strain and stress of rapid readjustment. The sudden leap from the lower to the upper levels of life was a feat of social acrobatics that can hardly be repeated under more orderly scheme of development. The life of subsequent generations will be better ordered, and therefore we may expect that the resulting effect will be seen in the family life. The birth rate of the mass of the race is not affected by like considerations. They feel little or nothing of the stress and strain of the upper class, and multiply and make merry, in blissful oblivion of these things. The rate of increase of the upper class is scarcely a third of that of the bulk of the race, as is clearly indicated by the relative prolificness of the Howard University faculty as compared with that of their parents. The higher or professional class in the negro race will not be recruited from within its own ranks, but must be reinforced from the great mass below. This will produce healthy current throughout the race which will serve somewhat to bridge the chasm produced by the absence of a mediatory class.

The whole question suggests the importance of a more careful and extended study in this field of inquiry which is as fruitful as any other in its far-reaching effect upon the general social welfare.

**Source:** Kelly Miller. "Eugenics of the Negro Race." *Scientific Monthly*, July 1917.


### Virginia's "Act to Preserve Racial Integrity" (1924)

*During the Jim Crow era, there were a number of attempts to keep people classified as white from marrying members of other racial groups. Virginia's "Act to Preserve Racial Integrity" was particularly draconian insofar as it defined whites as those who had "no trace whatever of blood of another race, except that one with one-sixteenth of the blood of American Indian, unmixed with other race, may be classed as white." Enforcement of the Act to Preserve Racial Integrity included requiring Virginians to complete and submit a "Registration of Birth and Color," which asked about the color of one's father and mother. Completion of the registration card also necessitated signing an affirmation stating, "I believe the statements as to color of parents on the other side of this card are correct and that I am signing this with the knowledge that the penalty for making a false statement as to color is one year in the penitentiary." The requirement that a physician also sign added an air of scientific validity to a subjective, arbitrary, and unscientific attempt at further racial stratification.*

REGISTRATION OF BIRTH AND COLOR—VIRGINIA

Full Name:

(Given Name First. Give Full Maiden Name if Married Woman or Widow.)

Place of Birth:
Date:
Sex:

Name of Husband
(If Married Woman or Widow)

Father
Full Name:
Birth Place:
*Color:

Mother
Full Name:
Birth Place:
*Color:

Remarks:

*A white person is one with no trace whatever of blood of another race, except that one with one-sixteenth of the blood of American Indian, unmixed with other race, may be classed as white. The date of birth may be omitted if desired.

I hereby affirm that I believe the statements as to color of parents on the other side of this card are correct and that I am signing this with the knowledge that the penalty for making a false statement as to color is one year in the penitentiary.

Person Registering
Signature
Address

Witness to Signature
Address of Witness

*Signature of Physician

If Not Signed by Person Registered State Kinship of Signer

Place of Filing
Date of Filing

If the person signing statement cannot write, he or she must make a mark between the given name and the last name. Thus:

his [her]
John X Doe
mark

*If the doctor present at birth signs, it will be accepted as to age for labor, school, etc.

**Source:** Library of Virginia, Shaping the Constitution. Available at http://edu.lva.virginia.gov/online_classroom/shaping_the_con stitution/doc/birth_registration.

## The Ringle Report (January 1942)

*The Supreme Court decisions in* Korematsu v. United States *(which upheld the internment of Japanese Americans) and* Hirabayashi v. United States *(which upheld the imposition of curfews on Japanese Americans) relied on justification from the Roosevelt administration that Japanese Americans posed a serious threat to the United States during World War II. However, the Roosevelt administration withheld the Ringle Report, in which Office of Naval Intelligence officer Kenneth Ringle argued that most Japanese Americans were at least passively loyal to the United States (opting, in most cases, to avoid doing active harm to America or Japan). Thus, the internment was justified and approved by the Supreme Court thanks to perceptions of risk that were largely inaccurate.*

The following opinions, amplified in succeeding paragraphs, are held by the writer:

That within the last eight or ten years the entire "Japanese question" in the United States has reversed itself. The alien menace is no longer paramount, and is becoming of less importance almost daily, as the original alien immigrants grow older and die, and as more and more of their American-born children reach maturity. The primary present and future problem is that of dealing with these American-born United States citizens of Japanese ancestry, of whom it is considered that [at] least seventy-five per cent are loyal to the United States. The ratio of these American citizens of Japanese ancestry to alien-born Japanese in the United States is at present almost 3 to 1, and rapidly increasing.

That of the Japanese-born alien residents, the large majority are at least passively loyal to the United States. That is, they would knowingly do nothing whatever to the injury of the United States, but at the same time would not do anything to the injury of Japan. Also, most of the remainder would not engage in active sabotage or insurrection, but might well do surreptitious observation work for Japanese interests if given a convenient opportunity.

That, however, there are among the Japanese both alien and United States citizens, certain individuals, either deliberately placed by the Japanese government or actuated by a fanatical loyalty to that country, who would act as saboteurs or agents. This number is estimated to be less than three per cent of the total, or about 3500 in the entire United States.

That of the persons mentioned . . . above, the most dangerous are either already in custodial detention or are members of such organizations as the Black Dragon Society, the Kaigun Kyokai (Navy League), or the Heimusha Kai (Military Service Men's League), or affiliated groups. The membership of these groups is already fairly well known to the Naval Intelligence Service or the Federal Bureau of Investigation and should

272 Racism in America

immediately be placed in custodial detention, irrespective of whether they are alien or citizen.

That, as a basic policy tending toward the permanent solution of this problem, the American citizens of Japanese ancestry should be officially encouraged in their efforts toward loyalty and acceptance as bona fide citizens; that they be accorded a place in the national effort through such agencies as the Red Cross, U.S.O., civilian defense, and even such activities as ship and aircraft building or other defense production activities, even though subject to greater investigative checks as to background and loyalty, etc., than Caucasian Americans.

That in spite of paragraph . . . above, the most potentially dangerous element of all are those American citizens of Japanese ancestry who have spent the formative years of their lives, from 10 to 20, in Japan and have returned to the United States to claim their legal American citizenship within the last few years. These people are essentially and inherently Japanese and may have been deliberately sent back to the United States by the Japanese government to act as agents. In spite of their legal citizenship and the protection afforded them by the Bill of Rights, they should be looked upon as enemy aliens and many of them placed in custodial detention. This group numbers between 600 and 700 in the Los Angeles metropolitan area and at least that many in other parts of Southern California.

That the writer heartily agrees with the report submitted by Mr. Munson . . . [The 1941 Munson Report—officially the "Report on Japanese on the West Coast of the United States"— was written by businessman Curtis B. Munson, who served as an intelligence agent for the White House. Munson agreed with Ringle's assessment of Japanese American loyalty, except to contend that a few were disloyal and could sabotage vital installations like dams, bridges, and power stations.]

That, in short, the entire "Japanese problem" has been magnified out of its true proportion, largely because of the physical characteristics of the people; that it is no more serious than the problems of the German, Italian, and Communistic portions of the United States population, and, finally that it should be handled on the basis of the individual, regardless of citizenship, and not on a racial basis.

**Source:** "Ringle Report on Japanese Internment." Naval History and Heritage Command. Available at https://www.history.navy .mil/research/library/online-reading-room/title-list-alphabeti cally/r/ringle-report-on-japanese-internment.html.

## Lyndon B. Johnson, "Special Message to the Congress Proposing Further Legislation to Strengthen Civil Rights" (April 28, 1966)

*Many associate Lyndon B. Johnson's administration with the passage of the Civil Rights Act of 1964 and the Voting Rights Act of 1965. However, the approval of landmark legislation like this is only the first step; implementation and enforcement can be just as difficult as the initial passage. In this important 1966 speech to Congress, President Johnson touts the progress made toward racial equality but also notes that certain "racial fanatics" continue to oppose the protection of equal citizenship rights for blacks. While downplaying the backlash as coming from "relatively few" people, he does demonstrate a recognition that continued violence toward blacks may deter them from exercising their rights. To combat such violence, Johnson proposes adding one hundred FBI agents to address civil rights crimes. He also calls on Congress to extend existing protections for racial minorities via a federal law against discrimination in the rental and purchase of housing.*

To the Congress of the United States: Last year I came before the Congress in an hour of crisis to recommend new and powerful guarantees of the right to vote. . . .

The fruits of the Voting Rights Act and of the Civil Rights Act of 1964 are already impressively apparent. Discrimination in places of public accommodation—perhaps the most unbearable insult to Negro citizens—has been made unlawful. The mandate of that law has spread faster and more effectively than its most optimistic supporters believed possible. Discrimination in employment is now illegal. Opportunities closed to Negroes in the past have begun to open. The discriminatory use of federal funds has been prohibited. The effect of that prohibition—strengthened by new federal procedures—is now being felt in schools, hospitals, welfare programs, and in many other areas once blighted by racial bias. . . .

Perhaps the most evident threat to civil rights in 1966 is the danger that recently secured rights may be violently denied by a relatively few racial fanatics. Citizens who honor the law and who tolerate orderly change—a majority in every part of the country—have been shocked by attacks on innocent men and women who sought no more than justice for all Americans. The effect of that violence goes far beyond individual victims. Every assault or murder that goes unpunished reinforces the legacy of violence—the knowledge that it is dangerous for a Negro to assert his rights, or even for others to stand up for those rights.

**Source:** *Public Papers of the Presidents of the United States. Lyndon B. Johnson, 1966, Book 1.* Washington, DC: Government Printing Office, 1967, 461–462.

### *Loving v. Virginia* (June 12, 1967)

*The decision in* Loving v. Virginia *struck down laws that forbade interracial marriage. Specifically, it held that Virginia's law to that effect was unconstitutional under the Fourteenth Amendment's Due Process Clause.*

There can be no question but that Virginia's miscegenation statutes rest solely upon distinctions drawn according to race. The statutes proscribe generally accepted conduct if engaged in by members of different races. Over the years, this Court has consistently repudiated "[d]istinctions between citizens solely because of their ancestry as being 'odious to a free people whose institutions are founded upon the doctrine of equality.'" *Hirabayashi v. United States*, 320 U. S. 81, 320 U. S. 100 (1943). At the very least, the Equal Protection Clause demands that racial classifications, especially suspect in criminal statutes, be subjected to the "most rigid scrutiny." *Korematsu v. United States*, 323 U. S. 214, 323 U. S. 216 (1944), and, if they are ever to be upheld, they must be shown to be necessary to the accomplishment of some permissible state objective, independent of the racial discrimination which it was the object of the Fourteenth Amendment to eliminate. Indeed, two members of this Court have already stated that they "cannot conceive of a valid legislative purpose . . . which makes the color of a person's skin the test of whether his conduct is a criminal offense." . . . The fact that Virginia prohibits only interracial marriages involving white persons demonstrates that the racial classifications must stand on their own justification, as measures designed to maintain White Supremacy.

**Source:** *Loving v. Virginia*, 388 U.S. 1 (1967).

This chapter provides resources for future research categorized by topical area. The following works address how race and racism operate in the context of consumer goods; the criminal justice system; cyber racism; education; employment, health, welfare, and socioeconomic status; housing and transportation; immigration; intersectionality; the military; political participation; racial construction and categorization; racial attitudes; racial progress; religion; reparations; science and pseudoscience; social psychology; sports; the arts; theory; and white supremacy.

## The Arts

Pinder, Kymberly N., editor. 2002. *Race-ing Art History: Critical Readings in Race and Art History*. New York: Routledge.

This edited volume includes a series of readings covering race and ethnicity in visual culture over the past 2,000 years (primarily in the Western world). Several of these readings address race and art in the United States, such as the stereotyping of Native Americans, the representation of black men as savage or docile, and the depiction of cowboys as usually white men. The volume also addresses

---

G. W. McLaurin at the University of Oklahoma in 1948. Thanks to the Supreme Court's decision in *McLaurin v. Oklahoma*, McLaurin was able to pursue graduate education at the University of Oklahoma. However, the university segregated him from white students. (Library of Congress)

how even art celebrating progress toward greater racial equality can service white supremacy. For example, the Emancipation Group statue in Washington, D.C., shows Abraham Lincoln towering over an unclothed black man crouching at his feet, representing the emancipation of the slaves as a great accomplishment of white Americans without simultaneously acknowledging white Americans' establishment of slavery in the colonies in the first place. Further, the volume discusses the demeaning way in which the art world has characterized work by racial minority artists, such as how black American Horace Pippin's work received praise but was described as simple, unsophisticated, and primitive.

## Consumer Goods and the Reification of Whiteness

Wonkeryor, Edward Lama, editor. 2015. *Dimensions of Racism in Advertising: From Slavery to the Twenty-First Century*. New York: Peter Lang.

This edited collection addresses a number of ways in which racism has pervaded American advertising from the colonial period to the present. It addresses the problematic caricatures made of blacks, Native Americans, and Chinese and Irish immigrants in advertisements and the lag in diversity in advertisement when the U.S. population became more diverse. It also addresses the extent to which corporate advertisers tend to focus on reaching white consumers with some exceptions (e.g., tobacco and liquor marketing) due to perceptions that blacks do not have enough expendable income to warrant focus. Thus, not only is blacks' purchasing power reduced by economic inequality but also their purchasing options are limited by the narrowmindedness of advertisers.

## Criminal Justice

Alexander, Michelle. 2010. *The New Jim Crow: Mass Incarceration in the Age of Colorblindness*. New York: The New Press.

 *The New Jim Crow* is predicated on a simple but important premise: where we used to discriminate overtly on the basis of race, we now label people of color as criminals and then overtly discriminate on that basis. Many forms of discrimination (in housing, employment, voting rights, access to public benefits, and the ability to serve on a jury) are entirely legal when directed at people who have been convicted of a felony. Given that people of color are stopped, searched, arrested, and imprisoned at disproportionately high rates, they are particularly susceptible to such repercussions. As Alexander notes, the United States actually imprisons a higher percentage of blacks than South Africa did during apartheid, but that high rate of imprisonment cannot be explained away by crime rates, as people of color are no more likely to commit a number of crimes (including drug crimes) than whites.

Butler, Paul. 2017. *Chokehold: Policing Black Men*. New York: The New Press.

 Referencing and expanding on the premise of Michelle Alexander's *The New Jim Crow* and other work on how the criminal justice system exerts racial control, Butler emphasizes two important points. First, racism in criminal justice does not represent a flaw in the system; rather, it is an intended feature. Second, targeting black men through the criminal justice system is primarily instrumental rather than emotional; it is done not so much out of racial animus as it is done to produce tangible economic benefits. Butler argues that the arresting of black men produces an economic stimulus package on two levels. It benefits cities (which rake in fines and court costs from arrested black men). It also benefits members of the white working class (who face less competition for employment if a number of black men are incarcerated, are avoiding arrest warrants, or are facing discrimination in their employment searches based on their criminal records). Butler demonstrates that the criminal justice system has picked up where slavery and Jim Crow left off in the economic exploitation of black men.

Greenfeld, Lawrence A., and Steven K. Smith. 1999. "American Indians and Crime." Retrieved June 15, 2019. https://www.bjs.gov/content/pub/pdf/aic.pdf.
Work addressing racial disparities in criminal justice frequently focuses on the extent to which people of color are disproportionately targeted by police. However, the other side of crime—who is victimized—is also worth considering. This report combines Bureau of Justice Statistics, FBI, and census data to explore Native American crime victimization. Greenfeld and Smith find that Native Americans are more than twice as likely to be the victims of violent crime even after taking into account age, housing location, income, and biological sex. They are also more likely than any other racial group to experience violence from members of other racial groups. However, blacks are still five times more likely to be murdered than Native Americans.

James, Lois. 2018. "The Stability of Implicit Racial Bias in Police Officers." *Police Quarterly* 21(1):30–52.
Given the discretion that police officers have in determining when to use deadly force, the higher likelihood that they will use deadly force if a suspect has a weapon, and the number of recent high-profile examples of unarmed black men being killed by police officers, the question of whether police officers demonstrate stable implicit racial bias situationally or constantly is an important one. James found that when they slept less, police officers

were more likely to make associations between black Americans and weapons. This article suggests that tiredness may catalyze recourse to stereotype in the presence of ambiguity when assessing a threat.

## Cyber Racism

Back, Les. 2002. "Aryans Reading Adorno: Cyber-Culture and Twenty-First Century Racism." *Ethnic and Racial Studies* 25(4):628–651.

Back is often credited with popularizing the term "cyber racism" and argues that the rise of digital technology has enabled new expressions of whiteness, and, specifically, new types of racist culture that did not exist previously. The increasing availability of the Internet has allowed white nationalists to not only spread their message more widely than ever before across large geographical spaces but also maintain a degree of anonymity. There are message boards dedicated to racist dialogue, opportunities for racial harassment via computer viruses and hacking software, and even racist computer games with simulated violence against various racial groups. There are also white supremacist dating sites where people seek partners who promote white power. However, Back suggests that the rise of racist material online is "also a sign of fragmentation and withdrawal," because those looking for racist cultures to participate in on a day-to-day basis are having increased difficulty finding them locally offline. As Back puts it, "The investment in digital culture is a corollary of the failure of racist extremism to mount a serious presence in non-digital political spheres" (Back 2002:648).

## Education

Byrd, W. Carson. 2017. *Poison in the Ivy: Race Relations and the Reproduction of Inequality on Elite College Campuses.* New Brunswick, NJ: Rutgers University Press.

*Poison in the Ivy* reveals evidence from twenty-eight prestigious universities that the intergroup contact brought about by diversity is insufficient to combat racism within these institutions. This is, in large part, because these institutions tend to foster highly individualistic views about merit and success that overlook or intentionally ignore race. Since individuals attending these institutions (and particularly white students) are more frequently praised for about their qualities and abilities rather than informed of the structural advantages they've accumulated, they tend to see racial inequality as an issue of some people not working hard enough rather than an issue of some people not having as many opportunities and resources. Byrd calls for an emphasis on inclusion rather than simply numerical diversity supported by structural changes to curricula and campus policies and programs rather than intergroup contact alone.

Ferguson, Ann Arnett. 2000. *Bad Boys: Public Schools in the Making of Black Masculinity.* Ann Arbor: University of Michigan Press.

Assumptions of black male criminality do not arise spontaneously in adulthood. *Bad Boys* provides a useful case study in how even elementary-school-age black boys are treated as potential criminals and punished far more frequently for violations of school rules. Through three years of participant observation at an elementary school, Ferguson uncovers evidence of how teachers and administrators openly talk about black boys as destined for prison. Ferguson contextualizes her findings among other literature on punishment in schools to make the case that these negative expectations for black boys are not uncommon throughout the United States and create negative expectations that undermine their prospects for educational success and their conceptualizations of their own self-worth.

Harris, Angel L. 2011. *Kids Don't Want to Fail: Oppositional Culture and the Black-White Achievement Gap.* Boston, MA: Harvard University Press.

> For years, a number of educational theorists have argued in favor of an oppositional hypothesis to explain African American underachievement in schools (largely thanks to the work of cultural anthropologist John Ogbu). In *Black American Students in an Affluent Suburb: A Study of Academic Disengagement*, Ogbu suggests that black students could be underperforming because academic success was stereotypically linked to whiteness, and they did not want to be perceived as "acting white" (i.e., they took on attitudes of opposition toward education). *Kids Don't Want to Fail* may not be the first contribution to the literature to undermine that hypothesis, but it provides perhaps the best counterevidence. Harris leverages longitudinal data from six different datasets to demonstrate that despite a history of discrimination, blacks students tend to value education no less than white students do.

Jencks, Christopher, and Meredith Phillips. 1998. "The Black-White Test Score Gap: An Introduction," pp. 1–51, in *The Black-White Test Score Gap*, edited by Christopher Jencks and Meredith Phillips. Washington, DC: Brookings Institution Press.

> In this introduction to an edited collection about black-white test score gap, Jencks and Phillips note that black Americans have noticeably lower average scores on vocabulary, reading, math, scholastic aptitude, and other standardized tests. They suggest that this gap is not inevitable, however, because nonverbal IQ test scores have risen dramatically over time (suggesting that environmental changes can impact the distribution of scores), the gap between blacks and whites on standardized tests has narrowed over time, and there is evidence that black children raised in white homes tend to have higher scores

in preadolescence (which may reflect trends like the differences in income between blacks and whites that could potentially be addressed via public policy). The authors also address the extent to which standardized tests might reflect biases that could disadvantage blacks, such as labeling bias, content bias, methodological bias, prediction bias, and selection system bias. Jencks argues in a later chapter that two of these biases contribute particularly substantial problems: (1) prediction bias (e.g., using instruments for admissions purposes that do not adequately predict performance but on which one group scores higher than another) and (2) selection system bias (e.g., selecting candidates based on performance on a test when the test is best at measuring attributes that favor one group over another even though both members of both groups could successfully perform in the position). This is another concrete area where policy changes could result in reduced inequality.

## Employment, Health, Welfare, and Socioeconomic Status

Misra, Joya, Ivy Kennelly, and Marina Karides. 1999. "Employment Chances in the Academic Job Market in Sociology: Do Race and Gender Matter?" *Sociological Perspectives* 42(2):215–247.

A major component of the study of sociology is stratification. Sociologists are well aware of the ways in which race, class, gender, and other sociodemographic characteristics differentiate life chances. Yet, as Misra and colleagues demonstrate, even within academia, stratification can persist. Drawing on data from surveys of sociology department chairs about the results of their hiring process through the American Sociological Association *Employment Bulletin*, Misra and colleagues found that only one of the jobs in their sample yielded a hire of a racial minority at advanced rank (i.e., as an associate or full professor). On the other hand, when administrations gave new lines to departments, they were three times more likely to go to minority faculty than to white faculty members, and minority candidates were also more likely to be hired to positions addressing the sociology of race and ethnicity.

Oliver, Melvin L., and Thomas M. Shapiro. 2006. *Black Wealth/White Wealth: A New Perspective on Racial Inequality.* New York: Routledge.

For many years, when racial differences in socioeconomic status were discussed, the focus was on income. Theoretically, if a significant income gap existed and public policies could be implemented to increase opportunities for racial minorities to raise their incomes, then socioeconomic status differences could be reduced. However, as Oliver and Shapiro demonstrate, changes in income are not sufficient in and of themselves to overcome the many years during which whites have benefited from slavery, Jim Crow laws, and other public policies in ways that have allowed them to amass wealth and pass that wealth on from generation to generation. The authors also note that there have been increased efforts to protect that wealth advantage for the already privileged via public policy. For example, some politicians have backed the elimination of the estate tax, when the estate tax is one of the few mechanisms by which accumulated wealth is redistributed.

Paradies, Yin, Jehonathan Ben, Nida Denson, Amanuel Elias, Naomi Priest, Alex Pieterse, Arpana Gupta, Margaret Kelaher, and Gilbert Gee. 2015. "Racism as a Determinant of Health: A Systematic Review and Meta-Analysis." *PLoS One* 10(9):1–48.

Paradies and colleagues conducted a meta-analysis of data from 293 studies spanning 30 years concerning the impact of racism on health. Although the analyses covered a variety of countries, the focus (81 percent) was on studies conducted in the United States. Generally, the authors found that racism is negatively associated with mental health (e.g., depression, anxiety, and stress), physical health (e.g., hypertension, heart disease, and high cholesterol), and general health. The association between racism and poor health was especially strong for Asian Americans and Latinos/Latinas.

Quadagno, Jill. 1994. *The Color of Welfare: How Racism Undermined the War on Poverty*. New York: Oxford University Press.

Quadagno makes the case for how poverty-reduction programs have been historically undermined by white Americans not simply because of classist ideologies but rather because of perceptions of such programs as particularly beneficial for racial minorities to their own detriment. For example, in 1964, the Task Force on Metropolitan and Urban Problems under President Johnson proposed rent supplements to give poor Americans the ability to live outside of stigmatized public housing options alongside people with more means to afford housing. However, rent supplements had the potential to offset housing costs enough for racial minorities to live in what had traditionally been all-white neighborhoods, angering whites who opposed integration. Quadagno usefully points out that even public policies with the potential to benefit whites may fall under white scrutiny if they also help racial minorities due to persistent racism.

Royster, Deirdre A. 2003. *Race and the Invisible Hand: How White Networks Exclude Black Men from Blue-Collar Jobs*. Berkeley: University of California Press.

In *The Wealth of Nations* and other writings, classical economist Adam Smith made the case for an "invisible hand" leading the rich to do things that are beneficial to society as a whole unintentionally through the pursuit of their own self-interests. Through an ethnography of working-class vocational school students in Baltimore, Royster interrogates the assumption of a different invisible hand in the job market—namely, that unseen forces ensure that those who work hard will have a relatively equal chance of achieving gainful employment. Royster provides evidence that calls such a meritocratic view into question by identifying a number of mechanisms that benefit whites even when it comes to accessing jobs that do not require a college degree. Comparing students with similar attendance, motivation, and grades, white students received more concrete job market support from teachers (e.g., apprenticeship opportunities or introductions to employers) than black students. Teachers were more willing to activate their social networks to benefit their white students.

Thomas, James, and David Brunsma. 2014. "Oh, You're Racist? I've Got a Cure for That!" *Ethnic and Racial Studies* 37(9):1467–1485.

The Implicit Association Test measures how quickly people associate various stimuli with one another. For example, if the respondent is asked to choose "good" each time a black man's face appears on a screen and "bad" each time a white man's face appears on the screen, does this take more time than when the respondent is asked to choose "bad" each time a black man's face appears on the screen and "good" each time a white man's face appears on the screen? If so, then that provides evidence of bias toward whites. Researchers at Oxford University found that white men given the beta-blocker drug propranolol no longer exhibited implicit racial bias on the Implicit Association Test. Contextualizing these findings, Thomas and Brunsma (2014:1479) offer a reply that racism is not consistent with the criteria for personality disorders or pathological disease and argue that drug therapy in response to racism only "masks, like a painkiller, the social, political and cultural conditions that perpetuate racism over time and across space."

## Housing and Transportation

Massey, Douglas S., and Nancy A. Denton. 1993. *American Apartheid: Segregation and the Making of the Underclass.* Cambridge, MA: Harvard University Press.

Massey and Denton trace the history by which American neighborhoods went from relatively integrated to strikingly segregated. Before 1900, as the cities industrialized, the economic disadvantages that blacks faced on average equated to fewer housing options, but it was not uncommon for middle-class blacks to live in integrated neighborhoods. However, by the early 1900s, violent white rioters were ransacking and burning black homes that were not in black neighborhoods. Increasingly, more economically successful blacks were moving closer to poorer blacks, and, as a result, blacks, in general, were becoming more spatially isolated from whites. This spatial isolation grew over the years through a combination of discrimination within communities (e.g., housing associations banning residents from selling their homes to blacks), by relators (80 percent of whom said they would not sell a home to a black person in a white neighborhood in one 1950s' survey), and by banks (which often refused to finance loans for homes in black neighborhoods). Government policies exacerbated the issue further: for example, in 1937, the Federal Housing Administration (FHA) began offering loans with guarantees on 90 percent of home collateral (meaning that people could buy houses with a down payment as low as 10 percent) and extended loan repayment to thirty years (instead of the previous twenty-five years) making monthly payments lower. However, FHA frequently rejected loan applications that would change the social class and racial makeup of neighborhoods in the interest of "security," meaning that blacks did not have the same opportunities to pursue better housing options through loans with lower initial costs.

Sanchez, Thomas W., Rich Stolz, and Jacinta S. Ma. 2003. "Moving to Equity: Addressing Inequitable Effects of Transportation Policies on Minorities." Retrieved May 2, 2019. https://www.racialequitytools.org/resourcefiles/sanchez-mov ing-to-equity-transportation-policies.pdf.

This report—a product of collaboration between the Center for Community Change and the Civil Rights Project at Harvard University—usefully places U.S. transportation policy into the context of American racism. It addresses topics ranging from the 1950s' and 1960s' practices of building large highways through minority neighborhoods to the present-day substantial difference in transportation accessibility between whites (who can more frequently afford their own cars) and blacks and Latinos (who together comprise more than half of public transportation users). The report also notes the extent to which potential solutions to transportation accessibility can have unintendedly negative consequences for racial minorities. For example, the extension of a rail line to a minority community that previously did not have one may increase accessibility in the short term but also make the area of greater interest to other parties. As the amenity of more accessible transportation increases property values to the point where rent or property taxes become unsustainable for current residents, those residents may then have to move to more affordable locations, often finding themselves even further away from city centers than they were before. Other topics include racial disparities in transportation construction hiring, institutional barriers to racial minorities seeking voice in transportation planning processes, and the lack of enforcement of the Civil Rights Act of 1964 and environmental laws as they pertain to transportation.

Seitles, Marc. 1998. "The Perpetuation of Residential Racial Segregation in America: Historical Discrimination, Modern Forms of Exclusion, and Inclusionary Remedies." *Journal of Land Use & Environmental Law* 14(1):89–124.

Seitles provides a parsimonious yet dense account of the history of housing segregation in the United States. The article includes coverage of institutional racism in housing (from the Federal Housing Administration's practice of "red-lining" to the Department of Housing and Urban Development's racist practices in housing project location and tenant procedures). It also addresses patterns of widespread personal discrimination through, for example, "steering" (showing and recommending different homes and neighborhoods to whites vs. other racial groups) and disproportionate denial of racial minorities' rental applications. The article then goes on to make a case for why increased housing integration would be beneficial to the nation and highlights programs that have been successful in combating housing segregation.

Tegeler, Philip D. 2005. "The Persistence of Segregation in Government Housing Programs," pp. 197–216, in *The Geography of Opportunity: Race and Housing Choice in Metropolitan America*, edited by Xavier de Souza. Washington, DC: Brookings Institution Press.

Tegeler examines how housing segregation perpetuated into the 2000s in government housing programs largely as a result of (1) a lack of enforcement of anti-segregation rules, (2) a lack of specificity in guidelines about site selection, and (3) the existence of incentives to continue building government housing in already–racially segregated spaces.

Tegeler points to how the statute for the Low-Income Tax Credit Program references the program's duty to provide fair housing only once, does not have any restrictions on site location for new housing, and prioritizes housing that will serve tenants with the lowest incomes for the longest possible period of time (which developers can do most cheaply by locating them in areas that already have a high amount of concentrated poverty). The Department of Housing also reduced access when it eliminated the requirement that public housing should be replaced on a "one-for-one" basis when a building is demolished.

## Immigration

Oppenheimer, David B., Swati Prakash, and Rachel Burns. 2016. "Playing the Trump Card: The Enduring Legacy of Racism in Immigration Law." *Berkeley La Raza Law Journal* 26(1):1–45.

Oppenheimer and colleagues offer an informative legal analysis of the racialized nature of immigration policy. They begin with an account of how German, Irish, Italian, and many other Eastern European and Southern European immigrants were initially racialized as nonwhite but eventually were able to assimilate into white identities. They next discuss Asian immigration, noting how Chinese and Japanese immigration were initially welcomed as they expanded access to cheap labor on the railroads in the West (in the case of the Chinese) and on the sugar plantations in Hawaii (in the case of the Japanese). It would not be long until both groups found their immigration opportunities curtailed or almost entirely banned (in the case of the Japanese after the passage of the 1924 Immigration Act), but, eventually, Asian immigrants would gain a degree of acceptance as well. The authors suggest that the trajectory was very different for Hispanics and blacks in America. They suggest that the former have been accepted or rejected largely based on the current state of the American economy, as Hispanic immigration have been essential to the fulfillment of important low-income jobs but, in times of economic downturn, have also been seen as providing competition to existing American workers. As for the latter, the authors argue that mainstream Americans "never fully accepted Black Americans economically or socially."

## Intersectionality

Davis, Angela Y. 1981. *Women, Race & Class*. New York: Random House.

Among other themes, Davis usefully reminds us that racism is intertwined with other forms of oppression (e.g., gender), and black women's experiences (particularly among the working class and poor) have often been over-simplified. In contrast to the relative breadth of variation in the stories of black men enslaved in America, accounts of similarly situated black women tended to focus on their sexuality or, as the controversial government study detailed in the Moynihan Report on black families in the 1960s did, on assumptions of their matriarchal roles in the absence of sufficient paternal influence. The Moynihan Report drew from evidence that slave owners often reported only the name of the mother on slaves' birth records (likely at least, in part, because they fathered some of the children themselves) to suggest that black inequality was largely the result of insufficient black male influence in the family. The Seneca Falls Declaration, while groundbreaking for women's rights, overlooked the differential experience of facing dual oppressions as a woman and as a racial minority. These are just a few of the areas in which Davis interrogates traditional accounts of history with an eye to intersectionality, noting how racism operates differently along gender and class lines.

Marable, Manning. 2000. *How Capitalism Underdeveloped Black America*. Cambridge, MA: South End Press.

Manning details the deliberate process by which the founders of the United States set up the basic institutions of the country with no intention of blacks having equal access to the rights they spoke of as sacrosanct in writing the constitution. From the three-fifths compromise to the Fugitive Slave Act of 1793, blacks were defined politically as lesser even while their labor was exploited for the economic benefit of whites. As time went on, housing, criminal justice, and other policies further diminished black economic opportunities. However, rather than treat black Americans as a monolithic group in which disadvantage has proceeded homogeneously, Manning importantly details how the experience of being black in America differs by social class. He details how even as members of the black working class struggled to decrease the wage gap they faced relative to whites, more economically stable black Reaganites pushed for de-unionization, denounced affirmative action, called for a reduction in spending on social programs, and opposed minimum wage laws. It's a useful acknowledgment of how the status quo is often reinforced by disadvantaged people willing to trade the more difficult prospect of something approaching full equality for the immediate and more possible prospect of short-term personal benefit (however precariously obtained).

McLeod, Jay. 1995. *Ain't No Makin' It: Aspirations & Attainment in a Low-Income Neighborhood*. Boulder, CO: Westview Press.

McLeod's classic ethnography details the life experiences of two groups of lower-class, male adolescents: the "Hallway

Hangers" and the "Brothers." The former are primarily white, while the latter are primarily black. Members of both groups end up facing underemployment and other difficult life circumstances, but their experiences are importantly differentiated by race. For example, the primarily black Brothers discuss being called racial epithets and beaten by police, while one of the white Hallway Hangers confessed to having assaulted multiple police officers but ended up having all charges dropped against him. As a result, while both groups hold themselves at least partially responsible for their trouble in reaching economic stability, the Brothers also acknowledge the role of structural racism. The book is a useful case study for how class disadvantages may operate across racial groups but manifest differently (and, in many ways, more acutely) for members of disadvantaged racial groups.

Patillo-McCoy, Mary. 1999. *Black Picket Fences: Privilege and Peril among the Black Middle Class*. Chicago, IL: The University of Chicago Press.

When it comes to discussions of race and class, racial minorities (with the exception of Asian Americans) are often described in terms of their relative socioeconomic disadvantages compared to whites. Before *Black Picket Fences*, few scholarly works focused on unique challenges of the black middle class—a group that has presumably "made it" but still faces a different set of circumstances. In this ethnography, Patillo demonstrates that even being ostensibly part of the same class position (in this case, middle class) can mean something different for blacks than for whites. For example, given that many neighborhoods remain racially segregated and blacks are more likely to be poor, members of the black middle class are more likely to live near poor neighborhoods, exposing them to higher crime rates, schools with lower-performance ratings, and lower access to resources than would typically be expected in a middle-class community.

## Military

Christensen, Don, and Yelena Tsilker. 2017. "Racial Disparities in Military Justice: Findings of Substantial and Persistent Racial Disparities within the United States Military Justice System." Retrieved June 14, 2019. https://www.protectourdefend ers.com/wp-content/uploads/2017/05/Report_20.pdf.

Christensen and Tsilker produced this report (based on Freedom of Information Act requests to each of the military service branches on the military justice system) for Protect Our Defenders. Protect Our Defenders is a group self-described as "dedicated to exposing and eradicating bias within the military justice system and to ensuring that all service members are afforded a fair, efficient, and impartial system of justice" (Christensen and Tsilker 2017:i). The authors found that blacks in the military were as much as 2.61 times more likely than their white peers to face judicial action in a given year, while Asian service members were less likely to face military justice. This report details racial differences in disciplinary action for the air force, Marine Corps, navy, and army and covers data from 2006 to 2015 (except in the case of the navy for which full-year data was available only for 2014 and 2015).

## Political Participation

Piven, Frances Fox, Lorraine Carol Minnite, and Margaret Groarke. 2009. *Keeping down the Black Vote: Race and the Demobilization of American Voters*. New York: The New Press.

Piven and colleagues provide an extensive account of how blacks have been targeted for disenfranchisement from the literacy tests, poll taxes, and violence of the 1800s to the voter suppression of the modern era. The authors note a variety of modern strategies used to keep blacks from voting, such as the cancelation of voter registrations for people who have not voted in recent elections, the removal of polling places, challenges to blacks as they arrive at polling places, and voter ID laws that target racial minorities.

## Racial Attitudes

Kelley, Robin D. G. 1997. *Yo' Mama's Disfunktional!* Boston, MA: Beacon Street.

It's one thing when an average person on the street displays a misunderstanding or deliberate misinterpretation of black culture. It's quite another when black culture is intentionally maligned by academics, journalists, political leaders, and others whose negative racial assumptions can influence the public. One example occurs when social scientists explain black culture solely in terms of "coping mechanisms, rituals, or oppositional responses to racism"—as reactionary rather than valuable in its own right (Kelley 1997:35). Another is when conservatives suggest that providing any form of reparations for past abuses faced by racial minorities undermines their ability to help themselves and renders them dependent on the government as though self-help and external assistance are mutually exclusive. Kelley also takes aim at liberals who dismiss identification with black culture and community as undermining of class solidarity. Importantly, the book identifies how the mischaracterization of black culture has not been a matter of theoretical disagreement alone but, rather, has had tangible effects on public policy.

Picca, Leslie Houts, and Joe R. Feagin. 2007. *Two-Faced Racism: Whites in the Backstage and Frontstage*. New York: Routledge.

In *The Presentation of Self in Everyday Life*, Erving Goffman discusses the differences in how people talk in the "front stage" (where we try to give off certain impressions from our choice of setting, clothing, manner of speech, and other details) and the "back stage" (where we feel less guarded and can potentially be more authentic, as we are no longer giving a performance of the self to the same degree). In *Two-Faced Racism*, Picca and Feagin discuss how, when we look at survey research over time, we can see that whites are giving less blatantly racist answers, but the reason for this may not be as straightforward as racial attitudes have simply improved. Picca and Feagin raise the possibility that more blatant forms of racism—rather than disappearing entirely—have instead shifted to the back stage where whites can have an outlet for such attitudes without facing condemnation in the front stage. To investigate this, the authors examined journal reflections on racial "interactions, accounts, events, and comments" written over the course of six to nine weeks by 626 white students hailing from 28 different colleges and universities throughout the country. The students documented over 7,500 examples of racist statements and actions— most of which they observed in back-stage settings where their family members, friends, acquaintances, and strangers allowed themselves greater latitude. This suggests that the reduction in blatant racism observed in research may be reflective more of a change in public transparency than a real change in racial attitudes.

## Racial Construction and Categorization

Baum, Bruce. 2006. *The Rise and Fall of the Caucasian Race: A Political History of Racial Identity*. New York: New York University Press.

Baum provides an elaborate history of how colonists invented the Caucasian race to justify the slave trade. Although ancient people noted differences in skin tone, these differences were not necessarily translated as indicative of superiority or inferiority. For example, Baum discusses how the ancient Greeks and Romans demonstrated a primarily positive view of Ethiopians. On the other hand, slaves had been viewed negatively by most societies. When black Africans were transported to America for slavery, the negative stereotypes about slaves, in general, became synonymous with views of black Africans. The pseudoscientific establishment of "Caucasian" as a supposedly objective descriptor of superior people and its application to whiteness reinforced racism as a primary mechanism for stratification in America.

Daniel, G. Reginald. 2002. *More Than Black? Multiracial Identity and the New Racial Order*. Philadelphia, PA: Temple University Press.

A historical casualty to the "one-drop rule" and academia's focus until more recently on whites and blacks when discussing race has been a lack of attention to the nuances of multiracial identities. Daniel usefully explains the origins of focus on the black-white binary and resistance to it from the "multiracial consciousness movement." Resistance to the strict dichotomization of race had implications for self-identification (e.g., whether questions on the census about race should include an "other" category, categories for "biracial" or "multiracial," or allow respondents to choose more than one race by which to self-identify to best reflect racial statistics). Recognizing multiracial identities reflected in the census also had the potential to introduce ambiguity regarding whether the data would continue to be reliable in demonstrating the existence of racism. Imagine, for example, two groups of people. The first identifies as multiracial but is perceived by others as black, while the second identifies as multiracial but is perceived as white. That broad range of inclusion within the category of "multiracial" introduced the possibility that multiracial people could look like they experienced a medium amount of discrimination across the board, when, in actuality, individuals with darker skin tones or phenotypical features presumed to be indicative of being black could be facing substantially more than individuals with lighter skin tones or phenotypical features associated with whiteness.

Davis, F. James. 1991. *Who Is Black? One Nation's Definition.* University Park: The Pennsylvania State University Press.

Davis thoroughly explains how the category of black was racially constructed in the United States. He addresses the origins of the one-drop rule and the court cases and census procedures that reified it. He continues to trace the way the one-drop rule influenced public policies surrounding interracial marriage, transracial adoption, and even identity as those impacted by the one-drop rule struggled with how to perceive themselves. *Who Is Black?* notes that not only did whites create and sustain the one-drop rule in order to benefit themselves but also a number of black people contributed to the maintenance of the one-drop rule by discouraging passing as white and intermarriage with whites. It's an important reminder of how oppressive social systems may eventually gain buy-in even from those who are being oppressed.

Ignatiev, Noel. 1995. *How the Irish Became White.* New York: Routledge.

*How the Irish Became White* imparts two important lessons. The first is that racial construction can change substantially over time. Irish immigrants left a country in which they experienced the low end of a caste system and were largely antislavery having experienced some degree of oppression themselves. They came to America largely poor, looking for work and living in the neighborhoods where free blacks were doing the same. As a result, they often ending up marrying, working with, and living next to black Americans and were even labeled by whites as "white Negroes" or "smoked Irish." Yet they eventually became accepted as white and racially distinctive from blacks. The process by which they managed that shift in status imparts the second important lesson of the book: mutual experiences of oppression may not necessarily lead to solidarity and cooperation in the future—particularly when resources are limited and subject to competition. Rather than work with blacks toward more equity, the Irish chose to separate themselves by with the Democratic Party to sustain racial segregation and even directly engaged in riots and other forms of violence to intimidate blacks. In so doing, they reduced competition for the jobs they wanted. Ignatiev provides a thoughtful case study for how race operates not as something innate, biological, or fixed but, rather, as something socially constructed, amorphous, and political.

Mora, G. Cristina. 2014. *Making Hispanics: How Activists, Bureaucrats, and Media Constructed a New American*. Chicago, IL: The University of Chicago Press.

The process by which the pan-ethnic category "Hispanic" became institutionalized was complex, involving the sometimes cooperative and sometimes conflicting goals and actions of a variety of groups and organizations from the National Council of La Raza to Univision to the U.S. Census Bureau. It was a process further complicated by racial identification. Mora notes that, on the one hand, Cuban Americans largely thought to differentiate themselves from other racial minorities, whereas Mexican Americans and Puerto Ricans were more likely to eschew being classified as white and to demonstrate unassimilated pride in their heritages. Yet the Hispanic label successfully gained widespread recognition and use—largely, as Mora argues—because it was just ambiguous enough that those who used it could do so for their own strategic purposes. In *Making Hispanics*, Mora usefully provides a practical case study for the sometimes-nebulous theoretical concept of the social construction of race and ethnicity.

Rodríguez, Clara E. 2000. *Changing Race: Latinos, the Census, and the History of Ethnicity in the United States.* New York: New York University Press.

This book is part of New York University Press's *Critical America* series—a series with a strong critical race theory bent given its general editorship by Richard Delgado and Jean Stefancic. While the focus is on shifts in racial categorization among Latinos, *Changing Race* addresses a number of other racial groups as well and the real consequences that follow decisions made to classify people into one group or another. Rodríguez reminds us that racial categorization has real consequences, pointing to examples such as when Native Americans marrying African Americans were consequently categorized as black, complicating the question of whether they should be counted as Native American by the federal government for the purposes of tribal recognition. This was important, because with tribal recognition comes access to certain rights and privileges as determined by previous treaties. Underlying all of the political and social shifts around racial categorization described in the book is the undeniable fact that how one self-identifies racially or is identified racially by the government and other institutions is primarily meaningful because of racial stratification— because racial identities are not all created equally.

## Racial Progress

Anderson, Carol. 2017. *White Rage: The Unspoken Truth of Our Racial Divide.* New York: Bloomsbury.

Anderson's book is a stark reminder of how, for every step forward toward racial progress, there is a backlash from those who see equality as a loss of personal opportunities and privileges. *White Rage* provides numerous examples of when blacks had the opportunity to advance, and whites angrily sought to block that advancement from President Johnson's rejection of Sherman's Special Field Order No. 15 (which would have provided land for blacks after the Civil War) to the backlash against school desegregation after the Supreme Court's decision in *Brown v. Board of Education*. The book concludes with a more recent example of white rage—the backlash against Barack Obama's two-term presidency. The response to the first black president was the election of a leader of the birther movement who claimed (despite a lack of evidence) that President Obama wasn't even born American. Anderson reminds us that progress is not always a straightforward path toward a better destination—there are often potholes, twists, and turns along the way.

DiAngelo, Robin. 2018. *White Fragility: Why It's So Hard for White People to Talk about Racism*. Boston, MA: Beacon Press.
    In this New York Times best-selling book, DiAngelo fleshes out the term "white fragility," which she coined in a previous essay. She argues that, having perpetually benefited from white supremacy, whites are unused to situations in which they experience "racial stress" (DiAngelo 2018:2). When they do experience such stress (e.g., when they are informed of the privileges they continue to enjoy via their racial categorization), they react in defensive and angry ways to restore the assumption that the hierarchy by which whites are benefiting is fair and reasonable. This includes withdrawing from potentially informative and productive conversations and situations. The book is especially directed toward "white progressives" who believe that they are already aware of the problems of structural racism and, thus, are defensive in the fact of arguments that they are continuing to contribute to racism and "put

[their] energy into making sure that others see [them] as having arrived" rather than into potential solutions. Di-Angelo challenges white readers to consider the ways in which white fragility impedes racial progress.

Lee, Stacey J. 1996. *Unraveling the "Model Minority" Stereotype.* New York: Teachers College Press.

Asian Americans occupy a unique position among racial minorities in America. Despite facing discrimination from initial immigration to the present (including such extremes as the internment of Japanese Americans during World War II), Asian Americans have often been stereotyped as hardworking, industrious, economically advantaged, good at math, and other descriptors that may appear complementary on their face but carry with them unfair generalizations and expectations. In this ethnography, Lee digs into the model minority stereotype among self-identified identity groups ("Asian American," "Asian," "Korean," and "Asian new wave") and demonstrates the diversity among them. For example, she finds that "Asian new wavers" were more interested in peer approval over family approval and less invested in school than respondents from other Asian American groups. They also gained a reputation for wearing flashy clothing and partying. Not only does Lee's evidence suggest that the model minority stereotype is not universally applicable to Asian Americans, but she also notes the problematic effect that such a stereotype carries for other racial minorities. Lee provides examples of how some white teachers used the model minority stereotype as a benchmark for racial minorities' potential for progress and as evidence of a meritocracy. They argued that if Asian Americans could be successful, then blacks and Latinos could do, and, by extension, if blacks and Latinos were not as successful, then they must be to blame for it.

## Religion

Shelton, Jason E., and Michael O. Emerson. 2012. *Blacks and Whites in Christian America: How Racial Discrimination Shapes Religious Convictions.* New York: New York University Press.

> Drawing from in-depth interviews and focus groups with Christian laypeople and pastors, Shelton and Emerson note a number of differences between white and black Americans' religious experiences based on the two groups' differential historical trajectories. Black respondents noted the impact of the legacy of slavery, Jim Crow, and other systems of oppression on their faith—driving them to rely more on God even for day-to-day stresses and concerns. They described their worship practice in more practical and experiential terms that included working through experiences of suffering. In contrast, white respondents prayed to God in more general and generic terms and framed their worship in terms of formality and attention to doctrine. The book provides interesting insights into how experiences of racism can impact wide-ranging aspects of a person's life—even including how they experience and practice religion.

Tisby, Jemar. 2019. *The Color of Compromise: The Truth about the American Church's Complicity in Racism.* Grand Rapids, MI: Zondervan.

> Although Christians have pushed back against racism at various points in American history, Tisby (president of The Witness: A Black Christian Collective) provides a streamlined historical survey of the number of times in which they've compromised with or actively catalyzed racism. The book addresses how Christian slave owners allowed missionaries to engage slaves in religious instruction insofar as it reinforced their ability to maintain their labor force. Missionaries, seeking to evangelize, capitulated to slave masters and focused on the spiritual liberation of God rather than

the possibility of earthly freedom. As time went on, factions in American Christianity formed over racism (e.g., when the Southern Baptist Convention formed through the unification of churches supporting slavery). Many Christian universities remained segregated more than halfway into the 1900s, and one (Bob Jones University) did not lift its ban on interracial dating until the year 2000. In more recent years, church leaders have often been hesitant to call out racism within their congregations. Noting this history, Tisby calls on Christian churches to confront the racism that they have often ignored or stoked.

## Reparations

Darity, William, Jr., and Dania Frank. 2003. "The Economics of Reparations." *American Economic Review* 93(2):326–329.
 Debates have long raged about whether or not African Americans should be given economic reparations to partially address the injustices they had faced under slavery, Jim Crow, and other periods of legal abuse and disenfranchisement. Aside from the moral and political implications of these debates, a critical aspect is feasibility, for which Darity and Frank provide useful insights, in this article. The authors provide criteria for how to identify who would receive reparations (i.e., those with sufficient evidence to demonstrate that at least one ancestor was a slave in the United States who identified as black, African American, colored, or Negro on a legal document at least ten years before the reparations programs began), various estimates of the cost of implementing reparations (in trillions of dollars), and how reparations payments could be financed (e.g., via taxes on nonblacks, government bonds). They also importantly point out the need to be careful in implementing reparations to avoid accidentally increasing racial inequality; if, for example, reparations payments incentivized the purchase of goods and services from

nonblack Americans, then these payments could actually result in a decline in blacks' relative economic standing.

## Science and Pseudoscience

Blauner, Robert, and David Wellman. 1973. "Toward the De-colonization of Social Research," pp. 310–330, in *The Death of White Sociology: Essays on Race and Culture*, edited by Joyce A. Ladler. Baltimore, MD: Black Classic Press.

This essay proceeds from the premise that "the relationship of the researcher to his subject has been defined as being similar to that of the oppressor to the oppressed" (Blauner and Wellman 1973:310). For many years, white social scientists entered segregated spaces to study racial and ethnic minorities in order to further their own careers or to advance institutional goals that were often disconnected from the goals of their respondents. The researchers would retain control over question selection and interpretation of the data, and they would publish with an academic audience in mind, creating end products that were not necessarily accessible or relevant to their respondents. They would expect trust and openness from respondents but would not be expected to leave themselves vulnerable in the same way. Having identified these problems with social scientific research, Blauner and Wellman suggest a "decolonization" that includes (1) ensuring that participants are paid for their time (with the payment framed as a wage rather than a bribe for information) and (2) being honest about the actual goals of the study as well as whether the research will actually benefit those being studied in any concrete ways.

Zuberi, Tufuku. 2001. *Thicker Than Blood: How Racial Statistics Lie*. Minneapolis: University of Minnesota Press.

Tufuku explains how much of the progress made in the development of statistical methods occurred because proponents of eugenics were attempting to demonstrate white supremacy with the veneer of scientific legitimacy.

On the other hand, an important counter to eugenics became possible because of the development of new statistical techniques. Scholars like Du Bois fielded their own surveys to demonstrate how the disadvantages faced by racial minorities stemmed from historical mistreatment rather than from innate differences in ability. Thus, good fruit has been harvested from the poison tree.

## Social Psychology

hooks, bell. 1995. *Killing Rage: Ending Racism*. New York: Henry Holt and Company.

Beyond the clear material disadvantages of experiencing racism, there is the deep personal struggle to reconcile one's own emotions, identity, and perceptions with the negative picture painted by widespread stereotypes and the damage done through discrimination. hooks discussed how black people who have achieved some degree of economic success become adept at controlling the feelings of anger that reasonably accompany experiences of discrimination in order to avoid (sometimes violent) reprisals. hooks shines a light on how white rage is condoned, but black rage is framed as dangerous and condemned to render black people passive and accepting of their continued persecution. She suggests that, by killing rage, black Americans are also killing their capacity for revolutionary action. In a spirit of avoiding such a surrender, *Killing Rage* continues through a collection of essays that engage in frank and honest race talk that also acknowledges intersectionality (as when hooks discusses sexism in black life and "black on black pain" stemming from class divisions among black Americans).

Steele, Claude M. 2011. *Whistling Vivaldi: How Stereotypes Affect Us and What We Can Do*. New York, NY: W. W. Norton & Company.

*Whistling Vivaldi* proceeds from an example of the negative repercussions of racial stereotypes: namely, how people tend to grow nervous or even walk on the other side of the street when they see a black man coming toward them at night. Steele references a story from now *New York Times* columnist Brent Staples, who recalls how his presence as a black man walking down the street generated fear, but he was able to dispel that fear by whistling Vivaldi's *Four Seasons* (a marker of cultural refinement and, possibly, upper-class status). Steele is perhaps best known for his work on stereotype threat, and, although stereotype threat is applicable to stereotypes about a variety of sociodemographic factors, it was first studied in reference to racial stereotypes. Stereotype threat occurs when one is in a situation in which one expects to face a context-relevant negative stereotype based on group membership and, therefore, experiences anxiety. That anxiety can then result in one actually underperforming (thereby confirming the very stereotypes one was attempting to avoid). In his initial work on stereotype threat, Steele found that when black students are asked to provide their race on a standardized test, they achieve lower scores (presumably because thinking about their race in the context of taking a standardized test makes them think about the negative stereotypes regarding black students' performance on such tests). This book synopsizes that work as well as a variety of subsequent extensions.

## Sports

Carrington, Ben. 2013. "The Critical Sociology of Race and Sport: The First Fifty Years." *Annual Review of Sociology* 39:379–398.

Although the sociology of sports has not been particularly mainstream to the discipline, sporting provides a great medium for the study of race. Carrington notes how sporting, games, and physical fitness were connected to ideas about race in America even during initial colonization.

Sporting represents an important area of inquiry for the sociology of race, as it has been a venue for racial segregation and racial integration, for racial empowerment and racial discrimination, and for the reification and the breaking of traditional stereotypes about race. In this article, Carrington usefully frames how sociologists have studied race within sports by highlighting two key periods: (1) the period from the 1960s to the 1990s, when the emphasis was on how racism impacts people within sports (e.g., racial gaps in pay, hiring, and firing); and (2) the period from the mid-late 1990s on when the emphasis shifted to how the operation of race in sports impacts broader society. Underlying this shift has been a broader recognition that sporting represents a microcosm of society with the capacity to not only reflect how race operates in broader contexts but also impact race relations in ways that reverberate throughout the rest of society.

## Theory

Anderson, Elijah. 2011. *The Cosmopolitan Canopy: Race and Civility in Everyday Life.* New York: W. W. Norton & Company.

Through ethnographic work in Philadelphia, Anderson presents modern race relations as a combination of ostensible diversity coupled with less obvious racial boundaries. He describes people engaging in diverse public spaces who "see but don't see" each other under a "cosmopolitan canopy" stitched together with "the fabric of civility." Anderson notes that this civility may be conditional and subject to unspoken rules (e.g., black vendors selling their wares may be left alone on certain streets but accosted by police on others). It is also subject to periodic tears when whites treat blacks with overt disrespect, revealing that the surface niceties of the cosmopolitan canopy can still be covering continued prejudice beneath.

Bell, Derrick. 2005. "The Chronicle of the Space Traders," pp. 57–72, in *The Derrick Bell Reader*, edited by Richard Delgado and Jean Stefancic. New York: New York University Press.

In this science fiction story, Bell poses the hypothetical of what would happen if the U.S. government was visited by aliens from outer space who offered gold, chemicals to reverse environmental pollution, and completely safe nuclear energy in exchange for everyone identified on a birth certificate as black. As the story progresses, the characters behave in ways that are disturbingly realistic even if posed via fiction. The administration, seeing widespread support among whites for the trade, seeks to convince blacks of their patriotic duty to participate and solicits a prominent black conservative economics professor to help sell the idea in exchange for helping to smuggle him and his family out of the country prior to the trade. Bell (2005:57) describes the story as reflecting "the contradictions and dilemmas faced by those attempting to apply legal rules to the many forms of racial discrimination" and allowing him to share views from the critical race theory perspective that would be less accessible to a general audience via traditional academic means.

Bonilla-Silva, Eduardo. 2017. *Racism without Racists: Color-Blind Racism and the Persistence of Racial Inequality in the United States*, 5th ed. Lanham, MD: Rowman & Littlefield.

Bonilla-Silva makes a strong case that more overt forms of racism—though by no means absent—have become less common than "color-blind racism." Color-blind racism is presented as a stance by which whites can claim to be nonracist while continuing to reinforce structural racism. Someone invested in a color-blind approach might avoid using racial slurs, disagree with negative racial stereotypes on a survey, express a desire for equality, and claim not to see race in favor of focusing only on people's objective qualifications. At the same time, the color-blind person might oppose policies like affirmative action for racial minorities, seeing them as "reverse discrimination" that unduly privileges race over merit. While seemingly race neutral on its face, such a view overlooks the continued influence of structural racism. If whites have, on average, more income, more wealth, and other structural advantages compared with most other racial groups, then they are not competing with racial minorities on an even-playing field. A large part of color-blind racism consists of pretending like the playing field is even when it's empirically and demonstrably not. Color-blind racism allows whites to conform to changes in what constitutes adhering to social norms of acceptability while continuing to safeguard their structural advantages. Bonilla-Silva provides compelling evidence of color-blind racism primarily via interview data.

Analyzing interviews with college students and data from the 1998 Detroit-Area Survey, Bonilla-Silva identified four key frames by which whites perpetuate color-blind racism: abstract liberalism, naturalization, cultural racism, and minimization of racism. Abstract liberalism involves an emphasis on values like equal opportunity and individualism while ignoring differences in material condition. Imagine, for example, that black students and white students are treated the same way in the college admissions process but as a result of the repercussions of slavery, Jim Crow, and other policies that have accumulated more wealth into white hands. The white students would have been better positioned (on average) to afford test preparation classes for their standardized tests, private tutoring, and other advantages, ensuring that equal opportunity could not be achieved in any real sense. For example, it allows one to argue against affirmative action—despite its potential to help alleviate traditional barriers to college entry for underrepresented minorities—because it appears to represent reverse discrimination against whites (even though the effect of this "reverse discrimination" would be a course correction aimed to increase actual equality) (Bonilla-Silva 2017).

Although Bonilla-Silva identified abstract liberalism as the most important frame of color-blind racism, he also discussed three other frames as important. Naturalization involves whites arguing that occurrences contributing to racial inequality are biological or traditional or otherwise not the product of their intentional, self-promotional actions (e.g., saying that there is residential segregation because people simply like to live with people who are more like them) while ignoring structural processes (e.g., bank redlining) that have led to segregation. Cultural racism is a form of victim-blaming that occurs when racial inequality is explained not as the result of discrimination but rather as the result of prevailing cultural influences (e.g., claiming that blacks face higher poverty rates, because they are irresponsible in the realm of family planning). Finally, minimization of racism, as the name implies, regards suggesting that discrimination is now so uncommon compared to previous eras that something else must be to blame for the disadvantageous position of racial minorities in America today (Bonilla-Silva 2017).

Mills, Charles W. 1997. *The Racial Contract*. Ithaca, NY: Cornell University Press.

In eighteenth-century France, Jean-Jacques Rousseau wrote *The Social Contract*, a book claimed by some to have inspired the French Revolution. In its famous opening line, Rousseau (1762) writes, "Man was born free, and everywhere he is in chains." The line harkens back to the work of philosophers like John Locke and Thomas Hobbes, who spoke of pre-societal people living in the freedom of the "state of nature." That freedom was not without cost; Hobbes saw it as allowing for perpetual war, as there was no centralized power to keep people's selfish wants (and the violent acts committed to secure them) in check. Through the social contract, people gave up their ability to exact punishment on their own behalf in return for the security and control of laws and institutions (Henderson, James [Sákéj] Youngblood. 2000. "The Context of the State of Nature," in *Reclaiming Indigenous Voice and Vision*, edited by Marie Battiste. Vancouver, BC: UBC Press).

In *The Racial Contract* (1997), Charles Mills makes the case for how the contract presupposed by philosophers like Locke, Hobbes, and Rousseau was inherently a racial one—abstractly applicable to humankind but, in actuality, conferring its benefits to whites who proceeded to engage in the conquest and subjugation of others. The contract, then, enables stability among whites from which they can collectively impose white supremacy on other racial groups.

Wilson, William Julius. 1973. *Power, Racism, and Privilege.* New York: The Macmillan Company.

In this book, Wilson focuses on how power influences interracial behaviors. He argues that when racial minorities conform to predominant white norms, they may be doing so not from a lack of agreement with those norms but, rather, because they do not have the material resources to successfully challenge them. Even decisions about whether or not to engage in violent conflict to overturn an existing system of racial stratification are subject to conditions of power; potential revolutionaries gauge not only whether the dominant group has the resources to stop a revolution but also whether the dominant group is willing to use those resources to stop significant changes to the stratification system. The dominant racial group is also not immune to power shifts, as Wilson argues that whites generally become more racially intolerant when they face economic hardship, as poverty can limit their ability to advance and force them to compete with racial minorities more for employment. Power also comes into play intra-racially. Wilson suggests that black business leaders with primarily black customers have sometimes wanted racial segregation to continue so as to avoid competition from white businesses. He applies these ideas about the essential role of power to an analysis of slavery, Jim Crow segregation, and competitive race relations.

Winant, Howard. 2000. "Race and Race Theory." *Annual Review of Sociology* 26:169–185.

Winant traces the history of the study of race in sociology from the early assumptions of race as biological through the recognition of race as socially constructed to the present era in which race is investigated in an atmosphere increasingly dismissive of the continued presence of racism. He notes how the successes of the civil rights movement, the end of colonization in a number of places around the globe, and the rollback of Jim Crow laws have necessitated new theorizing about how race operates. The concept of race and the analysis of racism are presented as malleable and subject to change from social, political, and economic events. Accordingly, Winant offers notes on racial formation theory as a way forward in this "postcolonial, postsegregationist (or at least post-official segregation), and racially heterogeneous (if not 'integrated')" present in which we face the "persistence of racial classification and stratification in an era officially committed to racial equality and multiculturalism" (Winant 2000:171, 180). This article provides a logical application of Winant's previous theoretical work around racial formation theory with Michael Omi in their 1986 book *Racial Formation in the United States: From the 1960s to the 1980s* to the evolution of the sociological study of race and racism.

## White Supremacy

Smith, Andrea. 2016. "Heteropatriarchy and the Three Pillars of White Supremacy: Rethinking Women of Color Organizing," pp. 2–6, in *Color of Violence: The INCITE! Anthology*, edited by INCITE! Women of Color Against Violence. Durham, NC: Duke University.

In this chapter, Smith argues that white supremacy relies on three logics: the logics of slavery, genocide, and orientalism. The logic of slavery normalizes keeping black people in captivity—whether through formal enslavement, sharecropping, or imprisonment via racially biased laws and criminal justice processes. The logic of genocide champions the rights of nonindigenous people to claim any land they desired and the expectation that indigenous people standing in the way should step aside or literally disappear. The third logic—of "Orientalism"—says that Western civilizations are superior to Eastern ones and Eastern civilizations constitute threats to Western empires that must be checked and controlled (via, for example, anti-immigration policies). The term "Orientalism" originated with Edward W. Said in a 1978 book by the same name and focused on European views of the Middle and Near East, but the presence of this third logic has become even clearer in America with the passing of time. In the wake of such events as post-9/11 militarism in the Middle East and the Trump administration's travel ban targeting primarily Middle Eastern countries, those racialized as Arab (even if American citizens) have been similarly "othered."

## Arrival in North America

**40,000 to about 12,000 years ago**   Humans arrive in North America.

**985**   The Norse found the first-known European settlement in North America under Erik the Red.

**1492**   An estimated more than 5 million American Indians live in the area that will become the United States of America. This number will decline to about 600,000 by 1800 and to about 250,000 by the nineteenth century.

**1513**   European exploration of the area that will become the continental United States begins under Spanish conquistador Juan Ponce de León.

**1585**   The English attempt to found their first permanent settlement in Roanoke, Virginia.

**1619**   Dutch traders bring the first African slaves to colonial America, arriving at Jamestown, Virginia.

---

Volunteers aiding travelers impacted by President Donald Trump's discriminatory travel ban at Dulles International Airport in Dulles, Virginia, on January 27, 2017. Food and drinks were set up for travelers whose arrival in the United States was blocked by Trump's executive order banning immigration from several primarily Muslim countries. (Courtesy of Lauren Thomas)

## American Colonization

**1787**   In the midst of the constitutional convention, delegates agree to what becomes known as the Three-Fifths Compromise, which indicates that a slave will be counted as three-fifths of a person in determining population for the sake of governmental representation and taxes.

**1793**   The Fugitive Slave Act of 1793 guarantees slave owners the right to recapture runaway slaves and compels officials and citizens even in free states to comply.

**1798**   President John Adams signs the Alien and Sedition Acts into law, allowing the federalist government to deport immigrants more easily. A major motivation behind their passage is restricting the immigration of the Irish (who were racialized as black and seen as supporters of the opposing Democratic-Republican Party). Although the acts will be repealed or will expire without renewal, they will lay the groundwork for future legislation targeting immigration in a racialized context.

**1808**   Under the Act Prohibiting Importation of Slaves of 1807, no new slaves are allowed to be imported as of January 1, 1808.

**1830**   President Andrew Jackson signs the Indian Removal Act, giving him the authority to negotiate the relocation of indigenous people from land wanted by the American government to lands further west. When a number of tribes object, the American government forcibly removes 100,000 indigenous people from southeastern America and marches them to designated land on the other side of the Mississippi River. A few thousand people die on the way on what becomes known as the Trail of Tears.

**1831**   Nat Turner, a slave in Southampton County, Virginia, leads the most effective rebellion in the history of American slavery, recruiting about 75 other slaves to join him in killing 51 white people (including the family that enslaved him).

**1850**   President Millard Fillmore signs the Fugitive Slave Act of 1850 into law. The act increases the enforcement of the Fugitive Slave Act of 1793 and adds new penalties for helping fugitive slaves. Anyone who interferes with the extradition of a slave to his or her master can be fined up to $1,000 and sentenced to up to six months in jail. Moreover, federal agents are paid to return suspected slaves to their masters, and slaves are denied the right to a jury trial.

**1854**   In *People v. Hall*, the California Supreme Court rules that the testimony of Chinese immigrants against white citizens is inadmissible.

**1857**   *Dred Scott v. Sanford*—The Supreme Court rules that black people whose ancestors were brought to the United States in slavery are not American citizens and, thus, cannot sue in federal court. This leaves in place a Missouri court ruling that Dred Scott could not be free even though his master moved him to Illinois—where slavery was illegal—for years before moving him back to Missouri.

## The Civil War

**1861**   The Civil War begins as Southern states secede in order to preserve their ability to enslave black people.

**1863**   President Abraham Lincoln issues the Emancipation Proclamation, in which he declares all slaves in the Confederate states free. He framed it as necessary to win the war, because slaves were aiding the Confederate army by digging trenches, cooking meals, and contributing other forms of logistical support. The Emancipation Proclamation was largely symbolic but made the abolition of slavery a goal of winning the Civil War.

**1865**   Union general William T. Sherman issues Special Field Order No. 15, which confiscated Confederate land and offered it to black freedmen and white Southern Unionists for settlement.

## The Reconstruction Era

**1865**    President Abraham Lincoln is assassinated.

**1865**    The Thirteenth Amendment to the U.S. Constitution is ratified. The amendment outlaws slavery and involuntary servitude except in the case of imprisonment for a crime.

**1865**    Confederate veterans return to Pulaski, Tennessee, and form the Ku Klux Klan (KKK), a violent American hate group opposing equal rights for blacks. The KKK go on to raid the homes of blacks as well as whites who advocated for equal rights and commit a number of murders, assaults, and acts of vandalism and intimidation. They also stand in opposition to a number of other groups, including religious, ethnic, and sexual minorities. In 1871, they are dangerous enough to warrant the passage of the Ku Klux Act, which gave President Ulysses S. Grant the ability to impose martial law on several counties to control the threat.

**1865**    Congress establishes the Bureau of Refugees, Freedmen, and Abandoned Lands within the Department of War. The Freedman's Bureau, as it becomes more popularly known, provides basic provision to recently freed slaves but is undermined by funding revocation federally under President Andrew Johnson and at the state level by Southern Democrats and by the actions of the KKK.

**1866**    The Civil Rights Act of 1866 sustains that all U.S. citizens have equal protection under the law. It is the first federal law to do so.

**1868**    The Fourteenth Amendment to the U.S. Constitution is ratified. The amendment establishes equal protection under the laws for all U.S. citizens and will be used as the basis for school desegregation in *Brown v. Board of Education*.

**1870**    The Fifteenth Amendment to the U.S. Constitution is ratified. The amendment extends the right to vote to black men, although that right will be routinely infringed upon indirectly through measures like poll taxes and literacy tests that technically did not target blacks but disproportionately impacted them given that former slaves likely had little money and may have been prevented from learning how to read.

**1870**    Although the Fifteenth Amendment gave black men the right to vote, that right was frequently interfered with. The Civil Rights Act of 1870 gave the president the ability to use military force to guarantee the right to vote.

**1875**    Although its enforcement was limited, the Civil Rights Act of 1875 represented an attempt by President Ulysses S. Grant's administration to protect black citizens' rights to equality in transportation, public accommodations, and jury service.

## The Jim Crow Era

**1882**    Signed into law by President Chester Arthur, the Chinese Exclusion Act barred citizenship to Chinese Americans for sixteen years and ended Chinese immigration for sixty-one years.

**1886**    The American Federation of Labor (AFL), a precursor to what will become the very influential American Federation of Labor and Congress of Industrial Organizations (AFL-CIO), is founded. Its advocacy on behalf of American workers features calling for the exclusion of Chinese immigrants specifically and supporting literacy tests for immigrants, in general.

**1887**    The Dawes Severalty Act threatens to jeopardize indigenous ways of life by dividing communal tribal land up into individual properties and offering people an individual plot of land and citizenship in return for leaving their tribes. Moreover, the act empowers the government to sell any remaining tribal lands to anyone—indigenous or not.

**1888**    The Scott Act allows the U.S. government to prevent Chinese workers who leave the United States from returning.

**1889**    The Supreme Court upholds the legislature's ability to determine immigration policies and override international treaties in *Chae Chan Ping v. United States*. As a result, the Scott Act of 1888 (see earlier) is allowed to remain in force.

**1896**  *Plessy v. Ferguson*—The Supreme Court establishes the "separate but equal" doctrine, ruling that white-only facilities were allowable as long as other facilities were available to other racial groups. The Court argues that the Fourteenth Amendment was intended to prevent political equality but did not protect social equality.

**1898**  President William McKinley signs the Curtis Act into law, taking away around ninety million acres of tribal communal lands from the Choctaw, Chickasaw, Muscogee, Cherokee, and Seminole tribes and eliminating tribal courts and governments to allow the United States to take over the territory that would be admitted into the Union as the state of Oklahoma.

**1900**  Black Americans in a variety of places temporarily stop using streetcars in a series of protests against public transit segregation laws. Boycotts take place throughout the South and into the Southwest from Virginia to Texas over the next several years. In addition to walking or riding bikes, protesters organize an alternative form of public transportation via passenger vans, wagons, and carriages.

**1904**  The formal eugenics movement is in full force in America. Match-making services use health certificates to suggest potential love interests from "good stock." Thinking along these lines would lead to decisions like the Supreme Court's in *Buck v. Bell*, which upholds Virginia's Sterilization Act of 1924 and allows the forced sterilization of mentally ill persons who were institutionalized. A major part of the discussion of eugenics includes anti-immigrant sentiment and arguments about white superiority.

**1909**  The National Association for the Advancement of Colored People is founded by a diverse group of activists striving for civil rights.

**1917**  Congress passes the Immigration Act of 1917 over President Woodrow Wilson's veto, which imposes a literacy test on prospective immigrants and categorically bans immigration from most of Asia and the Pacific Islands. The Act paves the way for the Immigration Act of 1924, which imposes strict immigration quotas that saved most slots for northern Europeans while maintaining the ban on immigrants from Asia.

**1938**    Intended to increase food prices for farmers by limiting crop production, the Agricultural Adjustment Act authorizes payment to landowners to leave land untilled. Most of these owners were white, and intentionally leaving land untilled meant displacing thousands of black sharecroppers who had previously worked on that land.

## The Civil Rights Movement

**1941**    President Franklin D. Roosevelt releases Executive Order 8802, which prohibits discrimination based on race and ethnicity in government positions and in companies working on war-related jobs. It also creates a committee to look into allegations of discrimination (the Fair Employment Practices Committee).

**1942**    President Franklin Roosevelt issues Executive Order 9066, and the United States interns 117,000 people of Japanese descent into camps. In *Hirabayashi v. United States*, the Supreme Court upholds a curfew violated by a student of Japanese descent at the University of Washington but does not take up the constitutionality of the relocation order that he also violated. The internment process is affirmed by the Supreme Court in 1944 in *Korematsu v. United States*. The United States did not apologize for this until 1988, when President Ronald Reagan offered a formal apology and compensation under the Civil Liberties Act.

**1948**    President Harry S. Truman releases Executive Order 9981, which prohibits discrimination based on race, color, religion, or national origin in the armed forces.

**1949**    The Urban Renewal Act is passed—ostensibly to "clean up" areas of cities deemed to be "slums." In practice, the act brings about the mass demolishment of existing neighborhoods so that housing for higher-income groups can be built in their place. This leads to rising housing prices that make it difficult or impossible for former residents to return to their former neighborhoods.

**1954** *Brown v. Board of Education*—The Supreme Court strikes down public school segregation and overturns the precedent from *Plessy v. Ferguson* allowing for "separate but equal" facilities for different racial groups.

**1955** J. W. Milam and Roy Bryant (white men) murder fourteen-year-old Emmett Till (who is black) for allegedly whistling at a white woman. Despite strong evidence of their guilt, they are acquitted by an entirely white jury, and they later brag about having been guilty all along in a magazine interview.

**1955** Black activist Rosa Parks refuses to give up her seat to a white passenger and move to the back of a Montgomery, Alabama, bus. Her arrest prompts a year-long bus boycott, reprising the tactics employed to push back against streetcar segregation in the early 1900s.

**1956** A district court rules in *Browder v. Gayle* that Alabama laws segregating buses are unconstitutional. Despite Rosa Parks's involvement, she was not included as a plaintiff, because she had been convicted of violating city law with her bus protest, and there was concern that this might be a distraction. The Supreme Court declines to hear an appeal, and the buses desegregate, ending a bus boycott that had lasted over a year.

**1957** Martin Luther King Jr., Charles K. Steele, and Fred L. Shuttlesworth found the Southern Christian Leadership Conference (SCLC), which actively pursues an agenda of nonviolent resistance to racially discriminatory policies.

**1957** Central High School in Little Rock, Arkansas, becomes one of the first schools to integrate when nine black students (the "Little Rock Nine") arrive. However, that integration becomes tenuous when Governor Orval Faubus sends the Arkansas National Guard to block their entry. The students are not able to enter the school until President Dwight D. Eisenhower sends 1,200 of the army's 101st Airborne Division to take charge of the National Guardsmen there. They are subject to harassment and, in some cases, violence throughout the rest of the school year.

**1957**    The Civil Rights Act of 1957 makes it possible to federally prosecute anyone trying to prevent a qualified voter from voting, making it easier to defend minority voting rights.

**1960**    Black students from North Carolina Agricultural and Technical College in Greensboro, North Carolina, are refused service at a Woolworth's counter but stage a sit-in, remaining in their seats in protest. The event inspires similar sit-ins in several states.

**1960**    Black students at Shaw University in Raleigh, North Carolina, form the Student Nonviolent Coordinating Committee (SNCC), launching a variety of endeavors to further civil rights.

**1961**    Student volunteers (who become known as "Freedom Riders") begin to take interstate bus trips in the South to see whether new laws desegregating interstate public transportation have been effectual.

**1963**    Martin Luther King Jr. writes "Letter from a Birmingham Jail," defending the morality of violating unjust laws.

**1963**    The "March on Washington" brings 200,000 people to the Lincoln Memorial, where Martin Luther King Jr. gives his famous "I Have a Dream" speech.

**1963**    Riots break out in Birmingham, Alabama, after KKK members kill four girls at Sixteenth Street Baptist Church as part of a series of bombings targeting black civil rights leaders.

**1964**    The Twenty-Fourth Amendment to the U.S. Constitution is ratified, making poll taxes illegal. Poll taxes—requiring payment in order to vote—were originally implemented in former Confederate states after the Civil War to make it harder for blacks (who, as former slaves, did not have a lot of money) to exercise their rights.

**1964**   In a time that becomes known as the "Freedom Summer," a variety of civil rights groups affiliated with the Council of Federated Organizations (COFO) launch voter registration drives to recruit black voters to help oust Southern Democrats.

**1964**   The Civil Rights Act of 1964 is passed, prohibiting discrimination based on race, color, religion, sex, or national origin in voting, public education, employment, and other venues. It also creates the Equal Employment Opportunity Commission (EEOC) to enforce civil rights protections.

**1964**   The Federal Bureau of Investigation's Counter Intelligence Program (COINTELPRO) sends incriminating evidence to Martin Luther King Jr. and a note suggesting that he kill himself.

**1965**   On a day that will be known as "Bloody Sunday," nonviolent protesters marching from Selma, Alabama, to Montgomery, Alabama, are beaten and teargassed.

**1965**   The Voting Rights Act is passed, making it illegal for states and localities to use discriminatory measures (like poll taxes or literacy tests) to bar racial minorities from voting.

**1965**   Civil rights leader Malcolm X is assassinated.

**1965**   Executive Order 11246 directs companies with government contracts to take racial diversity into account in hiring, providing the first federal enforcement of affirmative action.

**1965**   President Lyndon Johnson signs the Hart-Celler Immigration Act of 1965 into law, eliminating the draconian quota system of the Immigration Act of 1924, liberalizing immigration policies, and allowing for chain migration (by which immigrants could sponsor their relatives for acceptance into the United States once they themselves naturalized).

**1967**   The Supreme Court strikes down laws banning interracial marriage in *Loving v. Virginia* on the basis that they violate the Equal Protection Clause of the Fourteenth Amendment to the U.S. Constitution.

**1968**   President Lyndon B. Johnson signs the Fair Housing Act into law. It prohibits housing discrimination based on a number of factors, including race.

**1968**   Civil rights leader Martin Luther King Jr. is assassinated.

**1971**   The Supreme Court upholds busing policies to integrate public schools in *Swann v. Charlotte-Mecklenburg Board of Education*. The busing plans will continue to be enforced as late as into the 1990s in some cities.

## The Modern Era

**1978**   In *Regents of the University of California v. Bakke*, the Supreme Court rules that, while a college cannot reserve a certain number of spots for a specific racial group in an incoming class, race can be considered among other factors in college admissions, upholding affirmative action.

**1980**   The Supreme Court rules (in *United States v. Sioux Nation of Indians*) that the United States violated the Treaty of Fort Laramie and illegally took Sioux land and orders the government to pay more than $1 billion. The Sioux demand return of their land instead.

**1988**   Congress passes the Civil Rights Restoration Act over President Ronald Reagan's veto. The act forces private institutions receiving federal funds to adhere to civil rights legislation in the same manner as public institutions. This was required not only in programs funded by the federal government but also in all the practices of such institutions.

**1991**   President George H. W. Bush signs the Civil Rights Act of 1991 into law, making it easier for employees facing discrimination to successfully sue.

**1992** Four Los Angeles Police Department (LAPD) officers are acquitted of excessive force charges in the indiscriminate beating of Rodney King, leading to thousands of people rioting. The incident led the mayor to authorize an independent investigation by the Christopher Commission, which found evidence of excessive force with a racial bias in the practices of the LAPD.

**2003** The Supreme Court upholds the University of Michigan Law School's use of race-conscious admissions policies that benefit underrepresented minorities.

**2008** President Barack Obama becomes the first black person to be elected president of the United States.

**2013** Patrisse Cullors, Alicia Garza, and Opal Tometi co-found the Black Lives Matter (BLM) movement in response to George Zimmerman's acquittal on charges he faced for killing black teenager Trayvon Martin. Zimmerman reported Martin as suspicious to 911 and, ignoring the dispatcher's instructions, followed him, leading eventually to an altercation in which Zimmerman shot Martin to death. BLM activists would go on to protest the deaths of Michael Brown, Eric Garner, and other black people indefensibly killed by police as well as protest at candidate rallies during the 2016 presidential election to raise awareness about police brutality aimed at black Americans. The movement has spread internationally.

**2013** In *Shelby County v. Holder*, the Supreme Court strikes down a key section of the Voting Rights Act that includes the coverage formula used to determine whether a jurisdiction with a history of racial discrimination in voting has to submit proposed voting changes for approval before enacting them. As a result, a number of states move forward, with voting restrictions known to disproportionately disadvantage racial minorities, such as voter ID laws.

**2018** The Supreme Court upholds the Trump administration's travel bans against primarily majority-Muslim/majority nonwhite countries, citing the wide latitude of presidential powers in the area of immigration. Precedent for the decision includes *Chae Chan Ping v. United States*, in which the Supreme Court rationalized excluding Chinese immigrants based on the alleged dangers of people of other racial groups coming to the United States and failing to assimilate.

**affirmative action**    Refers to policies designed to prioritize opportunities for members of a group that has traditionally faced discrimination (such as in admission to a university or employment).

**Anglo-Saxon**    A term referring to the Germanic immigrants who inhabited modern-day Great Britain and became ancestors to most British people; colloquially used sometimes to refer to whites.

**anti-miscegenation laws**    Laws designed to keep whites from marrying people classified as members of other racial groups.

**Asian**    A term referring to ancestry from the Asian continent. Asia currently encompasses fifty-two countries, including forty-nine recognized by the United Nations.

**assimilation**    Occurs when a minority group starts to become more like the dominant group in a society (such as in terms of language, dress, or customs).

**bad blood**    A term used to refer to a variety of illness conditions threatening the health of African Americans. In the Tuskegee Study of Untreated Syphilis in the Negro Male, patients were told that they were being treated for bad blood when, in fact, their syphilis was left untreated so that the progression of the disease could be observed.

**black**    A term frequently used to refer to people with darker skin tones. In the United States, it is commonly applied to African Americans.

**blackface**   Darkening one's skin to impersonate a black person. In the United States, this has typically involved performing a caricature of African Americans relying on negative stereotypes.

**Caucasian/Caucasoid**   Colloquially used to refer to white people. Originally, the term referred to natives of the Caucasus mountains, who were believed by many eugenicists to be physically superior to other humans. Although often excused as a scientific classifier, the term furthers unfounded assumptions of white supremacy.

**color-blind racism**   Involves arguing for racial equality while ignoring the existence of institutional factors that sustain racial hierarchy (such as when someone says all lives matter in response to black lives matter, not acknowledging the fact that people's lives are often measured differently by the general public based on racial categorization).

**contact hypothesis**   The idea that, given certain conditions, increased contact with members of another group will diminish prejudice.

**critical legal studies**   A movement within legal academy questioning assumptions of the law's value neutrality and its tendency to overlook racial minorities, in general, and blacks, in particular.

**critical race theory**   Focuses on the extent to which racism is a core feature of society rather than a personal problem of certain individuals and pushes back against prevailing narratives that whites tell to justify their overrepresentation in privileged positions.

**discrimination**   Treating people unfairly based on perceptions of their membership in a particular category (e.g., a racial group).

**diversity**   Variety or, in the context of race, the representation of a variety of racial groups in a particular setting or context.

**eminent domain**    The ability of the government to confiscate private property and use it without the owner's permission after providing compensation.

**eugenics**    A movement attempting to find ways to refine humanity by weeding out hereditary traits seen as undesirable. Eugenic theories were used to justify everything from antimiscegenation laws to forced sterilization and often categorized racial minorities as having less desirable traits.

**implicit bias**    Refers to assumptions and stereotypes that operate at the subconscious or unconscious level. Via implicit bias, one can believe in racial equality but still harbor underlying negative views of other racial groups that one may not be fully aware of.

**institutional racism**    Racism that occurs through and within institutions (e.g., the government, banks, schools, companies).

**interpersonal racism**    Racism between individual people.

**intersectionality**    Recognition of how sociodemographic characteristics are connected, meaning that experiences of oppression or privilege differ based on the combination of one's identities and categorizations. For example, Asian women face gender discrimination but experience advantages in income compared to other racial groups. As a result, they make more, on average, than black men and Hispanic men but less than white men and Asian men.

**intrapersonal racism**    Racism you experience by accepting negative stereotypes and beliefs about the inferiority of your racial group.

**Jim Crow laws**    Laws passed throughout southern America to create and maintain racial segregation.

**model minority**    A framing of a minority group's success as a model to which other minority groups should aspire. (This idea has been applied to Asian Americans to place blame on other racial minority groups for not reaching a similar level of success rather than make institutions more equitable.)

**Mongoloid**   A term used by eugenicists to refer to people with primarily Asian and Arctic North American origins. It was used to negatively categorize people in comparison to whites who were framed as Caucasoid.

**Native American**   A term used to refer to indigenous people of North America.

**Negroid**   A term used by eugenicists to refer to people with primarily sub-Saharan African origins. It was used to negatively categorize black people in comparison to white people who were framed as Caucasoid.

**Occidental**   Refers to having origins in the global West (contrasted with oriental).

**Oriental**   Refers to having origins in the global East (contrasted with occidental). The term is often seen as offensive when directed at Asian people given its association historically with racist depictions.

**prejudice**   Assumptions (generally negative) about something or someone that go beyond actual experience.

**pseudoscience**   Ideas insufficiently supported by science that are espoused as scientific anyway.

**racialization**   Externally defining people or their situations in racial terms when the people themselves do not.

**racism**   Prejudice or discrimination directed at members of a different racial group based on assumptions of the superiority of one's own group.

**reparations**   Payment given to compensate for previous wrongs. For example, reparations have been proposed as a partial remedy to historical racism.

**social construction**   The idea that the meaning of anything in reality is not inherent but rather decided upon by people interacting with that reality and each other.

**stereotype**   An (often negative) assumption about an entire group based on ideas about individual representatives of that group.

**white**    A term commonly used to describe people with lighter skin tones. In the United States, the term has traditionally referred to people of European heritage.

**white privilege**    Refers to the advantages that people racialized as white enjoy regardless of individual merit. White privilege may include material benefits and assumptions of competency, trust, and respect.

**white racial frame**    A set of beliefs, emotions, and experiences assumed by the majority of white Americans that positions whiteness as normal, natural, and superior while denying the existence and/or prevalence of racism.

**white supremacy**    Belief that white people are inherently better than people of other racial classifications. White supremacy is used to justify illegitimate white domination and power.

**yellowface**    Altering one's skin tone to impersonate an East Asian person. Just as blackface involves a performance of negative stereotypes about black people, yellowface involves a performance of negative stereotypes about East Asians.

# Index

## About the Author

**Steven L. Foy** is assistant professor of sociology at the University of Texas Rio Grande Valley. His research primarily focuses on race/ethnicity (particularly regarding stigma, colorism, and the social psychological processes surrounding racial construction), medical sociology (particularly regarding mental health, medicalization, and the connection between religion and health), and social psychology (particularly regarding stigma, stereotype threat, and status characteristics theory). His work has been published in the *American Journal of Sociology*, the *Journal of Attention Disorders*, the *Journal of Religion and Health, Psychiatric Quarterly, Social Compass, Society and Mental Health, Sociological Spectrum, Socius*, and *The American Sociologist*.